EX LIBRIS

This is book   470

The Vancouver Club
First Century 1889-1989

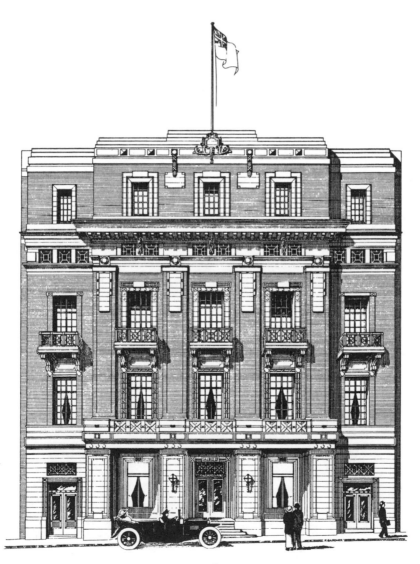

The Vancouver Club
First Century 1889-1989

Reginald H. Roy

Canadian Cataloging in Publication Data

Roy, Reginald H., 1922-
The Vancouver Club first hundred years, 1889-1989
ISBN 0-88925-921-6
1. Vancouver Club (Vancouver, B.C.) – History.
I. Vancouver Club (Vancouver, B.C.) II. Title.
HS2735.V35V32 1989   367'.9711'33   C89-091129-0

DEDICATION

This history is dedicated to the members of the Club and to the Staff whose energy, actions and decisions through the years of war, depression and prosperity contributed to its outstanding success.

Thomas E. Ladner, Chairman
History Committee

Table of Contents

PREFACE

Our Club, situated as it is in the heart of the business community, is a sanctuary from the rush and turmoil of life--a home where a man can enjoy a quiet hour or two, confident that the busy world outside cannot disturb him.

The minute a visitor enters the club he feels he is in another world, a kind of regency, elegant, hospitable, splendour. The beautiful staircase leading up to the dining room is a reminder that the premises date back to 1913. They say that nowadays more things happen in a year than happened in ten years in the 19th Century or in a score of years in the 18th Century.

Probably the major event since the opening of our building in 1913 has been the amalgamation of the University Club and the Vancouver Club on December 29, 1987. Both Ed Wallace, the then President of the University Club, and I were positive of the outcome of the amalgamation discussions from the start. Now, after just over one year as one, we find the meld is working extremely well and the club is being fully utilised again.

It is interesting to note that Charles H. Wills was the only member who had been President of both clubs, the University Club in 1958 and the Vancouver Club in 1977. It is also interesting that two men have been Secretary–Manager of both clubs. D. B. Robinson in the early '20s at the Vancouver Club and 1926–1939 at the University Club; George W. Smith 1977–1986 at the University Club and since then our Secretary–Manager here.

On behalf of the Directors, I wish to thank the History Committee under the chairmanship of Tom Ladner, also our Secretary–Manager, George Smith; Acting Secretary–Manager, University Club, Tom Marshall; our archivist, Fred Auger; Dr. Reg Roy who wrote the history and all members who gave so freely of their time to contribute to this book.

I also want to acknowledge and thank all the donors without whose contributions this history would not have been possible.

Hubert O. Chapman,
President, The Vancouver Club

INTRODUCTION

On May 11th, 1934, W. G. Murrin, then president of the Vancouver Club, wrote a letter to a number of older club members which
read in part:

> *There is a feeling among the Members that a History of the Club,*
> *which will be of interest to those who belong to the Club now and*
> *in the future, should be compiled and printed, and that the older*
> *Members should be asked to collaborate in the preparation of*
> *such a record.*

Later that month Murrin had a number of senior members to dinner at
the club. Some of the guests were instrumental in creating the Vancouver Club, most of the others had joined in the 1890s. Among those
present was F. M. Chaldecott, the club's president in 1907. As the
guests reminisced about the early days someone scribbled notes. Tape
recorders were a thing of the future. Chaldecott was asked to write the
club's history and it appeared, in pamphlet form of six pages in 1934
and was included in the club's publication of 1936 under the title "The
Vancouver Club, Historical Notes, Constitution and House Rules,
List of Members."

Club archives reveal what these men had for dinner, the seating
arrangement at the table, and what they drank. With respect to the
latter they polished off one bottle of gin, one vermouth, one sherry,
three sauterne, three scotch and one port. There were twenty-one at
the table, and the total cost, meal, liquor, wine and cigars, came to
$77. The result of the dinner conversation was five and a half pages of
scribbled notes on some of the major points made by the founding
members. The notes were brief and, for the historian, tantalizing. It
was like reading the diary of a man who had just broken the Bank at
Monte Carlo to find that he had recorded the event as: "Had an
interesting day." This was an early indication to the author that the
club's archives might be found wanting.

In 1970 the Vancouver Club once more considered the writing of its history. Two years earlier it had been approached by Paul Bissley, formerly Secretary–Manager of the Union Club of Victoria. He had just completed his manuscript of the history of the Union Club and sent it to the General Committee with the proposal "to publish an historical record of both clubs under the one cover." This was declined, but later Bissley was asked to write the Vancouver Club history. He completed it early in 1971 but it was not considered ready for publication until later that year, just in time to be included in one of the centennial publications marking the anniversary of British Columbia becoming a province of the Dominion of Canada.

Over a decade later George Hungerford, a member of the General Committee and later club president, suggested that Bissley's history should be updated and reprinted in time for Expo '86, but that a revised history should be prepared in time for the club's own centennial in 1993. During 1984 and 1985, an attempt was made to encourage one of the club members to take on the task but to no avail. In April 1986, Hungerford, now president and T. E. Ladner, a past-president, were anxious to see some action. This time it was to be more than a rewrite. "The project," Ladner said, "should be a completely new book with the endeavour to relate the history of the Vancouver Club with the history and activities of the City of Vancouver and the Province of British Columbia." It was also agreed that a professional historian should be asked to undertake the task.

I was asked if I would be interested in writing the book by a former committee member, the Honorable Robert G. Rogers, at the time Lieutenant–Governor of British Columbia. In June 1986, I met with Thomas Ladner who had accepted the chairmanship of the History Committee. The meeting went well and I was able to start serious work on research and interviewing members in September. The object was to complete the book in two years.

It did not take long to find that the club's archives were very limited. The minutes of the annual meetings were available, and the minutes of the General Committee had been preserved. The correspondence of the club's presidents is almost non–existent. The "dead files" of the members reveal very little about the members themselves. There are few newspaper items about the club because the club itself shunned publicity of any sort. The death of a prominent member would be noted, sometimes quite fully, in the local papers and these proved to be quite useful. In general, however, the club's archives have been neglected.

This, in turn, made it necessary for me to interview as many club members as possible. I started with the older members and staff and worked my way down to those who had joined in the post–Second

World War era. These taped interviews and the transcripts of them are now part of the club's archives. They are not available to the public without the permission of the person interviewed. Periodically I have quoted from them with the permission of the person interviewed. In the goodness of time these interviews will provide an excellent source of information for social and business historians sometime in the middle of the next century. For the present they are not open. It is because much of the material for this book was given to me in confidence, or because the sources are held privately in the club, that I have not used the usual display of footnotes in this history. Many of the sources are quite obvious; my fellow historians will just have to accept my word that other quotations and sources do exist in the club's archives.

I owe a great many thanks to those who have been so very patient with me when I was interviewing them either in the club, in their office or in their homes. Without their cooperation this would have been a much poorer book. They helped put flesh on the skeleton provided by the archives. I might add that one could write another volume about the members of the club quite easily. The hardest task was not what to include, but what to leave out. Conscious of both time and space limitations, I had to make hard decisions about individual accomplishments which could not be told as fully as I would have liked, and some not at all. I can truthfully say I have never interviewed what I have thought to be a dull club member. Indeed, they have been the liveliest, most interesting and most entertaining group of people I have ever met.

The History Committee has been a tremendous help in the preparation of this book. As chairman, Thomas Ladner has injected some naval discipline into the committee's meetings and kept his crew steadily on course. Hubert Chapman, as president of the club, has attended almost all the meetings and has been particularly helpful in describing the negotiations then underway respecting amalgamation. David R. Blair, A. D. (Peter) Stanley, George Hungerford and Lawrence Dampier, all past presidents of the club, were able to provide me with information during their own tenure on the General Committee as well as when they served as presidents. Their suggestions respecting people to be interviewed, both members and staff, were always most useful, and the long hours they spent reading the draft chapters and, later, the galley proofs, always added to the improvement of the final product. Fred Auger, who was co-opted onto the committee in 1987, brought with him a fund of information on fine art in the club as well as the experience of a former editor.

During the last two years the club's office staff transcribed many of the taped interviews I had with the members. We owe them a debt of thanks. George Smith, who sat in with the History Committee, has been his usual courteous, cheerful and efficient self in assisting the committee and this author despite the many other demands on his time, particularly when the clubhouse was being renovated in 1988. Certainly he made my task much easier in many ways.

Finally, I want to thank Mrs. Gloria Orr who typed the greater part of this manuscript. This is the third or fourth book she has typed for me and she still manages to smile when I go into the office. At home, my wife, Ardith, has exhibited much patience as my desk and then the den floor became strewn with files, minutes, correspondence, newspaper clippings and much more. The only one who seemed to enjoy that was "Bagpipe," our cat, who thought it great sport to dive into these papers and scatter them all over the place. Sorry, Bagpipe, but it's time to tidy things up.

Reginald H. Roy
University of Victoria

CHAPTER I

THE ORIGINS

It had been a devastating fire. On June 13th, 1886, just two months after the "city" had been incorporated, a fire had swept through the community leaving only a few buildings standing where there had been hundreds. On the morning of the 15th, a contemporary reported,

> ... *numerous tents and small huts were to be seen dotting the townsite, which gave it the appearance of a military encampment. It was a grotesque scene never to be forgotten by those who participated in it.*

No time was lost in rebuilding the city. Within six months over five hundred buildings were erected, "many of them substantial two and three story frame blocks, and a large number of them built of brick." By the end of the year the city boasted about 14 office buildings, 23 hotels, 51 stores, nine saloons, one church, one roller rink and more than 8,000 people. Most of the principal streets had been planked and, that done, work began on planking Water, Cordova, Carrall, Hastings, Cambie, Powell and Oppenheimer Streets.

One of the main reasons for this burst of activity was the decision of the Canadian Pacific Railway to extend its western terminus from Port Moody to Vancouver. The decision to do so was both logical and profitable. The company had been given a large land subsidy to extend its railway and, consequently, had acquired thousands of acres of land in what was to become the downtown core of the city as well as large stretches of future residential property. Thus while the pioneer citizens of Vancouver were rebuilding what was then little more than a village, the directors of the C.P.R., according to a report written at the time,

> . . . have been actively engaged with a staff of over 200 men, clearing their land, grading streets, building wharves, and making every preparation for the immense volume of trade which will pass over their line during the present year. They have in course of erection a large hotel, which when completed will rival anything of the kind on the continent. The ground is being prepared for a large passenger depot, and also for round–houses, workshops, workmen's houses, freight sheds and warehouses.

In mid–May, 1887 the first Hotel Vancouver opened. Some people felt that its location on the corner of Georgia and Granville Streets was too far from the centre of town. About a week later, the first passenger train from Montreal arrived, to be greeted by H. B. Abbott, the C.P.R.'s general superintendent. In June, the C.P.R.–chartered **Abyssinia** arrived––the first passenger ship to come to Vancouver from Japan. Early in August the bustling city saw the first street lights––all 53 of them––turned on and, three years later, the Vancouver Electric Railway and Lighting Co. sent its first tramcar for a test run along Main, Cordova, Granville and Pender Streets.

By 1890, the city's population had reached 12,500. A Board of Trade had been formed, the magnificent Stanley Park had been opened by Mayor David Oppenheimer and a young man from the United States, B. T. Rogers, was completing his plans to establish on the waterfront a sugar refinery which was to become a city landmark. Another entrepreneur, H. O. Bell–Irving, formed the Anglo–British Columbia Packing Co. in December, 1890 and within a year or so the firm was producing more than one–quarter of the province's total salmon pack.

Vancouver was booming and there was no doubt that the C.P.R. connection was transforming it from a frontier logging town into a potentially major seaport city which would rival and might even surpass Victoria. By 1892, Hastings Street was paved from Cambie to Granville Streets, the first street in the city to advance beyond wooden planks. Two years later St. Paul's Hospital was founded, and in 1895 not only was mail delivery started in parts of the city, but the first letter boxes were installed on city streets. Traffic still moved on the left-hand side of the road and the noise and smell of an automobile would become a nuisance only after the turn of the century. Despite all these signs of growth and prosperity, of building and construction, as late as 1896 the city council still found it necessary to pass an ordinance limiting to two the number of cows permitted each family.

The prospects for growth and development in Vancouver and British Columbia brought to the city a large number of men interested in sharing and enlarging the business potential which presented itself. The Canadian Pacific Railway had a number of their senior staff involved not only in strictly railway and transportation matters but in land development as well. The lumber and fisheries industries were on the brink of a vast expansion, and when additional railroads and feeder lines were built, mining was to flourish as well. To service these industries and the growing population, banks, insurance companies, law firms, investment companies, professional men, wholesale and retail companies and a host of others were established. Canadian, British and American businessmen and entrepreneurs brought with them the drive and energy which was to develop the city and its environs, but quite naturally they also anticipated creating a social life with which they were familiar in their home province or country.

The origins of the Vancouver Club are somewhat obscure. It would be natural for a group of men, similar in outlook, taste and interest, to meet together, enjoy each other's company over a meal, and discuss matters relating to their business, political or social concerns. They would be familiar with the men's clubs in Britain as well as those in Eastern Canada. Some would be familiar with, and somewhat envious of, the Union Club in Victoria which had been established in 1879. Such a club offered not only a pleasant social environment for its members, but with its dining room, library, bar, billiard room and other amenities, it provided a "downtown" home away from home where members could dine well in congenial company or relax in a pleasant atmosphere. It was a place where they could invite their friends to dine or where they could arrange for visitors to stay for several weeks. A club was also convenient for entertaining important dignitaries visiting the city in an ambience not to be found in even the best hotels. Moreover, a club could be used for various social occasions whether it be entertaining the officers of a visiting naval vessel or for a summer or winter ball where ladies would be invited to dine and dance and share the pleasure of the club with their male partners. A club could also be a home for a single member, one where he could find more comfort, congeniality, friendship and service than if he were forced to live in a hotel or boarding house. Belonging to such a club assumed certain obligations as well as privileges. A member would have to help maintain the costs of operating the club over and above the financial obligations he would incur either at the bar or the dining room. It did not mean that a member had to be wealthy or rich, but certainly he would be expected to have an above-average income.

In the summer of 1889 a group of men in Vancouver decided to form a club which, they decided, would be called the Vancouver Club. The name, incidentally, was not unique. There had been a club started with the same name in Victoria in the 1860s, but for some reason it had only a short life. There must have been a considerable amount of work put into the formation of the Vancouver Club and evidently the members were determined it would be worthy of the new city growing around them. On February 7th, 1890 the Vancouver "Daily World" reported:

> *Within a few weeks the Vancouver Club will occupy a splendid set of rooms in the Lefevre Block, fronting on Seymour Street. The club was organized in July last with a membership of about 50 citizens. To acquire rooms adapted to their requirements, an agreement was reached with Dr. Lefevre by which they could secure a part of his new block. The northern portion of that fine building was turned over to them to fit up as they chose. . . . The Clubrooms will occupy the upper three stories . . . fronting on Seymour Street. Considering the wealth and standing of the members and the requirements of such a city as Vancouver, it is unnecessary to say that the furnishings throughout will be most comfortable and luxurious. . . . Entrance is had to the clubhouse by a hall and stairway leading to the first floor. Just at the top of the stairs is a cosy little reception room for strangers who desire to speak to a member. The greater part of this floor will consist of the coffee and dining room, and a lavatory and cloakroom adjoining. The next floor will be occupied by the general dining room, reading room and smoking room. On the upper storey will be a finely finished billiard room, private smoking room and the steward's room. The club have control of the ground floor but have let it to Mr. W. J. Meakin who will fit it up as a first class restaurant, with a bar and dining room, fronting on Seymour Street. One storey of the whole Lefevre Block will be occupied by the rooms for guests. Mr. Meakin will have direction of the club*

*dining room and refreshments, the edibles being taken to the
rooms by means of a heist.*

*Since their organization, the club has held no meetings. Mr.
H. Abbott is the president and Mr. G. R. Major secretary and
treasurer who, with a committee of seven, constitute the officers
for the present year.*

Three months later, on May 3rd, the same newspaper reported
that the Vancouver Club would be informally opened that evening.
Once again the reporter described the rooms on the various floors,
mentioning that they are all "handsomely carpeted" and that the table
in the billiard room cost $900. He went on to say: "The furniture is so
beautifully upholstered and the curtains of the latest style. . . . Rich
pictures of all kinds are hung around the walls, while the chandeliers
are an ornamention in themselves." He suggested that in time it might
vie "in comfort and fame with the great St. James's Club of London," and added that "the club's fittings and furnishings are a great
credit to the energy and enterprise of the gentlemen who have so
energetically and so satisfactorily carried to completion all the
arrangements connected with this organization."

However, evidently some changes had taken place since February. The May newspaper article stated: "Mr. Meakin, who will run the
bar, is to take charge of the whole building. . . ." In the earlier report,
H. Abbott and G.R. Major were mentioned as being president and
secretary–treasurer of the club. In May these two gentlemen remain in
their position and members of the committee are listed as J. C. Keith,
J. M. Browning, F. C. Cotton, A. St.G. Hamersley, R. H. Alexander,
R. P. Cooke and C. Sweeny.

It is unfortunate that no records of this first attempt to form a
club appear to exist, especially as its presence in the Lefevre Block was
so brief. There is a note in Sweeny's diary, dated July 13th, 1890,
stating "a proprietary club, started by Meakin in the Lefevre Block in
May, closed by him on 12th July." The earliest history of the club is in
pamphlet form, written in 1935 by F. M. Chaldecott, one of the
earliest members of the club. His description of the short–lived club is
very brief. He states the club "materialized" early in 1890 when
"arrangements for quarters were made with W.J. Meakin, proprietor
of a restaurant and boarding house . . . situated in the Lefevre Block. .
. ." The contradictions in the newspaper accounts written at the time
with what has been written since leave many questions unanswered.
Chaldecott writes, "Owing to some disagreement with their landlord
the members one morning found themselves 'locked out'. The restaurant took over the cutlery and crockery, on the latter of which was
emblazoned 'Vancouver Club', and same was used in the public
dining room of the restaurant for a number of years afterwards."

Downtown Vancouver, July, 1900. Vancouver Club in centre near the shoreline.
(City Archives)

The mystery surrounding the events between May 1889 when the club was "organized" and mid–July, 1890, when members were 'locked out' from "their" quarters, poses many questions. One wonders if the luxurious furnishings actually belonged to the club, or was there some sort of a rental agreement which, owing to so few members––even if they were prominent––could not be met. Why did the first newspaper report state that the club had reached an agreement with Dr. Lefevre, yet within a few months Mr. Meakin, who originally was to sublet, ends up apparently dominating the scene? If Meakin took over the club's "crockery and cutlery", there is a strong suggestion of unpaid bills, either for meals, wages or rent, or perhaps all three. In any event, the members had their fingers burned, and if the club was to continue, it was apparent that it would have to be properly organized, registered, and provided with a very sound financial base.

There must have been several meetings of the club's membership in the late summer of 1890. The club had not been formally registered and therefore still had no legal existence. As far as is known, there was no constitution, no regulations and no house rules. In fact there was no house, and it appeared that a logical first step to take, was to build a clubhouse and so avoid the humiliation of being evicted or locked out. As a first step a piece of property had to be purchased and, that done, a suitable building erected which would be designed by an architect and built to satisfy the needs of the club.

There was one site which caught the eye of the members at the foot of Hornby Street. It was on a location which gave a sweeping view over the harbour to the snow–capped mountains beyond. To the west lay Stanley Park with its virgin forest while to the east one could look over the harbour for miles up to Second Narrows. Immediately north of the site, but not offering any obstruction to the view, was the new C.P.R. terminus and docks. The selected site was also in a fashionable residential area yet close to the business centre. The club's first historian described it as follows:

> At that date, and for a number of years afterwards, West Hastings Street... was a first class residential district where many of the members resided.... Harry Braithwaite Abbott and family lived in a house built on the north–west corner of Hastings and Howe Streets....
>
> W.F.Salsbury and family resided on the south east corner of Hastings and Hornby Streets..., and David Simpson, manager of The Bank of British North America, lived on the south–west corner of the same streets....
>
> The south–east corner of Hastings and Burrard Streets was occupied by J.D.Townley, and opposite... F.C.Innes, of the firm of Innes and Richards, had a nice residence, later occupied by

William Murray, Manager of The Bank of British Columbia. The north-west corner of Hastings and Burrard Streets (now the site of the Marine Building) was owned by F.M.MacIver-Campbell, who sold same to Edward Mahon....

*   *   *   *

On Seaton [now West Hastings] Street, between Thurlow and Bute Streets, the following members resided or shortly after came there, viz: William McC.Hutchinson, E.P.Davis, Dr.- Duncan Bell-Irving, A.St.G.Hamersley, J.P.McRoberts, J.M.Spinks, Captain C.C.Bennett, C.B.MacNeill, J.P.Nicholls, George McL.Brown... and later F.M.Chaldecott purchased the house of G.C.Webster which... was one of the first houses built in the West End after the fire of 1886.

The site approved, the next thing was to buy it from its owner, the Canadian Pacific Railway. It was decided to approach the president of the company himself, probably the idea of several of the club members who knew him and who felt the direct approach might be the best. On October27th, 1890, the following letter was sent to W.C.Van Horne in Montreal:

Dear Sir:
Several of our prominent citizens have been talking over the very great advantage the city would derive from the foundation of a first class social club. Under these circumstances, a number of us--some forty or fifty--are prepared to advance sufficient capital, $20,000 to $25,000, to put up suitable buildings and purchase a site; and feeling sure you would take a lively interest, and would be anxious to assist us in anything that would be a permanent benefit to Vancouver, we have thought it well to apply to you to give us the plot of ground on Hastings Street, part of Block130, lying between Mr.Ferguson's and Mr.Innes' house, as a site, and we would suggest that, under these circumstances, $50.00 a front foot would be a fair price.
We all feel that we are at a considerable disadvantage as compared with Victoria in this matter. This was particularly noticed during the last season when we had frequent visits from the naval squadron, as well as from European and American travellers, to whom we were unable to offer the advantages offered by Victoria, and there is no doubt a good social club tends to attract and retain visitors and travellers who now rarely pass through the city.
In [the] event of our suggestion meeting with your approval, we suppose you would not mind a portion of the purchase money

remaining out a 6% interest for a few years, until the club gained strength to pay it off.

> *Your obedient servants,*
> *F. C. Cotton, J.C. Keith,*
> *Robert G. Tatlow, James Whetham*

All of the men who signed this letter were interested in its growth and progress. F.Carter Cotton was the publisher of the "Daily News-Advertiser" and Keith, the manager of the Bank of British Columbia. Tatlow, a former militia officer, had first come to the province with Major Strange on a tour of inspection of its defences. At the time the letter was written he was engaged in various financial enterprises as a broker and real estate agent. Later, as a politician, he was to be finance minister under Sir Richard McBride. Dr.Whetham, aside from his professional career, was also interested in business matters.

The letter to Van Horne was a good one and struck a responsive note. He would be aware of the value of a club, and if it would benefit the businessmen of Vancouver, it would benefit the C.P.R. owing to its very large landholding and transportation interests. Unoccupied land and empty freight-cars were the last thing Van Horne wanted. The tremendous costs involved in pushing the railway through the mountains and across the Canadian Shield had to be recovered, and thus anything that would stimulate east-west trade should be encouraged--even a social club.

On December24th, 1890 Van Horne wrote to J.M.Browning, the C.P.R.'s Land Commissioner and, to look ahead, the club's first president. He expressed his sympathy for the idea of a club, but hedged on the suggested price for the lot. He pointed out the considerable depth of the lot, ranging between 215 and 233 feet. He felt that the western section of the lot should fetch between $150 to $175 per foot front, and the eastern portion, somewhat deeper, ought to be valued even higher. However, he did agree that the site could be purchased at around $100 per foot front which took into consideration a building rebate of twenty percent. As far as payment was concerned, Van Horne was prepared to be generous. "If a satisfactory building is to be erected upon it," he wrote, "the trustees will not object to let the whole or greater part of the purchase price stand over a reasonable term of years at 6 percent interest. I don't think they would object to 7 years or even 10 years."

This letter, written the day before Christmas, would probably reach Browning early in 1891--possibly earlier--or about the same time it would take a letter from Montreal to arrive in Vancouver today. In April a meeting of the "Promoters of a new Social Club" was held in the Hotel Vancouver. H.O.Bell-Irving was in the chair. He informed the group of the prospects of obtaining the new site and discussion then turned to the means to be employed to establish a club on a firm foundation. At this meeting a list of names willing to become members was submitted and it was decided that these should be interviewed. If they were interested in promoting the club, a guarantee was to be secured from each "to subscribe for $1000 in shares of a company to be formed, the number of subscribers to be limited to fifty."

The canvass of potential club members was successful. Between forty and fifty men had indicated their strong interest in the previous year. This interest was to be tested by a potential payment of $1,000, a sum one should multiply by about fifteen to appreciate what it would be almost one hundred years later. The intent was not that it would be paid all at once, but rather that each shareholder could be called to pay a portion of it on demand as the payments for the site and building became due. From a strictly financial point of view, it would form a pool of capital deemed necessary to get a club house started.

Within a month, on May7th, a second meeting was held. This, apparently, was a meeting of men who had agreed to become members of the club. They agreed unanimously to form a company known as the Vancouver Club Company Limited. It was to have a capital of $50,000 in fifty shares of $1,000 each. To arrange for the initial organization of the company, the meeting nominated the following trustees: J.M.Browning, John Hendry, David Oppenheimer, J.C.Keith, H.O.Bell–Irving, E.E.Rand and G.G.Mackay.

The trustees acted with dispatch. Early in June the company was registered with the provincial government. In its statement it noted that it was to exist for fifty years, that no shareholder would be held responsible for more than the $1000 share he had subscribed, and that there would be four, not seven, trustees--Mackay, Rand, Oppenheimer and Bell–Irving. The object of the company, in brief, was to buy land, erect a club house, furnish it and carry out all necessary business relating to it. In a word, it was to become the financial agent for the club, a task it would turn over to the Granville Club Co. in due course.

On June19th, two days after the certificate of incorporation had been filed with the provincial government, a meeting of the "Subscribed Chartered Members of the Vancouver Club," as they called themselves, met in Meakin's Restaurant. The club's former quarters had been taken over by the St.George's Club. Evidently the relationship between Meakin and the early members of the Vancouver Club had been patched up, or perhaps the combination of his good food and central location overcame what reluctance might have existed to patronize Meakin's establishment. The club members were anxious to push on with their plans, and at this meeting it was decided to appoint C.O.Wickenden as architect. His charges were not to exceed more than four percent for the cost of the plans and would include his supervision of the construction of the building. He must have been requested to get to the drawing board as quickly as possible, and one can assume, also, that he must have been subjected to numerous suggestions respecting the approximate cost of the club house and what the members would anticipate respecting the functions of the rooms in the building.

It is unlikely that Wickenham, an original club member himself, could have produced the architectural drawings so quickly if he had to cope with the building code standards today. With remarkable energy he was able to have them ready for the General Meeting of Subscribers on July24th. After examining his proposals, and probably after making various changes and amendments, the architect's plans were approved and Wickenham was instructed to call for tenders.

During the Autumn of 1891 and Spring of 1892 there were numerous meetings of the trustees and several of the members themselves. About a month after the architect had called for tenders he had a meeting in his office and described the tenders received. The lowest bid was accepted. On September15th, almost three weeks later, a meeting of subscribed members was called for an evening meeting at the Hotel Vancouver. Those attending were D. Oppenheimer (Chairman) H. T. Ceperley, Thomas Dunn, H.A. Jones, J. M. Browning, B. T. Rogers, J. A. Russell, Captain Powers, H.Bell-Irving, R. Casement, L. G. McPhillips, I. Oppenheimer, W.E. Green, Dr. J. T. Carroll, E. Mahon, A. St.G. Hamersley, E. E. Rand, G.E. Bertaux, G.M. Callender, T. O. Townley, C. O. Wickenden, J. Wullfsohn, and (by proxy) J. C. Keith, O. G. Evan-Thomas, John Campbell, J. T. Williams and C.D. Rand.[1] At this meeting the chairman reported that land had been purchased, plans had been made, tenders called for and, presumably, he informed the group that the trustees favoured the lowest bidder. According to the newspaper report in "The Daily World," "After some discussion the contract was awarded and as soon as details are arranged work will be commenced."

It was also at this meeting that the first directors were elected. These were J. C. Keith, D. Oppenheimer, E. Mahon, H. Bell-Irving and E.E. Rand. Whether these directors replaced the former trustees is not clear. In any event, when they met three days later in the Bank of British Columbia building, David Oppenheimer accepted the position

[1] It is interesting to note that of those listed, only three--Powers, Bertaux and Callender--are not among the names of the Vancouver Club members published as an appendix to its Constitution, Rules and Regulations in 1893.

of President of the company and G. M. Callender was elected Secretary-Treasurer. They decided to ask the subscribed members to pay ten per cent of the capital stock as of October 1st. Additional calls would be made as required and as the preparation of the site and the construction of the club house progressed.

The final cost of the club property itself was estimated at $10,000, and the C.P.R. was generous in that the amount was to be made payable over a period of ten years with a six per cent interest rate. The tender for completing the building by Mr. Cook was $22,452 with $276 for extras. During February 1892 the "Daily News–Advertiser" reported that the foundation of the Vancouver Club building should be completed early in March, and it assumed building would start shortly thereafter.

As it turned out, it would be another year before the building was ready for occupancy, and the reason for this appears to be primarily financial. In October 1891, when the building contract was decided, it was originally given to a Mr. MacKinnon who agreed not to exceed the $23,976 price the directors imposed on him. For some reason it would seem that MacKinnon must have withdrawn his offer during the winter of 1891–92, and as a result the contract was awarded to E. Cook late in March for approximately $1,000 less than MacKinnon. At their October meeting in 1891, the directors had decided to issue a series of first mortgage debentures for a total of $50,000 at an attractive rate of eight per cent, but by the late summer of 1892 the club was running into financial difficulties. It was one thing to offer mortgage debentures, it was another thing to sell them, especially if the building concerned was a club house.

Meanwhile the club house itself was not progressing as quickly as had been hoped. One thing that was needed was to form a club. This decision reached its culmination early in 1893 when the subscribers decided to organize themselves into the Vancouver Club. On March 25th, 1893 they adopted a constitution and agreed on the rules and regulations for club members. It would be interesting to know more about the discussions that went on when the constitution and rules were being drawn up, but there is no record of them. When it was resolved by the subscribers in February 1893 to form a club, J.M. Browning was elected the first president. He had a committee to help him, and it must have been this group which presented the constitution for adoption in March.

It might be advisable to summarize the club's progress at this point even though the club house itself had not opened its doors. It should be remembered that the early records and minutes prior to 1893 are not available. In brief, the Vancouver Club was first mentioned as being organized in 1889 but it was not registered under the province's

The first clubhouse, finished in 1893, showing West Hastings Street with wooden sidewalk and dirt road. *(City Archives)*

"Companies Act" so had no legal existence. What it lacked in legality it made up in drive and enthusiasm. After the "Meakin affair," the men involved decided to purchase land and build their own club house. This decision in itself demanded a legal existance, and thus the Vancouver Club Company Limited Liability, to give its full name, was incorporated on May 27th, 1891 and registered a few days later. This company, with its "subscribed members," continued to exist legally until it was struck off the provincial register of companies on June 7th, 1914. It did not dissolve itself, rather it sunk into desuetude and the provincial registrar of companies struck it off the register since the company officers for years had failed to file any annual report.

The Vancouver Club, as we have seen, was organized and adopted its constitution in March 1893. Its membership was virtually the same as the Vancouver Club Company. The Vancouver Club itself, however, was to lead a thriving existence without bothering to register itself since its finances were being looked after by the company. This, initially, was satisfactory, but early in 1894, as the club was nearing completion, bills were mounting and additional money was needed and not too easy to come by. For example, late in 1893 an approach had been made to the B.C. Land and Investment Co. for a loan of $30,000. Writing for advice to its office in Victoria, the manager of the Vancouver office wrote in part:

> *I believe Mr. D. Oppenheimer, on behalf of the Club, has already opened negotiations with you for the loan. They are very anxious to know as soon as possible if the matter will go through and at what rate of interest.*
>
> *For many reasons, of course, the loan would be very desirable. There are some good names in connection with the concern and it would no doubt help business in many ways. . . . On the other hand I do not consider the property very first class security in itself, [and] should be afraid that it is too soon for Vancouver to support well an institution of this kind, but by requiring something additional in the way of a bond with ten or fifteen good names, it perhaps might be good enough.*

The route chosen to raise capital and secure loans was for the members of the club to create the Granville Club Company Limited Liability. It, in essence, was to be the new fiscal agent for the Vancouver Club and was to remain as such for many years to come. It was incorporated on March 8th, 1894 and continued its existence until 1928 when the Vancouver Club took over complete charge of its financial affairs. The purpose of the Granville Club was to borrow and raise money, to acquire land and all rights pertaining to it, to build and maintain a club house, to acquire all manner of personal property, to obtain necessary franchises, licences and so forth needed by the club and to agree with, by mutual agreement, a body--the Vancouver Club--for the carrying on of a club.

To raise money, the Granville Club issued debentured stock for a total of $100,000, divided into 1,000 shares at $100 each. Each member who joined the Vancouver Club was required to purchase one share. It was to hold title of the Vancouver Club's land and property. It would execute any mortgage for monies borrowed on the club's property. Looking ahead, it could and did demand from the Vancouver Club an accounting. The Vancouver Club paid rent to the Granville Club (and was ticked off if it fell in arrears), and if the Vancouver Club wanted to make certain changes in the club house, the executive of the Granville Club wanted to hear about it. When the Vancouver Club wanted to buy additional land, the Granville Club bought it for them.

It was a complicated way of carrying out the financial affairs of the club, but there was rarely any friction because the executive of the Granville Club were all members of the Vancouver Club and not infrequently were on the General Committee as well. Its creation served the purpose in 1894. In 1907 the legal relationship between the two clubs was brought to the Supreme Court of British Columbia to clarify the rights of the Vancouver Club, but it would be another twenty-one years before the Granville Club, by this time little more than a name, closed its books and officially handed over to the Vancouver Club all its financial responsibilities.

By the Spring of 1894 the club house was nearing completion. In March the first annual meeting of the members was held there at which time the president announced that the building would be ready for occupation by the end of May. A large amount of money had been spent furnishing the club house. President Browning estimated the cost of the grounds, building and furnishings at $60,000. The property itself, legally conveyed by the C.P.R. to the Granville Club on April 5th, 1894, cost the members $12,500 or $125 per front foot. It straddled part of Lots 3 and 4 in Block 16, a subdivision of Lot 541, and ran an average depth of about 225 feet. If the cost of the building remained close to the estimated $23,000--and this is rather doubtful --the cost of furnishing the club must have been almost as much as it cost to build the club. In 1901, the Granville Club figures estimated the real estate and buildings as about $47,000 and the furnishings at a little over $9,000. Whatever the actual price when the members occupied the club in the Spring of 1894, there can be little doubt that the 75 members who attended the first annual meeting in their new home must have been well pleased. There may have been a dirt road and a plank sidewalk outside, but once through the arched entrance one entered into a different world.

At this general meeting, Browning was re-elected president. According to the club's constitution, the president, vice-president and treasurer were to be elected annually. There was to be a General Committee of nine members, three of whom would retire in rotation. Thus, to quote the original constitution, "The three members elected in 1894 shall hold office for three years, and of the other six members, three shall be selected by the Committee to retire at the Annual Meeting, 1895, and the remaining three shall retire at the Annual Meeting, 1896."

With the club built, furnished and new staff getting accustomed to their work, it was natural for the members not only to invite their friends (and possible future members) to the club, but once things were in place and running smoothly, it was decided to have a ball. The price was set at $7.50 which allowed the member to bring two ladies, but did not include the price of wine served at the table. This glamorous affair occurred on August 10th. Many years later the balls given by the club were recalled by both men and women who, by that time, were in their fifties or sixties. Through their descriptions to newspaper reporters about the festivities at the club at the turn of the century and prior to the Great War, one can capture something of the atmosphere of the time. In January 1930, one reporter wrote:

> *A glimpse of the guest list for any of the affairs held at the old Vancouver Club reveals, naturally, the names of innumerable men of affairs. But, more intriguing from the social standpoint, are the many girls "among those attending," who are now some of our most prominent hostesses.*
>
> *One visualizes them, in their picturesque frocks, being just as much 'belles of the ball' as their own attractive daughters are.*
>
> *There is a breath of fragrance about the visions those olden times in Vancouver, comparatively new town as it was, conjure up. There was Hastings street with its muddy dirt road, along which the cabs would roll in an effort to be dignified before a building so austere. There were the gentlemen who wore frock coats and side-whiskers, and who were moulding the infancy of a town still in its clumsy days of early growth. And then there were the women themselves--women of the gay nineties--who decked themselves in all their frills and furbelows, whose eyes shone the brighter and whose excitement was the keener, for any one of those rare and gala nights when the clubhouse doors were thrown open to guests and the ladies were allowed to storm the fortress.*
>
> *What hosts they were--those Vancouver Club members of some three decades ago! How they excelled themselves to come up to the expectations of the most imaginative lady guest.*
>
> *Usually there was a mid-summer dance, held early in July, and a mid-winter dance on New Year's Eve. At these elaborate affairs some prominent visitors in the city were usually entertained, and it added to the thrill for the ladies that the young naval officers of ships were almost certain to be invited.*
>
> *On many a scene of splendor have those old walls, now half demolished, looked down. How they must have thrilled to see a young gallant handing out his lady fair from a high-wheeled vehicle, with prancing, well-groomed horses in front. Gay parties were always in a setting of the utmost decorative elegance--here a complete bower of roses, there a country garden, a courtyard, or a fairyland world in itself. It is often said now by those who were fortunate enough to attend these functions, that, never since, have their decorative schemes been equalled in Vancouver. And that was the whole thing--souvenirs, wines, champagne, flowers for the ladies--everything was included for the modest admission charge of $5.*
>
> *Will ever an ivy-covered building, in all its wisdom, know again the ravishing beauty of a great bouquet of roses embalmed in a huge block of gleaming ice? Will ever a Vancouver ballroom be privileged to see a masquerade such as the Vancouver Club*

gave years ago, when a Turkish atmosphere, with all its alluring romance, was reproduced for the guests--even silk-draped divans adding their charm?

The "Vancouver Sun" reporter, writing on the club's social activities at the turn of the century, gave his description of the late Victorian and Edwardian parties at the club as follows:

Every aspiring mother in the province believed her life's ambition satisfied if [her] daughter made her debut at one of the Vancouver Club's balls during mid summer or at the Christmas holiday season. In those days to cross the threshold of the Vancouver Club meant social recognition.

Through the eyes of some of the "old timers" who have contributed to the making of this article, one can vision those festivities. Apart from their significance as a community event, they were brilliant.

There is the summer affair, held at the end of June. The night is starlit, warm and there is just enough breeze to cool excited brows. The facade of the building is festooned with flowers. On the lawn at the rear, looking out on Burrard Inlet, a great tent has been set up. Beneath the canvas and under tthe watchful eyes of Rod McLeod, a battery of stewards prepare for the evening.

Theirs is an important task. They are polishing glasses and tenderly placing champagne bottles in position. For this is a ball of the nineties when the hip flask is not yet with us.

The cabs are arriving, their wheels deepening the ruts in the soft bed of Hastings Street. Coach horses paw impatiently as the guests descend. Hoop-skirted debutantes, accompanied by their chaperones, trip up the walk to the club's doorway. Young bloods of the town with gardenias in their buttonholes, men of the army and navy in glittering dress uniforms. The girls are a-flutter at the sight of the naval officers, for their coming from Victoria is indeed an event.

The hilarity starts. Its note quickens through the evening. It has not diminished as the guests depart in the dawn.

But what of the club building itself? There are numerous photographs of it, but once more we must rely on a newspaper reporter who describes the interior of it a week after the club's first ball.

THE VANCOUVER CLUB
A Credit to the City both in Design and Finish Description of the Arrangements and Furnishings of the Interior--Quiet Elegance Combined with Comfort

"The cut of the Vancouver Club building, which appears in this issue, shows the Hastings Street elevation, the steps leading up to the main entrance which faces that thoroughfare. This

institution is one of the main things in Vancouver that have gone on with a rush. The idea originated in the minds of conservative men of a class who want a thing good and who are willing to have the patience to abide their time in order to secure the fulfilment of their desires. When it is said that such men as J. M. Browning, H. Abbott and D. and I. Oppenheimer were among those who originated the idea, the force of the foregoing remark will be felt. The Club is now an accomplished fact and is open to those eligible from this time forward. In fact, the writer has been told that a ball for members and friends was held in the club rooms a few evenings ago, but that is only hearsay.

"The building may be judged as regards architecture from the picture. It is club style since it was designed with an eye single to having it answer well the purpose for which it is intended. A run through the interior will convince anyone that this object has been attained. Refined elegance, combined with solid comfort, reigns everywhere. Why that term solid comfort is so popular is a question, and it is also a question if it suits exactly in this case because the things most suggestive of comfort in the institution under consideration are not exactly solid. They are the soft, yielding carpets that make one feel like walking on air, and the big, leather covered chairs that soothe one into remaining longer than his good wife may deem strictly proper.

"Entrance to the building as stated is made from Hastings Street. Facing the door is a huge fireplace that when logged up on a winter's night will send a thrill of pleasure through all who enter. Over it is a noble stag's head, which will prove a splendid suggestion for tales of hunting prowess among the members of the long winter evenings when the toddy is steaming in the mugs.

"To get a proper idea of the interior of the building, let us, as Steward Holmes suggested to the reporter, start at the ground floor and work up.

"On that floor is situated the billiard room. Here are found two Burroughs and Watts' English tables, with all the latest improvements. The room is also supplied with the famous Robertson championship cues, with numerous lacquered cue holders for members who wish to have a tool for their own special use. This apartment is fitted up with both gas and electric light, with the most improved designs of shades over the tables. Leather cushioned settees provide comfortable accommodation for spectators. Adjoining is a lavatory and other conveniences. Just at the rear of the billiard room is the bowling alley, finished with cushions, pins and balls by Reid Bros. & Co. of Toronto. The floor was laid by Para & McPhalen of this city, and a truer surface could not be asked for. This firm has also done all the other carpenter work in connection with the alley. Access is gained from both the billiard room and the bowling alley to the bowling green at the rear, which is not ready for use, but which promises to *be the finest on the coast. Three feet of the surface was taken off and refilled with choice earth, the upper foot of which has been screened. This has been sown with a combination of grasses which experience has shown to provide the best and most lasting surface. In other apartments on this floor are to be found the cellar, the cold storage room, the furnace room, and a couple of other rooms which may be used for storage and other purposes. The hot water heating system has been put in, and the furnace will only require filling twice or thrice a day.*

"Passing up again to the first floor, there is found to the right of the entrance a reception room. This is furnished with arm chairs and settees covered with a greenish brown silk pile with Wilton carpet to match and a cosy fireplace. To the left of the entrance is the writing room, which is neatly and appropriately furnished. On this floor the other smaller rooms are the wine room and a cloak room and lavatory. There is no bar whereat drinks will be served, but the wine room is fitted up with all the modern conveniences appertaining to the dispensing of hilarity water in its multiform combinations. Chief among the fittings of this room is the refrigerator, which was built by Robertson & Hackett specially for the Vancouver Club, on designs by Steward Holmes. It is exceedingly commodious--a good feature--and works on the cold storage principle. Electric bells connect this department with all the other rooms, and all the corners of all the other rooms in the house, so that all a member has to do is to agitate the annunciator and convey to the mercury, who will respond with what particular brand of coffin nail he desires, and it will be brought him on a silver tray done up in the highest style. The rear half of this room is given up to the reading room, and the fathers of the club have certainly done everything that could be done to cultivate a literary taste among the members. The room is spacious, comfortable, bright; is prettily carpeted and most comfortably furnished. The large leather covered chairs, which are the prominent feature of the furnishings, are of the kind that a man of any shape and any degree of avoirdupois can take comfort in. All the latest periodicals and leading newspapers are on file.

"On the second floor, which is reached by way of a wide and softly carpeted stairway, are the card rooms, two in number. These are fitted in the ordinary way and may be used for entertainments with Jack and his sister Kitty, or for the more sober game of whist. There is also on this floor the main dining room. This, like the reading and billiard room, is 43 x 23 feet. It is carpeted in a medium shade in keeping with the wood work and oak furniture. It, like the reading room, opens on to a wide balcony that commands a magnificent view of the harbor. This balcony on a summer's evening will be one of the most desirable spots imaginable, and with a genial companion and a choice Havana, it will be like a taste of the bachelor's idea of Elysium.

On this floor is also a private dining room fitted in oak. Each of the dining rooms has a separate entrance from the kitchen which is also on this floor. The ventilation of the kitchen is so arranged that it will be impossible for any of the odors therefrom to reach any other parts of the house. Connected with the kitchen is a pastry room and a complete scullery department, each of which is fitted with all the latest improvements to secure cleanliness and perfect sanitation.

"The third floor contains on the one side the bedrooms and bathrooms for help, and on the other side the bedrooms and bathrooms for the members who choose to live in the building or for persons who are accepted entirely as the guest of the club.

"From the wine room, lifts run to the top of the building, so that no time will be lost in serving orders. The salvers, beer mugs, etc., are all English electro plate and bear the monogram of the club.

"The architect of this creditable structure was C. O. Wickenden. It has a frontage of 74 feet and a depth of nearly 53 feet, exclusive of the balconies. The site could hardly be improved on, and as a whole from a club habitue's standpoint, as near perfection has been attained as can be expected in matters mundane."

During the first two decades of its existence, the Vancouver Club flourished. By 1896 club membership had increased to 206 resident members and 12 supernumary members, the latter mostly officers from the passenger liners which had regular calls into Vanouver. By 1908 resident membership had increased to 314, and by the beginning of the Great War, the club was bursting at the seams with 414 members. Added to that was the number of non-resident members. The latter, initially, were members whose permanent place of residence was at least ten miles from the city of Vancouver. They had to pay the initial entrance fee of $25, but since it was anticipated as non-residents they would not make as much use of the club, their annual contribution was only $16, half that of a resident. By 1908 there were 117 of them, and by 1912 there were 166. The decision to extend the distance from the city to 25 miles to enjoy the lower non-resident rates was probably based on the fact that steadily improving transportation facilities were making it easier to travel between a member's residence and the club.

The increase in membership also reflected the tremendous growth of Vancouver during these two decades. When the club was in the process of formation, Vancouver had a population estimated at 15,000. By 1905 it had reached 45,000, and then doubled its population within five years. By the outbreak of the Great War the city was more than 130,000. This increase was due partly to natural birth, partly to amalgamation but in large measure to immigration. The advent of the Klondike Gold Rush in 1896 was a tremendous stimulus to business. One of the city's men's wear shops, Chapman's, immediately hung a banner across the entrance which read "Outfits for Klondike". Other businesses were doing the same and whether the prospector wanted a woolen coat or camping equipment, it could be obtained in Vancouver. In the years that followed there were signs of growth everywhere. By 1897 the B.C. Electric Railway was incorporated and four years later work was underway on the construction of the city's first major library. A year later Charles Woodward was building a large department store on Hastings Street. By 1905 not only had the Great Northern Railway reached the city but street lighting was extended, pay telephones had been in operation for almost six years and H. Hooper's Taxi service was well launched. By 1909, two years after the incorporation of the Vancouver Stock Exchange, the first Granville Street bridge was completed. A month later the city's first ambulance went on a test run during which it ran over and killed an American tourist. The city's first "skyscraper", the Dominion Trust Building, was being completed on the corner of Hastings and Cambie Streets and in the following year construction began on the courthouse and the Vancouver Block. The C.P.R. began to build Piers "A" and "B" which club members could watch from their vantage point on Hastings Street. By 1913 Kingsway, the major road link between Vancouver and New Westminster was completed, construction had started on a new Vancouver Hotel and the World Building, touted as the tallest in the British Empire, was ready for occupation.

The involvement of members of the Vancouver Club in the growth of Vancouver in these, and indeed later, decades was pervasive. Between 1906 and 1913, for example, F. C. Wade, Dr. A. Monro, F. R. Russell, J. Ellis, W.Malkin, W. Hart McHarg, W. Godfrey, E. Buchan, J. D. Stuart and R.H.H. Alexander--all club members--were either presidents or vice-presidents of the Canadian Club. Seven members--C. D. Rand, R. B. Johnson, W. F. Germaine, C. Loewen, F. J. Proctor, H. E. Robertson and J. Waghorn--were among the founders of the Vancouver Stock Exchange. On the Vancouver Board of Trade twenty of the club's members served as presidents or vice-presidents between 1887 and 1914, while between 1886 and 1929, four Vancouver Club members--D.Oppenheimer, C.Tisdall, F. Buscombe and W. Malkin--became mayors of the city.

Among the most powerful institutions involved in developing the city was the Canadian Pacific Railway. It was closely tied in with the Bank of Montreal and the Royal Trust Co. When it moved its tracks into the city, the C.P.R., as mentioned earlier, had been given massive land grants which included a good slice of what is now the central business district of Vancouver together with much of Fairview, Shaughnessy, Little Mountain, Oakridge, Arbutus Ridge, Kerrisdale and Marpole. The C.P.R.'s land commissioner, J. M. Browning, was not only a founding member of the Vancouver Club but served as its president in 1893 and 1894. The general superintendant of the C.P.R.'s Pacific Division was H.B. Abbott who served as club president from 1898 to 1901. The treasurer of the railway's Pacific Division, William Salsbury, was president during 1911 and 1912. It was the C.P.R., as has been seen, that owned the property on which the Vancouver Club had been built.

To some extent the C.P.R. also determined where many of the club members resided. As the city began to develop, the West End became the preferred area for businessmen. Here they built their large houses on spacious lots with carriage houses, tennis courts and gardens. By 1908 almost three-quarters of the club members lived in the West End, about 13 per cent resided between Hamilton and Burrard Streets and others were scattered across Kitsalino, Mount Pleasant, Fairview and elsewhere. The C.P.R. opened Shaughnessy Heights in 1912 and there was a massive movement to this preferred area which started almost immediately. By 1914, although 244 members were still living in the West End, 76 had moved to Shaughnessy. This migration was to continue after the Great War and, of course, as the city grew, and especially with the completion of the Lion's Gate Bridge, members' choice of their residential area tended to spread further afield.

From the very beginning of the club, its members frequently have been referred to as "prominent citizens", "men of influence", "wealthy businessmen" and so forth when reference has been made to them in the newspapers. It might be interesting at this point to select some of the early members and attempt to outline their origins and background as well as some of their accomplishments, particularly as they relate to both the city and the province.

David Oppenheimer, a well-known entrepreneur in British Columbia, worked hard to bring the Vancouver Club into existence. Born in 1834, in Germany, he and his brothers immigrated to the United States in 1848. They came to British Columbia ten years later during the gold rush and set up a dry goods business in Yale to serve the Fraser River gold miners. As gold strikes were made further inland their business flourished, and later they moved to Victoria. In 1855 David and his brothers, Isaac and Solomon, moved to Vancouver to establish a wholesale grocery business and soon they were involved in various enterprises ranging from real estate to brick building.

David Oppenheimer has been called the "father of Vancouver". Both he and his brother, Isaac, were elected city aldermen in 1887 and David became mayor in 1888, a post he held for the next four years.

He served as mayor without salary, entertaining guests at his own expense and using his own office as the City Hall. As mayor he organized the water supply service of the city, built sidewalks, helped establish Stanley Park, organized the Parks Board, built bridges to improve transportation within the city and advertised the city far and wide. He personally guaranteed funds for the construction of the first YMCA in Vancouver as well as the Alexandra Orphanage. He donated part of his own extensive land holdings for public parks, and in a variety of other ways did a great deal for the growing city which he helped to mold.

Oppenheimer's business interests were wide ranging. He was president of the Board of Trade, of the Vancouver Improvement Co., of the Burrard Inlet and Pitt Meadows Canal Co., of the B. C. Dredging and Dyke Co., and of the Vancouver Shipbuilding, Sealing and Trading Co., of the B. C. Exhibition Assn., of the B. C. Fruit Growers Assn., of the B. C. Agricultural Assn., and of the Burrard Inlet Rowing Club. His brother, Isaac, was president of the Vancouver Club for two years (1895-96). David Oppenheimer died in 1897 and it is quite fitting that the city decided to erect a monument to him near the entrance to Stanley Park.

Another club member, and later club president for four years (1898-1901) was H. B. Abbott. Born in 1829 in Abbottsford, Quebec, he became an engineer under the tutelage of the famous Colonel Gzowski. As a young man he was deeply involved in pioneer railroads in Eastern Canada. In fact when the American Civil War broke out, and British regiments were landed at Saint John, N.B., it was Abbott's task to see to the troops' transportation from Saint John to Riviere du Loup before these cities were connected by rail. Three years after he joined the Canadian Pacific Railway in 1882 he was faced with a somewhat similar task. The Riel Rebellion had broken out and Abbott, by that time, was in charge of completing the construction of the main line west of Sudbury. It was Abbott who arranged the transportation of Canadian forces over uncompleted sections of the railway, sometimes using horses and sleighs to carry them over the ice until they reached the railhead to Winnipeg.

Abbott first came to British Columbia in 1885. He was present at the ceremony when Lord Strathcona drove the last spike at Craigellachie connecting the eastern and western sections of the C.P.R. and in January 1886 he was appointed the railway's General Superintendant of the Pacific Division.

It was Abbott who let the contract for the clearing of the new townsite of Vancouver, and during the next decade he was involved in supervising and constructing a variety of pioneer railway endeavours which helped to develop the province. There may not be a statue of

C.P.R. Station, c.1895, showing early tracks and docks.   *(City Archives)*

him in the city, but one of the busiest streets in downtown Vancouver bears his name as does a mountain in the Selkirks and a town in the Fraser Valley.

Another early member of the club was James F. Garden. Born in New Brunswick in 1847 of United Empire Loyalist stock, he became a surveyor. Apparently he had been surveying on the prairies when the Riel Rebellion broke out so he joined the Intelligence Corps formed from Dominion Land Surveyors by Captain J. S. Dennis. He was wounded at the Battle of Batoche in 1885 and in the following year came to Vancouver to practice surveying. With two partners, the firm of Garden, Hermon and Berwell did a lot of the primary surveying in and around the city, including the first survey for construction of the B.C. Electric Railway. Both Garden Drive and Garden Park are named after him.

Aside from his work as a civil engineer, Garden was elected mayor of Vancouver in 1898, remaining in office for three years. He also represented Vancouver as a member of the legislative assembly for nine years.

A Vancouver Club member who had a remarkable range of interests and who worked for the betterment of Vancouver was

William F. Salsbury who was elected club president during 1911 and 1912. Born in England in 1847 (and it might be noted that about one-third of the club's membership in this era were of British birth) he came to Canada in 1870 after working with a British railway. After working for the Grand Trunk Railway, he joined the C.P.R. and came to British Columbia with the first through-train in 1886. He became treasurer of the C.P.R.'s Pacific Division, secretary of the Esquimalt and Nanaimo Railway and vice-president of the Columbia and Kootenay Railway. He was one of the pioneers in organizing what was to become the B.C. Telephone Co.

Aside from these and other business interests, Salsbury's influence was widespread in other areas. He served as city alderman for two years and later was president of the Board of Trade. He played a major role in securing Stanley Park for the city and later pushed through the construction of a road around the park. He was influential in the creation of the Brockton Point Athletic Grounds and helped to organize the Vancouver Rowing Club. He was a founding member of the Vancouver General Hospital, was chairman of its board for years, and held the same position with the Tranquille Sanitorium. A devout Anglican, he worked energetically to build Christ Church Cathedral on Georgia Street. The editorial in the Vanocuver "News-Herald" put it nicely when commenting on his services in 1938: "Mr. Salsbury needs no statue to keep his memory green. Vancouver itself is his monument."

One enterprising young man who was among the early members of the club was B. T. Rogers. An American, he went to work in the sugar business in his teens. In due course he came to Vancouver and was struck with the possibilities of establishing a sugar refinery in the city. The combination of importing the raw material by sea, refining the sugar, and shipping it by rail to a growing market in Western Canada seemed to be a profitable venture. The city wanted the refinery, various executive members of the C.P. Railway were willing to venture the capital, and young Rogers was able to have the plant in operation by 1891. His enterprise flourished and expanded into the largest refinery in Western Canada.

During its first two decades, a number of club members resided in Victoria. Most were members of the capital city's Union Club but had full membership in the Vancouver Club as well. Frank S. Barnard was in this category. His father had come to the colony to establish the famous Barnard Express which played a major role in supplying the gold miners during the gold rushes. Young Frank, as a boy, could remember seeing the Royal Engineers come to Yale when they were helping to build the road to the Cariboo. After being educated in

Ontario, Barnard returned to British Columbia where he entered his father's business.

His interest in transportation, together with his appreciation of Vancouver's potential growth, led him to form the Consolidated Railway Co., which later became the B.C. Electric Railway Co. As president of the former and managing director of the latter, he played a major role in establishing a transit system which materially helped in the growth of the city. He was president of other firms both in Victoria and Vancouver. Shortly after the outbreak of the Great War he was appointed Lieutenant–Governor of the province, a position he held for an unusually long term. He was created a knight in 1918 in recognition of his services to the province. He was the first member of the club to receive the vice–regal appointment in British Columbia.

Among the members of the Vancouver Club at the turn of the century, there were probably few who knew the province as well as Henry J. Cambie. Born in Ireland in 1836, he came to Canada as a 16 year old and began working for Eastern Canadian railroads. He became a surveyor and construction engineer. He first visited Vancouver in 1874. As he said later "the coach brough us from Westminster through the tall timber which had been corduroyed for a great part of the way to Hastings where a small steamer met and took us first to Moodyville and then to Hastings Mill. These two mills, with their yards, comprised all the improvements then existing on the harbour of Vancouver, each having a clearing around the mill of two or three acres."

During the 1870's Cambie began a series of explorations and surveys on the mainland. One of his main duties was to find a terminal site for the projected cross–Canada railway. It was a challenging task, but it was largely due to his work that the C.P.R. reached Port Moody and Vancouver.

Cambie was given the job of constructing the Fraser River Canyon section of the railway, possibly the most difficult secton of the entire line. "Quite a stretch of it," he recalled later, "was laid out by a very small portion of our engineering staff, consisting of two sailors who strung ropes from rock to rock or from tree to tree, and a few engineers who, steadying themselves with these ropes, went along on their bare feet to lay out the work." Cambie, of course, was one of the engineers, and with the surveying done he directed the blasting, bridging and tunnelling which followed. He, like Abbott, was another club member who attended the ceremony of driving the last spike marking the completion of the railroad. Shortly after he was appointed Chief Engineer of the Pacific Division and when the townsite of Vancouver was being laid out, a street was named after him. He moved to Vancouver and built a home on the corner of Thurlow and Georgia

Streets. Cambie was also one of the men instrumental in building Christ Church Cathedral and when he died after serving as a consulting engineer for many years, a marble tablet was placed in the church which read: "The last and one of the greatest of the pathfinders of the new Dominion. His name is inseparably identified with the construction of the Canadian Pacific Railway through the Rocky Mountains." In 1957 the Engineering Institute of Canada placed another metal plaque in his memory in the main station of the C.P.R., just a stone's throw from the Vancouver Club. It was a well deserved tribute.

Cambie was a good friend of one of the founders of the club, Henry O. Bell-Irving, who also played a considerable role in the development of Vancouver and the province. Bell-Irving was born in Scotland in 1856, qualified as an engineer in Germany, and with his brother came to Canada where, in 1882, he joined the Canadian Pacific Railway. He was involved in the hard work of pushing the railway through the Rocky Mountains, and it is claimed that he was the man who posted the sign "The Great Divide" when the site was determined by the surveyors. With the eastern section of the line completed, Bell-Irving shouldered his pack to walk the 50-mile gap to the western section still under construction. It was at a work camp that he met Cambie. Bell-Irving continued on to the coast, was robbed on the Cariboo Trail, and arrived in Granville in 1885 with only his surveying instruments.

In Vancouver he established himself as an architect in partnership with Walter Graveley, another club member. When the fire of 1886 destroyed his drawing instruments, Bell-Irving went into the merchandising business with R.G. Tatlow, who was to be an early club member and R. P. Patterson. It was through this export-import enterprise that Bell-Irving became involved in the export of sockeye salmon. This, in turn, led to the formation of the Anglo-British Columbian Packing Co. with its headquarters in London but with H. Bell-Irving and Co. Ltd. as its managing agents in Vancouver. It was one of the first and in its day the largest of the salmon canning companies in the province.

While Bell-Irving was bringing canneries in British Columbia, Alaska and Washington under the wing of ABC Packing Co., he was also involved in other business interests. He served as president of the Vancouver Board of Trade for two years, served as a city alderman, promoted the formation of the 72th Regiment (Seaforth Highlanders), was a commodore of the Yacht Club and worked hard to establish the Vancouver Club.

Henry's brother, Duncan Bell-Irving, was trained as a scientist in Germany and later took his medical degree in London. He came to Vancouver in 1884 and was the medical officer at Hastings Mill for a short time. He took up permanent residence in Vancouver in 1888 and later became closely associated with his brother's firm. Both men were active in the growing community. Duncan became chairman of the Medical Association and organized the first Rifle Association in Vancouver. He became president of the St. Andrew's and Caledonian Society and of the Vancouver Pipers Association. He was instrumental in the formation of what became the Jericho Golf Club and his efforts on behalf of the Vancouver Club resulted in his election in 1902 for a three year term as its president. Descendants of both men continued to be active in the club--and still are today.

* * * *

The early members of the Vancouver Club, and only a few have been mentioned here, came from a variety of backgrounds. A considerable number were born and educated either in Eastern Canada or Great Britain. There were few native Vancouverites, and the obvious reason for that, of course, is that the club was formed so shortly after the city itself was founded. A club rule stated that no person could become a member until he was 21 years of age, so even the youngest member would have to be born in 1872 in Vancouver even to be considered as a "native son" when the club was formed.

As one might expect in a city that was expanding by leaps and bounds, many club members were associated with each other in various business enterprises. At the same time there could be and were keen business rivalries among members. But business was not the main aim of the club, then or now. It was basically a home away from home, a place where one could relax, enjoy good food and service, meet friends, indulge in some modest sports, and entertain acquaintances or visitors from abroad. One could anticipate in the club a code of conduct, dress and behaviour which, added to the opportunity to meet new and interesting friends, gave the club an ambience which made membership attractive to an increasing number of men.

CHAPTER II

A NEW HOME AND A NEW CENTURY

During the first two decades of the club's existence the pace of the world seemed to quicken. The death of Queen Victoria in 1901 not only marked the close of what has been termed the Victorian era but it ushered in a century of tremendous growth and development. Some of the club members had taken part in a few of the wars and skirmishes that marked her reign. There were veterans of the Riel Rebellion, and several young men, such as Victor Spencer, were members-to-be who had recently returned from the Boer War. The age of iron and steam was changing the transportation systems both on land and at sea, and the comparatively new internal combustion engine was introducing even more changes every year.

Although railways and steamships were instrumental in making Vancouver a burgeoning metropolis, new inventions and technological advances would have their impact as well. In the year the club was formed, Henry Ford, built his first automobile. Two years later Marconi invented wireless telegraphy and the club was five years old when Count von Zeppelin built his first airship. Several of the oldest members of the club today were in their pre–school years in 1903 when the Wright brothers flew a powered aeroplane. In the following year work began on digging the Panama Canal. Its completion was to have a beneficial effect on the growth of Vancouver's trade and served as another stimulus to the city's growth. In 1909 and 1911, respectively, club members would read in their newspapers about Peary reaching the North Pole and Amundsen reaching the South Pole. Scientists were beginning to write about radio waves and physicists were theorizing astounding concepts capped by Albert Einstein's general theory of relativity in 1915.

In Vancouver there were signs of progress everywhere. Electric tramways were extending their lines and more people were getting telephones. The Vancouver High School affiliated with McGill University to become Vancouver College––the origins of the University of British Columbia. The C.P.R., having pushed its rails across the country, began to be linked with feeder lines which tapped rich resources of ore and timberland in the interior and allowed the produce from orchards and farms to be shipped to the coast. Labour unions were flexing their muscles and in 1909 there was a strike of longshoremen who wanted thirty–five cents an hour for day shift and forty cents for the night shift.

Members of the Vancouver Club not only took part in the growth of the city but many helped to generate that growth. Sometimes progress came a little too close for comfort. In January 1910, for example, the club secretary "was instructed not to sign the petition now in circulation asking the City Council to favourably recommend to the B.C. Electric Railway Co. the running of streetcars on Hastings and Burrard Streets." The reason, presumably, was to avoid the noise of the tramcars disturbing club members and, perhaps worse, having a tramcar stop by the club house where people would line up.

Inside the clubhouse itself one can glimpse from the old Committee Minutes a little bit of the members' interests. Normally the club does not contribute to charities or to appeals of any kind. It was felt that it was up to the individual members to decide what they wished to contribute and what institution or causes they wished to support. This policy was circumvented in 1908 when word reached the city of a disastrous fire in Fernie, a town in the interior of the province, which left many families destitute. A contribution to the Fernie Relief Fund from club members was wired to the mayor of Fernie to help alleviate the distressed citizens.

From the earliest years, club members were interested in sports. Some were instrumental in establishing the Vancouver Rowing Club, for example, and among those promoting the Vancouver Lawn Tennis Club were C. Gardiner Johnson, H. J. Crombie, R. G. Tatlow, J. H. Senkler, Richard Marpole, the Malkin brothers, the Bell–Irvings, C. J. Marani, Andrew Jukes and A. P. Horne. Within the confines of the club there was a much used bowling alley which cost members five cents a game. This room, with a bar close by, continued in use until 1905 when pressure for additional space led to certain rearrangements. The servants' rooms on the top floor were converted into bedrooms for members. The bowling equipment was sold and the bowling alley was converted into servants' quarters. Lawn bowling behind the club was initiated about this time and, in 1908, the charge was ten cents per player per game. A squash racquet court was used frequently, one of the rules being that "strangers could not use the Racquet Court unless they had been entertained at lunch or dinner by a member." Later, when the ballroom was built, two members asked permission of the Committee to establish a fencing class there. The Committee agreed, but later (March 1909) warned the enthusiasts of the epee that the fencing class was for members only. A request that the ballroom be used as a minature shooting range was turned down.

The card rooms were always popular and remained so for over half a century. In the original "Rules and Regulations" of the club there was a no gambling rule which read:

> *No game of hazard shall be played in the club. Whist shall not be played for any higher stakes than one quarter of a dollar points; other games may be played for limited stakes; the limits of stakes to be fixed by the Committee. No bet on any game of cards or billiards shall exceed one dollar.*

How often that rule was quietly broken over the years it is impossible to say, and if a group of members wanted a private game, they could rent a small card room for one dollar a day. It seemed to be a common practice to continue the game far into the night and even the most tactful servant had difficulty getting the members to leave. Was it really midnight? Surely the servant's watch must be half an hour fast. The General Committee tried to solve the problem in January 1902 by passing the resolution:

> *. . . that the Hall Clock be the official time for the Club and that all members must be out of the Club by one o'clock (or twelve on Sunday evening) otherwise they will be fined two and a half dollars. If not out by two o'clock they will be fined an extra five*

*dollars and if not out by three o'clock each member will be fined
ten dollars per head.*

Billiards was popular, too; so much so that by 1905 there was a
request made to the General Committee for two markers to be on duty
between three and seven o'clock rather than one. That the Committee
agreed is some indication of the number of pool, snooker, pyramids
and billiards players in the club. As far as is known, the first challenge
cup (in this case for pyramids) within the club originated in the billiard
room.

The card players, in time, began to outnumber the billiard players and as the membership increased, so did the demand for additional
space. Four men playing a game of billiards would take up the same
floor space as twelve members at three card tables. In 1909, the
secretary was authorized to get another card table and place it in the
billiard room, and two years later a motion was passed that the private
dining room, when not engaged, could be used as a card room. A
month later, in January 1912, the General Committee passed a motion
stating that the silent reading room and the entire north end of the
billiard room could be used by the card players. The secretary had his
office shifted to the basement while his former office was made into
the silent reading room.

Space was becoming a problem in all parts of the club. One of the
early traditions of the club, for example, was to have a ball. The first
one, as has been seen, was held in August 1894 but as the club's first
historian put it,

> *In subsequent years the Annual Ball was held on the First of
> July in order to entertain the Admiral and Officers of His Maj-
> esty's Fleet stationed at Esquimalt, when the Squadron visited
> Vancouver during the Dominion Day celebrations. The atten-
> dance was so large that the Club premises were found inadequate,
> and it became necessary to erect a Marquee and suitable dancing
> floor on the tennis lawn, with sundry sitting-out annexes con-
> structed with sails borrowed from sailing vessels in port. . . . The
> interior of the Marquee was suitably decorated with flags from
> the ships, and the band of the Flagship provided a first class
> orchestra. These dances took place annually so long as Esquimalt
> was a naval station, and when the latter was abandoned, the date
> was changed to New Year's Eve, and a Children's Ball on New
> Year's Day.*

As early as 1903, a proposal had been made to build a large
pavilion ''on that portion of the club grounds north of the squash
racquet court and possibly including part of the old skittle alley.'' This
would mean purchasing another fifty feet of property, but the addition of a pavilion meant there would be room for dances, dinners,

smoking concerts, badminton and so forth. In July, the trustees of the Granville Club were approached and it was put to them that the club's finances were such that the additional fifty feet should be purchased. There was mutual agreement on the proposal. The price--$4,000-- seemed reasonable, the need was evident, and as a consequence plans were made and a building contract awarded that summer.

When completed the addition contained a billiard room, ball-room and an enlarged dining room. The club was particularly proud of the ball-room floor. It was "entirely free from the permanent structure, and was supported on pure rubber columns at 18-inch centres, which minimized the knee strain so that those dancing did not suffer from the usual stiffness resultant from the ordinary floor." "This quality was so appreciated," wrote one early club president, "that our Ball Room acquired a world-wide reputation."

The addition of the pavilion did give temporary relief to the call for more space and the enlarged dining room meant less waiting time for meals. There is no record of strictly club dinner functions at that time, but periodically the club would hold a banquet for some special group. The Kootenay Trail Blazers team was hosted in 1913, for example. Earlier, in 1909, the Committee had agreed "that on account of the international character of the function, the officers of the local Garrison (who are nearly all members of the Club) be permitted to hold their dinner to visiting Japanese naval officers in the dining room. . . ."

Now and then there are some brief references in the old minute books to events which are not explained or elaborated upon, but which deserve at least passing mention. One such occurred at the Annual General Meeting in March 1907. At that time a motion was passed, by a vote of 54 to 42, "that the Bar be abolished." At first glance it would imply that the members were overwhelmed by a temperance evangelist, but the problem, apparently, was the location of the bar, not the evil of drink. The motion led to the pro-bar members rallying their forces. A petition signed by thirty-three members later that month asked for a special meeting to consider the question. This was done and the earlier resolution was reversed by a vote of 48 to 15. It was explained that whatever the objectionable features of the bar were would be altered, and that a screen would hide the bar from the main passage. Meanwhile the bar would remain open. The barrels of whiskey would continue to arrive at the club and there were no complaints in the Suggestion Book when, four months later, the cost of a glass doubled to ten cents. Present members of the club will be a bit envious to know that until the beginning of the Great War not only could one purchase drinks at this price, but also buy sandwiches at the bar until 10:00 p.m. for five cents each.

In the decade prior to the Great War, membership in the Vancouver Club increased by more than twenty-five percent. In 1907 the General Committee was thinking seriously about improving and enlarging the club house and in May of that year permission was obtained to borrow $15,000 to upgrade and improve the building. The addition of a balcony to the dining room or new ranges for the kitchen did not solve the basic problem. The situation could not be allowed to continue. In the summer of 1909 a committee appointed to report on the club's future suggested that,

> . . . within a very few years the taxation on the property will be too burdensome and that it will be necessary either to sell a portion of the property and build a new club on the remainder of the land with the proceeds of the sale, or to build a commercial block on the whole land, reserving the top storey for club purposes.

While this matter was being considered, members were becoming increasingly aware of the inconvenience caused by burgeoning numbers. In 1904 the total membership was 304. A year later it increased to 347, jumped to 366 in 1907 and by 1908 it was over the 400 mark. By the summer of 1909 it was close to 450.

The increase in membership was not slowed by increasing fees and some minor restrictions. In 1905 the entrance fee was increased from $50 to $100, and the quarterly dues to $12. The motion increasing the fees also added the rider that "no resident candidate shall be eligible for election until he has been in the province of British Columbia for at least three months." The entrance fee was upped again in 1907 to $150 "until the number of Resident Members reached 375, after which the Entrance Fee shall be $500. . . ." When the new constitution came into effect on July 1st, 1908, the entrance fees were increased to $200, and the annual subscription dues were proposed at $72. This latter proposal, which was to come into effect in July 1910 brought forth a howl of protest from the membership. At the General Meeting held to confirm this increase, no agreement could be reached and as a result the president, vice-president and all the members of the General Committee resigned. They were persuaded to remain--but the annual subscription remained at $48 for at least a while longer.

The new constitution of 1908 also laid down that the total resident and life-resident membership of the club should be 350. This, at the time, did help matters somewhat but the attraction of membership did not slow down. By 1913 there were approximately 175 names on the waiting list, a situation which would not be repeated until the 1950s.

The first mention of building a completely new club house is in the minutes of the General Committee in Feburary 1910. It was in the same year the Terminal City Club began to build their club house next door. There was a certain rivalry between the two clubs and this may have inspired the Vancouver Club members to go one better. The proximity of the Terminal City Club led the Committee to ask the secretary to "obtain the written opinion of our Solicitors in respect to windows in [the] wall overlooking the Club's premises, in [the] building now in course of erection. . . ." The legal advice was that nothing could be done, "but, on the other hand, a barrier could be erected at any time in order to protect our own view." Perhaps it was better to move.

In December 1910 an extraordinary general meeting of the club membership was called. It was proposed that a new club house should be erected on the present site for $180,000, that a committee be struck, a loan negotiated, the entrance fee raised (to $300), yearly subscriptions increased and that each member should pay $100 towards a building fund. A meeting of this nature can lead to a considerable amount of debate and amendments were proposed with some relish and considerable heat. Basically the main argument was whether to sell the present site and buildings and move elsewhere, or rebuild on part of the club's property selling the older building and the land on which it stood. No decision was reached at this meeting, the members declaring they wanted more information. A committee was struck to report back as soon as possible and, considering the number of leading realtors in the club, it was not difficult to appoint experts for the task.

The main thing to be determined was the site, for this would determine the architect's plans and the financial arrangements to be made. A preliminary report was ready by January 4th, 1911 and it was based on the alternatives which emerged at the earlier meeting. The committee stressed that they had looked upon the two proposals as impartially as they could and hoped the membership would reach a decision "only after mature and deliberate consideration, because whatever programme is decided upon will in all probability have to stand during the life of most of us. . . ."

The Building Committee, chaired by Harry Abbott, had met several times in December and, as it explained in a printed report to the members, had come to the conclusion that other waterfront sites available were either unsuitable or not on the market. This left the alternative of using part of the present site or building completely anew on an available property on Georgia Street overlooking the new Court House. The report gave both the advantages and disadvantages of both propositions. To remain on the site was to retain the magnificent view the club enjoyed. It also had a central location, and it was felt that the new building "could be placed so that the present two-storey building of the Terminal City Club" would not interfere with

Downtown Vancouver, corner of Granville and Georgia Streets, at the turn of the century.
(Vancouver Public Library)

the view to the east. The disadvantages of the site were the possibility of buildings being constructed both east and west of the new club and the annoyance of smoke from ships which were changing from coal to oil-burning engines. It was also pointed out "that the district we are now in may, and probably will, become ere long either wholesale or retail business, and the Vancouver Club will necessarily become a 'down-town' club."

The second proposition was to buy a corner lot on Georgia Street over-looking the new Court House. The advantages would be obtaining more money from the sale of all of the club's present site and although the harbour view would be lost, so, too, would the occasional nuisance from steamer and railway smoke. The new site would be closer to the city centre and tram service and there would be the open space of the Court House grounds. The disadvantages listed were losing the view of the harbour and, as with the Hastings Street site, "the probability of its surroundings becoming retail business property...." In conclusion, the majority of the committee recommended building on the present site but noted that "there was considerable divergence of opinion" among the committee members.

The report of the committee led to further questions and further answers later in the month. The committee reported it could get $2,000 per foot (average depth--120 feet) if they sold 140 feet of the property, reserving the rest for the club (i.e., about 23,000 square feet) which would give the club $225,000 after paying off $59,000 owing, or they could get $2,500 per foot ($442,500) if they sold the entire property. The Georgia Street corner lot (15,000 square feet) could be bought for $125,000, leaving $317,500 for the building.

At about this time another factor came into consideration. The north-east corner of Hastings and Burrard, known as the Cotton corner, appeared to be available. The owners of five lots on this corner had a purchase price of $125,000 and a syndicate of club members took an option to buy the lots, an option they would be willing to turn over to the club until March 10th, should the club decide to buy. This, in turn, resulted in the members being called to another Extraordinary Meeting on March 7th. Once again there was considerable debate but on a motion it was agreed that the complete site of the club should be sold for a price not less than $440,000 and the site on the south-west corner of Georgia and Hornby Streets be purchased. The motion passed with a roughly three to one majority.

Such a thumping majority decision on what should be done would lead one to expect the General Committee to consider the matter settled. However, the club's constitution contained some very democratic clauses, one of which was that a number of members could petition for a special general meeting to consider a matter of particular consequence to the membership. There were about 140 members who attended the meeting when the vote was taken to move to another site. This was less than half the resident membership. A group of members quickly got together and another special general meeting was called for March 31st to reconsider the decision made three weeks earlier. About 200 members turned out this time, and one can assume there must have been a considerable amount of lobbying done in the meantime. In any event, once again the question to sell and move was put to the members and this time it lost--but by a narrow margin of six votes. The decision to stay where they were was not challenged seriously again, but the road ahead was not particularly smooth as groups within the club were to keep a critical eye on every phase of the building process for the next two years.

The next step for the General Committee was to consult with various architectural firms regarding the best use of the buildings and grounds they owned, the possible disposition of part of the property and to gather some ideas with respect to a club building which should contain facilities for around 600 or 650 members. Informal consultation on these matters went on during the summer of 1911 and by December of that year once again a special meeting was called to resolve certain matters which required attention.

The first resolution was straightforward. When the new club house was built, it was obvious the old regulation limiting membership to 350 would have to be changed. This was accepted. The second resolution asked for the formation of a committee of seven with sweeping powers to carry out the task of getting the club house built. They were to be given the authority to sell the land, raise a mortgage, obtain plans and estimates, enter into a contract for building the club house, call a meeting of the membership if they wanted advice, co-opt members to serve on their committee and, in brief, "to do all other acts and things . . . to provide a new Club House in any manner they may deem most suitable and expedient in the best interests of the Club." The club's governing authorities, the General Committee and the Granville Club Co. Ltd., were to be authorized to carry out the Building Committee's instruction, the only limitation being that the club property, or that part of it to be sold, must not be let go for less than $2,000 per foot.

They were sweeping powers but they were necessary if the job was to be done. The Building Committee could always be brought before a general meeting at any time, but at least action could be taken without having to call all the members together and getting involved in constant arguments.

The new Building Committee, chaired by F. J. Proctor, was elected and got to work at once. Estimates on the club's property ranged from $2,000 to $2,500 per foot so there was no problem there. The committee's powers were such that they had the opportunity to take one last look around to see if there might be a building site available better than their own. They looked but preferred to remain where they were. The size of membership was difficult to estimate, but it was felt the new building should be able to service about 600 resident category members with a possible expansion to 1,000.

As far as the actual building was concerned, arrangements would have to be made with the buyer of the old club house building and property to allow the members to occupy it until the new club house was ready for occupancy. As it turned out the sale was made with the club remaining in their building for one year after the sale had been concluded with the further option of paying a monthly rental should there be any delays. As for financing, the committee felt that aside from the amount raised from the sale of their property, a loan of $100,000 could be obtained and, they hoped, another $150,000 raised by debentures at 7% taken up by members.

Early in 1912, as a result of a competition, seventeen sets of plans had been received. After examination the committee selected the best five. Expert opinion was sought and the number was reduced to three and the final selection was made late in March to hire the firm of Sharp and Thompson as the club's architects. Two months later part of the club's property was sold to J.D. Cobbald.

A few words should be said about C. J. Thompson who had a major role in designing the club. Born in England in 1878 and trained there as an architect, he came to Canada in 1906 to work for the C. P. R. as an assistant architect. His work with them involved not only working on the designs of dozens of railway stations, but he also drew the preliminary designs for the Banff Springs Hotel, a wing of the Chateau Frontenac, and supervised the design and erection of the original Lake Louise Hotel. Sent out to Vancouver, he decided to leave the C.P.R. and go into partnership with a younger architect in 1908. Thompson's winning submission for the Vancouver Club was his first major job, but close on its heels came his designs for many of the buildings at the University of British Columbia. The partnership was to develop into one of the largest architectural firms in Vancouver and as Thompson, Berwick, Pratt and Partners it has completed projects from the B.C. Hydro Building to a vast variety of buildings from one end of Canada to the other as well as overseas. The firm continued to do work for the Vancouver Club for more than seventy years.

During the late spring of 1912 the architects worked hard on plans and drawings. These were shown to and discussed with the Building Committee, some revisions made but the basic work went ahead. Even by the end of March there was a great deal of racket as measures were taken to rearrange rooms in the club made necessary by the wrecking of the pavilion. This recent addition to the club stood on part of the property where the new club house was to be built, so it had to be pulled down before excavation could begin. Tenders for the building were called early in April and in June, the architect was instructed to lose no time in going ahead with the excavation after the pavilion was razed.

There had been some delay in completing the architectural drawings owing not to any lack of energy on the part of the architect, but apparently to the Building Committee members occasionally changing their mind. Late in June, Sharp and Thompson evidently had received a letter from the club secretary complaining about plans promised for an earlier date. The firm's reply indicates something of the pressure they were under:

> *You will doubtless remember that it was not until June 4th at the last Committee meeting that final instructions were received to have the billiard room above the dining room and one week was lost while this point was in abeyance therein. The adoption of the amended scheme for lessening the distance between the dining room and kitchen which was submitted then and approved, has necessitated the replanning of every floor at the last moment.*
>
> *The best is being done and if the drawings are required for exhibition, as stated by Mr. Salsbury, blueprints can be supplied in a week which will be complete with the exception of a few technical details.*

On July 12th, the architect had completed his plans. He was instructed to call for tenders at once, with August 21st given as the date for final submission. The excavation for the foundations was already underway. This was to cost $2300, and apparently it was done to save time and take as much advantage of the good weather as possible.

When the tenders were opened in August the prices quoted for constructing the building varied from $356,980 to $280,569. All were higher than anticipated so the Building Committee had to meet to consider what items could be reduced. This took place about two weeks after the tenders were opened with the architect in attendance. After much discussion, Thompson was asked to estimate the savings if the top storey of the building was eliminated and the depth of the building reduced by fifteen feet. He felt this would knock $42,000 from the price. A firm which had been a bidder on the contract, Messrs. Norton, Griffiths Steel Construction Co. Ltd., suggested they had ideas for reducing costs which might save $40,000. These figures were helpful but the total cost was still high. The committee did not want to skimp on the quality of the work, but the potential deficit was worrisome.

To add to its problems the Building Committee was asked to attend a General Meeting called by thirty-three members "owing to adverse criticism of the plans displayed in the Reading Room. . . ." They wanted a report "before taking further steps re completion of [the club house]," and although they felt the committee "had done everything in their power to make the plans suitable for club premises, . . . such is not possible owing to the size and shape of the ground." This was the last ditch stand of those who wanted the club moved elsewhere.

W. F. Salsbury had assumed the presidency of the club in 1911, having served the previous year as vice-president to Sir Charles Hibbert Tupper. He was thoroughly familiar with the divided opinion about the site and he kept himself informed of the week-to-week progress of work which went into the preparations for constructing the club. He was the one who wrote an open letter to the members in which he explained precisely what steps had been taken and why. As far as the site was concerned, he said that a thorough survey had been made of all potential properties so there was absolutely no chance of moving to a different site now. Of the $200,000 the club received for selling its property, over $30,000 had been expended and to switch site would mean a loss of this money. Respecting the architects plans, Salsbury pointed out that "expert assistance--entirely apart from the club architect--was obtained before a final decision was arrived at." Financially there would be a cost overrun of about $65,000. The total cost of the building was estimated at $358,628, but this included the contract price of the building ($227,066) as well as the cost of heating, plumbing, elevators, electric installation, architect's fees and all the rest of it. There would be no cutting down of height or depth if the club house was to accommodate an estimated membership of 600. Moreover, with 250 additional entrance fees (these were increased from $200 to $300 in 1913) the problem of the deficit should be taken care of.

Salsbury's reasoned argument and explanation had the desired effect. There were no more signed petitions or extraordinary or special general meetings. The contract was signed and during the winter of 1912-1913 work began on the new club house. The contract with Norton Griffiths was nine pages long and some of the conditions laid down would be interesting to a present-day contractor. One of the key paragraphs stated:

> *The contractor agrees to erect and complete in a fine, perfect*
> *and thorough workmanlike manner a building on the said prop-*

Early members assembled in front of first clubhouse, prior to the first demolition blow, January 9, 1930. (Club Archives)

Front Row: R.K. Houlgate, M.H. Leggatt, F.W. Rousefell, C.H. Gatewood, F.M. Chaldecott, J.G. Woods. Second Row: H.St.J. Montizambert, B.W. Greer, S. Henderson, D.S. Wallbridge. Back Row: J.D. Stuart, J.K. Macrae, E.J. Coyle, D. Robertson, C.B.

erty . . . and to find and provide such good, proper and sufficient materials of all kinds whatsoever as shall be proper and sufficient for the said work.

Other paragraphs stated that the contractor should "proceed with the said work of construction as fast as possible," that he would build on a cost basis (ten percent of the cost of the building) and that the building was to be completed on or before October 1st, 1913.

The Building Committee continued to meet regularly during 1913. Inevitably there were minor problems which came up and needed to be solved. As the year wore on the question of furnishing the club occupied more of the agenda. The committee was assisted by Mrs. Douglas Armour when choosing the drapes and carpets--and, incidentally, in later years advice from knowledgable women respecting the club's decor was not at all uncommon. An old English firm, Waring and Gillow, were favoured to provide most of the furnishings at a cost of over $32,000, but local firms were given orders also. There was a great number of items to buy--drapes, carpets, kitchen equipment, crockery, glassware, bedroom furniture and a hundred other items. Some, such as the doorplates, were specially made with the club logo on them. Six new billiard tables were ordered and the old ones sold. Bedroom bureaus, made of oak, were ordered from Weiler Brothers.

Sometimes changes were made. The interior dining room walls and pillars were being made for the club in Great Britain by expert craftsmen. When completed this pre-fabricated panelling would be installed and the final result would make this room one of the most admired rooms in the club. It would seem that one or two of the craftsmen would come to Vancouver to help install the woodwork. Not a nail was to be seen, and the joinery and workmanship was to be remarked on by visitors for years to come. What the cost of this feature of the club was is not known, and it is interesting to speculate if it might have entered into the decision to use "silent" strips of carpeting on the dining room floor rather than carpeting the entire area. Officially the reason was that a carpet was liable to get dirty and be more expensive to clean.

Each month the bills piled up. Silverware and cutlery--$3,500; glassware--$1,350; crockery--$2,350 (all from Buscombe and Co. Ltd.); linen--$2,500 (Johnson Bros. Ltd.); bathroom fixtures (McLennan and McFeely); liveries--estimated at $1,000; and so forth. A late additional expenditure was for a fireplace ($274) in the secretary's quarters on the fourth floor. Arrangements were made to install forty-six telephones in the club house--for a total of $75.20. Wash basins with hot and cold water were placed in eight of the twenty-four bedrooms. Those occupying other bedrooms would have to go to the washrooms and toilets at the end of the hall. Cuspidors were ordered for the lobby as well as for the smoking and card rooms on the third floor, and, of course, a good linoleum floor was chosen for the billiard room. Arrangements for furnishing the staff bedrooms and dining room in the basement had to be completed, and if their furniture was a bit Spartan, except in size they were not too different from the members' bedrooms on the upper floors. The members, depending on the price they paid, occasionally had a decent view from their bedroom windows. The same could not be said for those living in the basement.

To look ahead for a moment, the rates for bedrooms varied according to the floor they were on, the view they enjoyed and whether they had basins and running water. In 1918, the rates varied from $27.50 to $37.50 per month, or $1.25 to $2.00 per day. Room No. 14 was special. It cost $2.50. For visiting guests the rates were slightly higher and they varied from $40 to $55 per month and from $1.75 to $2.50 daily. These prices were a bit higher than the original prices. In the old club, a member could enjoy room **and** board for a month for about $70!

By the summer of 1913 the new club house was not finished nor would it be until the end of the year. Under the arrangements made, the club had to start paying $1000 a month in rent. This was annoying but it could not be helped. A suggestion that the members vacate the old club house and obtain the use of the ground floor of the new building was not practicable and was turned down. By November it became apparent that the move could be made in a matter of weeks. Since the rent had been paid for December, the committee decided that on the last day of the year there should be a farewell banquet at the old club and, on the stroke of midnight the members, led by their president, E. P. Davis, would parade the short distance to the new club house to open it with some show of ceremony. At midnight, as the club's "official" timepiece in the lobby struck the hour, the members left the club and entered their new home. It was a new year, 1914. A new era had begun.

*　*　*　*

The club members who welcomed in the new year had no idea that 1914 would see the beginning of one of the bloodiest wars the world had ever witnessed. Their primary interest in the first hour of 1914 was to examine the delights of the new club, to look into the freshly decorated rooms with their new furniture, try out the soft leather seats in the library and, in all probability, order their first drinks from the bars on the first and third floors. It must have been a great night; if nothing else it was probably the first time in twenty years that all the members were out of the old club house on time!

As the months went by, members who kept up with international affairs by reading any of the club's British and American newspapers must have felt some degree of uneasiness as events in Europe indicated increasing tension. The naval race between Germany and Great Britain showed no signs of let-up and relations between Germany and France had been deteriorating steadily. Russia, beaten by the Japanese a decade earlier, had become more determined to pose as the protector of the Slavs in the Balkans, an area where Austria–Hungary felt it must play a dominant if not decisive role. This "powder-keg of Europe," as it was termed, only needed a spark to set off an explosion. This occurred in June 1914 with the assassination of the heir to the Austrian–Hungarian empire by a terrorist. This act, coupled with bungling diplomacy, rigid mobilization plans, marble-headed monarchs with awesome powers, and a public accustomed to short wars, resulted in a world wide conflict which broke out in August, 1914.

The members of the Vancouver Club had a more than passing interest in military affairs. Many were from the United Kingdom and one can assume some had served with British regiments during the numerous colonial wars at the turn of the century. The club library subscribed to the Army List. The club made a point of inviting officers from the Royal Navy squadron at Esquimalt. A number of members had served with the Canadian forces in the Riel Rebellion and a few in the Boer War. Others, such as the Bell-Irvings and Leckies, were active in local militia regiments and indeed had been instrumental in creating a militia battalion, the Seaforth Highlanders of Canada, in 1910. In a word, club members during the summer of 1914 were becoming more interested in overseas developments. No one had any idea of what the scope and length of a major war might be. In the colonial wars the army might be vastly outnumbered by the natives, and up until the Boer War British or even Canadian soldiers might take comfort in the couplet "Whatever else, we have got, the Gatling gun, and they have not." The conflict about to break over the world was to change the face of warfare and, indirectly, it was to have an impact on the club.

From the declaration of war until its end, a large number of members volunteered to join the services. Those who remained set out to help the war effort. On September 2nd a special meeting was called to consider the raising of a Greater Vancouver War Relief Fund as other Canadian cities were doing. Hearing of this Frank Barnard, who held dual membership in both the Union and Vancouver Clubs and was the Lieutenant-Governor at the time, wrote to say that the Governor-General had started a Canadian Patriotic Fund. Incorporated by an Act of Parliament, its object was to obviate the overlapping which might occur in various relief organizations springing up in the country. Sir Charles Tupper, a recent past president of the club, also called to the attention of the club the urgent request of the British Red Cross Society for immediate funds "to supply medical necessities for the sick and wounded who are now at the front." The club president also read a letter from the vice-president of the Associated Charities who suggested that, whatever arrangements were decided on, the club "should amalgamate with other Societies insofar as the city was concerned."

In a situation of this nature the club usually decided to strike a committee to suggest the best course of action to be taken. This course of action was accepted but before the meeting broke up, H. Bell-Irving suggested that before they left, members as individuals might wish to contributed to the Red Cross. Over $2,000 was collected by the time the meeting ended.

The committee selected was a committee of one--C. S. Meek. His solution was to offer assistance to several groups, not only in cash but in volunteers to aid in organizing fund drives. A $2.00 voluntary addition to each member's monthly bill would help raise a suggested $100,000 goal in co-operation with other clubs in the city and a donation box in the club's rotunda for the War Fund was proposed as well.

Various other fund drives were started. In August 1915, for example, there is mention of an informal meeting of members who instituted the Vancouver Club Machine-Gun Fund. Apparently the idea was to present one or more of these weapons to a local unit but a telegram from Ottawa informed the fund raisers that "it would be impossible to specify guns for any special battalion, but gifts for that purpose would be equally divided between [sic] all units going to the front." This left the question of the disposal of the money already collected, and contributors were asked if they would agree if the money were given to another cause. This evidently reached the ears of Lady Tupper who wrote suggesting a donation to the 5th Base Hospital, C.E.F. The matter was left in abeyance.

There was at least one fund-raising dinner given at the club during the war when the famous cartoonist, Bengough, was entertained. He spoke on the topic, "Reminiscences of Canadian Public Men," particularly during the time of Confederation. As he talked, to quote a "Vancouver Sun" reporter, "his skillful hands were performing wonders in charcoal which were at once recognized as masterpieces of the art of caricature." The collection was put up for auction. Over $600 was collected and was given to the Patriotic Fund.

Contributions to the Patriotic Fund continued throughout the war. In the Spring of 1919 the club decided to change its contribution to the Returned Soldiers Club as an expression of the members' appreciation ". . . of the bravery and sacrifice of our Army and Navy," and ". . . of the debt we owe to those who have returned and have difficulties to overcome in resuming civilian life." It is interesting to note that club contributions to the Returned Soldiers Club continued until 1933. Members' wives were also involved in helping the war effort within the club's precincts. The Returned Soldiers Club, established during the war, had a Ladies Auxiliary. Late in 1917, F.W. Peters, the recent past-president of the club, asked on the ladies' behalf for permission to use the private dining room for Bridge. It was to be for a period of six weeks but only one day a week between three and six in the afternoon. The committee agreed, a profit was made and turned over to the Returned Soldiers Club, and it was so successful that it was done again in the late summer of 1918.

From the outset of the war the club decided to make special provision for its own members on active service and, within limits, to extend club privileges to serving officers in Vancouver. Six members signed a resolution in the Suggestion Book that the dues of members called away on active service should be remitted until they returned. A few months later it was suggested "that all officers of the 29th Battalion be made honorary members of the Vancouver Club," a request granted until the unit's departure for overseas. This, incidentally, was the first time ever that temporary "mass" honorary membership was granted. The use of the club (but not honorary membership) was extended to other military officers provided their units were mobilized for overseas as opposed to officers on duty in Vancouver. Officers returning to the city from overseas were given privileges of the club early in 1918 "... until such time as the formal application required has been submitted for consideration by the Committee." These privileges were reduced and later nullified several months after the end of the war. Members serving overseas were given two months grace after they returned before being charged normal dues.

Before the war there were a small number of German nationals who were club members and several of these made a rapid exit in order to fight for the Kaiser and Vaterland. In August 1917, the General Committee's minutes note:

> *A letter was read from E. von Campe (now a prisoner-of-war in England) requesting that his baggage, left at the club, be forwarded to him on payment by the Secretary of the Northern Trust Co. of Chicago, of the amount of arrears outstanding.*
>
> *It was resolved that E. von Campe's baggage be released on payment of the amount owing with compound interest added at the rate of 10 per cent per annum.*

Von Campe was not the only club member fighting for the Kaiser. Early in in 1920 the club secretary received a letter from the Swiss consul asking that he be given charge of certain trunks and effects left in the club by a W. von Freyburg. The secretary was ordered to turn over these effects--but only after collecting $111.25 von Freyberg owed in arrears.

The savagery of industrialized warfare, together with the tremendous casualties suffered as a result, led to the demands for a very harsh imposition of surrender terms, especially on the Germans. As early as January 1919, Dr. Duncan Bell-Irving suggested that in future Germans (but not Austrian or Polish nationals) should be excluded from club membership. This was found more than acceptable and in March of the same year the club's constitution was amended. Henceforth, no person of German birth who had not been naturalized as a British subject or as a subject of one of the Allied powers prior to August 1st would be eligible for membership. Furthermore such a person was not to be allowed to enter the club even as a guest! This rule continued for a decade and it was not until 1929 that the secretary "was instructed to write to Canadian Clubs, with which we are affiliated, asking their rule regarding the admission of Germans." Passions had cooled evidently and it seemed that Germany was on a democratic course. The amendments to the constitution were struck out on March 12th, 1930.

What about the "members at war"? One thing the war brought to the club was a new membership classification--members "On Active Service." An indication of the comparative youthfulness of members as a group can be seen when noting the number in this category during the wartime years. In 1914 there were 30, in 1915 - 66, in 1916 - 90, in 1917 - 89 and in 1918 - 75. Even in 1919, owing to slow demobilization or extended duty, there were still 21 members in this category. Aside from the members many of the staff had joined up, and in 1917 the General Committee agreed "that a separate Roll of Honour be placed on the Notice Board to include the names of all employees belonging to the Vancouver Club permanent staff who have left . . . the Club service to join His Majesty's Forces in defence of the Empire; and that upon receiving honorable discharge . . . they shall, as far as possible, be offered employment at the first opportunity."

Each month the number on the Active Servise List grew longer. Among those who left, and the following are only a sample, were Captain M. MacIver Campbell, Lt. C. W. Gamble, Lt. R. H. Tupper, Maj. C. H. D. Robertson, Capt. P. B. H. Ramsay, Lt-Col. R. H. Ker, Lt. R. C. Buchanan, Maj. J.H. Roaf, Capt. C. M. Marpole, Maj. F. W. Boultbee, Col. V. Spencer, and Lt. Robert Bell-Irving. They started out serving in the navy and army, and later a number joined the recently formed Royal Flying Corps as the war entered a new dimension.

In 1915 the club began to receive word of members who had been killed in action--Baron A. W. de Langsdorf, who served as a sergeant. Lt.-Col. W. Hart-McHarg, who was a world champion marksman and had won the King Wilhelm's Palma Gold Trophy in 1913, was commanding the 7th Battalion when he died. On the same day Major C. M. Merritt met his death, leaving behind him a small boy who, almost two decades later, was to win the Victoria Cross and be elected an honorary member of the club. Lt. Irwin Davis was killed, a sad blow to his father who was the club's president at the outset of the war. One could go on, but it is sufficient to say that the loss of friends and colleagues in the club affected all members.

Shortly after the armistice was declared the General Committee decided to have a war memorial created "in honour of those Members of the Club who in the Great War have given their lives for our Country." At first this took the form of an Honour Roll done in copperplate writing but a more permanent tablet was made in 1920. It was placed in the main lobby of the club where it remains today. On it are the names of 17 members and three from the staff.

During the war a number of members served with considerable distinction. It might be appropriate to mention a few at this time.

R. G. E. Leckie was a mining engineer working in Vancouver in 1914. A Nova Scotian by birth, he was a graduate of the Royal Military College. He served with several militia units in Eastern Canada and during the Boer War he commanded a squadron of the 2nd Canadian Mounted Rifles. When he returned to Vancouver he was one of several club members who were instrumental in organizing the Seaforth Highlanders of Canada. He became its first commanding officer and in 1914 was appointed the commander of the 16th Battalion (Canadian Scottish), C.E.F. He was in command when that unit was called upon to help stop the German break-through when poison gas was used for the first time on the Western Front. Awarded the DSO and CMG for his leadership and courage, he was later promoted to the rank of major-general. Invalided home, he was given command of Military District XI until 1920. A keen big game hunter, he was also president of the Vancouver Rifle Association and the B.C. Rifle Association.

Another Boer War veteran and club member was Victor W. Odlum. He had been granted a commission in the field in that conflict, retained his interest in the militia and was one of the original officers of the Irish Fusiliers of Canada when it was organized in Vancouver in 1913. He went overseas with the 7th Battalion (1st British Columbia

Regiment) and became its commanding officer early in 1915 when Lt.-Col. W. Hart-McHarg (another club member) was killed. Odlum was promoted later to Brigadier-General and remained in that command until the end of the war. After the armistice Odlum returned to British Columbia and resumed his interest in journalism and business, becoming publisher of the Vancouver Daily Star between 1924 and 1930. It is interesting to note that when the Second World War broke out, Odlum returned to active service, was promoted to major-general and had command of the 2nd Canadian Infantry Division for well over a year.

When A. D. McRae joined the Vancouver Club in 1909 he was in his mid-thirties and already a wealthy man. After making a small fortune in the United States he returned to Canada and organized the Saskatchewan Valley Land Co. in 1903. He and his associates ultimately bought hundreds of thousands of acres of land in the Canadian prairies and sold them to immigrants pouring into the country during the Laurier era. Moving to Vancouver he amassed greater wealth in fishing, forestry and land development. His tremendous organizing abilities were recognized during the war when he was appointed Quartermaster-General of the Overseas Forces of Canada in 1916. Later he was promoted major-general and loaned to the British Government to assist Beaverbrook organize the Ministry of Information. A staunch Conservative, McRae's abilities as an organizer were used by both the provincial and national Conservative party and some say he was in no small way responsible for arranging Premier Tolmie's selection as provincial party leader and helping to get R. B. Bennett and the Tories into power in 1930. Appointed to the Senate, McRae was to remain a powerful influence in provincial and national politics until his death in 1946.

Another club member whose civilian talents were used for wartime pursuits was J. W. Stewart. A Scotsman, he came to Canada in 1882. As a civil engineer he was engaged by the Grand Trunk Pacific Railway and was later involved in railway building both across the prairies and through the mountains. Although he was 52 years old when the Great War broke out, he volunteered his services to help construct, maintain and operate the expanding network of military railways needed in France and Belgium. Early in 1916 Lt.-Col. Stewart was requested by the British War Office to serve as Deputy Director of Light Railways. Less than a year later, and promoted to brigadier-general, he became Deputy Director General Transportation (Construction). As thousands more men joined the Canadian Railway Troops, Stewart's responsibilities increased until by the war's end he had under his command, as a major-general, over 20,000 troops who had laid some 2,500 miles of light and heavy track to help maintain the British, Canadian and other Imperial troops at the front. Stewart was awarded the CB, CMG and DSO for his remarkable achievements, frequently carried out in difficult and often dangerous conditions.

Few club members had a more distinguished military record than William W. Foster. Born in England, he came to Canada in 1895 and worked with the C.P.R. until 1909. From 1910 to 1913 he was the deputy minister of public works. In 1913 he and Captain A. H. McCarthy were the first men to scale the 13,000 foot Mount Robson and, in the same year he was elected president of the Canadian Alpine Association. A former president of the B.C. Conservative Association he was elected to the legislature in 1914 but temporarily ended his political career to join the 2nd Canadian Mounted Rifles as a captain. During the war he was given command of the 52nd Battalion and on several occasions was acting brigadier-general. He was wounded twice, mentioned in despatches five times, won the Distinguished Service Order with two bars (the equivalent of winnning it three times) and was also awarded the French and Belgian Croix-de-Guerre. These were the first of fourteen medals and decorations he was to be awarded in his long military career.

Foster's interest in military affairs had started in 1895 and did not end in 1918. After the war he became president of Pacific Engineers Ltd. He was one of the organizers of the Canadian Legion and served as both provincial and national president. In the militia he was promoted to command one of the reserve brigades and in the late 1930's he accepted the task of reorganizing Vancouver's police department as its chief. When the Second World War broke out in 1939, Foster went overseas again but returned to Canada to undertake a series of major appointments with the rank of major-general. For his work as a special commissioner for defence projects in northern Canada he was awarded the American Legion of Merit and made a Companion of St. Michael and St. George. When he died in 1954, an editorial in the Vancouver "Sun" referred to him as "one of the finest public servants in war and in peace that British Columbia has ever had."

* * * *

While club members were serving overseas in various parts of the world, what was going on in the Vancouver Club? Membership in the club had dropped from a total of 623 in 1914 to 514 in 1918. Although there were fourteen categories of membership (including the new Active Service members, dropped at the end of the war), the most important categories were the Resident and Resident Life. These were the men who lived in the city, paid full fees (except the Resident Life) and, most important, used the club and all its facilities on a fairly regular basis. There were fixed costs to be covered, and a diminuition in demand inevitably caused financial problems. In 1913 there were 414 Resident and 13 Resident Life members. By 1918 this had dropped to 310 and 11 respectively. The total loss of membership was in a category which added more to the financial strain on the club, especially as the new club building brought with it a mortgage which had to be paid.

Although there had been some renovations in the club during the war these appear to have been minor. As an economy measure the club's stock of cutlery, glassware, crockery and liveries had been greatly depleted, and help had been cut to a minimum. It was not until late in 1919, when club membership began to increase with the return of the veterans, that the General Committee instructed the secretary to submit requirements ''to place the Club on a normal basis'' and ''to obtain additional help.''

Aside from financial concerns, life in the club went on much as usual for the first few years of the war. The war news was followed very closely, the German submarine threat was worrying and one began to hear more about the exploits of Canadian airmen as yet another element was added to warfare. Moreover, with the establishment of a pilot training base near Vancouver, members would occasionally get a glimpse of the slow–flying aircraft in the sky--an indication of what was to come. In 1916, when the Terminal City Club suggested a series of billiard matches during the winter season the Vancouver Club replied that ''the present time is inopportune'' as so many of their players were serving overseas. (The billiard tournament was renewed in 1919).

There was one event looming up in 1916 which caused considerable concern among most club members, and that was the introduction of prohibition. In May 1916, a bill was passed in the Legislature which did not go into immediate effect owing to a controversy over the voting. In mid–August, 1917, however, the Prohibition Act was passed.

In the intervening months some steps were taken to moderate the proposed legislation. In October 1916, the Western Club suggested that combined action should be taken by the clubs in British Columbia to obtain amendments to the Prohibition Act ''favourable to the interests of property managed by Social Clubs.'' The Vancouver Club appointed a deputation to attend a meeting called to discuss the matter which was held in its own club house in November. Losses in revenue from the bar would be a serious matter. As early as September, members had been sent a circular letter informing them that

... in the event of the prohibition act coming into effect, the revenue of the club would be reduced to an amount necessitating an increase of approximately 35% over the present rates of subscription for each class of membership. As no other course presents itself, the committee is of the opinion that an increase of rates of subscription is inevitable.

British Columbia clubs faced a losing battle. The earlier vote in the Legislature was reinforced by a plebiscite which favoured the measure, and although there was a considerable delay owing to the time it took to gather and count the soldiers' votes, by 1917 it seemed inevitable that the club faced a stark and dry future.

There was some rear–guard action, however. In August, when the Prohibition Act was passed, the House Committee sought the advice of the club's solicitor, E. P. Davis, to find out whether the provisions of the new act overrode and repealed the provisions of the Club Regulation Act. Davis could not offer much hope and, since the new law was to come into effect on October 1st, it was decided to auction off the contents of the wine cellar to club members. Some samples of prices of the bottles put up for auction at the time are interesting:

Champagne	1 quart Bollinger (1906)	$ 4.00
	1 pint G. H. Mumm Extra Dry	$ 2.00
	1 quart St. Marceaus (1904)	$ 4.50
White Wine	1 quart Haute Sauterne	$ 2.25
	1 quart Niersteiner	$ 1.25
Claret	1 quart Chateau Lafitte	$ 1.75
Port	1 quart Grahams (1890)	$ 5.50
Sherry	1 quart Maderia, Fine Old Special	$ 3.00
Brandy	1 quart Monarch	$ 2.25
Gin	1 quart Gordon's Dry	$ 1.75
Rum	1 gallon Draught (36% O.P.)	$10.00
Liqueur	1 quart Benedictine	$ 3.75
	1 quart Grand Marnier	$ 3.75
Whiskey	1 quart Dewar's Special	$ 1.90
	1 quart Haig and Haig	$ 2.75

By the end of the auction there was only a few bottles left unsold, worth a total of $14.95. They were sent to the steward's house so that when the act became law, the club was officially dry.

The auction was on September 21st. A week later a subscription dinner was held at the club when Lt.–Col. H. St.J. Montizambert would be the guest of honour. Since prohibition would come into effect a few days later, it was decided "that the dinner would be the occasion for a farewell to the old order of things." There is no record of what went on at that dinner, but one can imagine that it continued well into the night with quite a few of the diners staying overnight at the club rather than going home in the small hours of the morning. It had happened before, and would happen again.

At the end of October, when the bar had been closed for a month, it was found that prohibition had resulted in a club deficit of $851 or about $2.80 per member. To help counter this loss, late in 1917 a resolution was passed to admit 100 new members at a $100 entrance fee. As a further precaution against losses, at an extraordinary meeting the membership voted (58to17) to assess all resident members an extra $3.00 per month as a temporary measure.

Although the club was to remain "dry" for the next four years, the same cannot be said of the members. How many took action to store up a supply of liquor in their home before prohibition came into force is not known, but there must have been a considerable number. There is the story of how one of the original members of the club made his preparations which is told by his grandson, a third generation member, Harry Bell–Irving. His grandfather was Dr. Duncan Bell–Irving who has been mentioned earlier in this volume. Harry Bell–Irving wrote in part:

> *It was well known that Dr. Bell–Irving respected the medicinal qualities of whisky and prescribed for his own health generous daily quantities. [He] was no supporter of Prohibition and viewed with amazement and disbelief those of his friends who adopted the attitude, and there were many of them that Prohibition was probably a good thing, and that they would not lay in an additional supply of whisky, but would simply have a normal supply on hand at the commencement of Prohibition and would do without as soon as this supply was exhausted.*
>
> *Dr. Bell–Irving, when he concluded that Prohibition was to become a reality, calculated his life expectancy, erring on the side of longevity, and then calculated his daily consumption of whisky and other alcohols, and having thus arrived at his lifetime supply, he multiplied the result by three and laid in this triple supply in his basement. I believe to accommodate the many cases of spirits it was necessry to create at least one additional room. At the time Dr. Bell–Irving lived on Seaton Street, just two blocks from the Club....*
>
> *In the last week before Prohibition my grandfather had some misgivings as to the accuracy of his calculations and so he purchased a final emergency reserve of twelve cases of Scotch Whisky and these twelve cases were stacked against a cement wall in his basement and a form was built around them and they were cemented solidly in so that there was no door or entry of any kind, his thought being that if all other supplies failed, this emergency*

reserve would remain safe and that to get at it the trouble of hammering and chiselling through the cement would be well worth while.

As the story goes, during the first few days and weeks following Prohibition many members of the Club, including my grandfather, followed their custom and met at the Club at the end of the day for a sociable hour. I do not know whether the supply of whisky in the Club was cut off immediately upon Prohibition or whether members were allowed to continue drinking until they had exhausted the supply in their lockers. In any event, it was not long until there was no more drinking in the Club.

Some of the doctor's friends became aware of his "ample" supply of whisky at home and it was not long until the doctor could be seen walking home from the Club escorted by one or two members, deeply engaged in conversation. Usually these friends were invited by the doctor to join him in a pre–dinner drink. The number of members who saw fit to escort the doctor home increased almost daily and soon it was not unusual for as many as ten men to see the doctor home and join him in an evening drink. Before my grandfather realized what was happening, the disaster he had feared came about and it was necessary to get the hammer and chisel and gain access to the emergency reserve.

To this point I am confident of the accuracy of the story. The following part of the story, which I was also told by my father, I have often repeated but have never confirmed. It appears that about the time my grandfather was broaching his reserve supply there were many British Columbians (including, I suspect, the vast majority of members of the Club) who recognized that a serious situation did indeed exist, and accordingly it was quietly rumored that during a certain weekend the chances were that those who brought whisky and other liquors to their homes through the harbor, provided they did so discreetly, could reasonably expect that the matter would not come to the attention of the authorities. As my father told the story, a day or two before the weekend in question a man with a discerning eye might have noticed that there was a larger number than usual of odd small craft in the harbor. From one of these craft a delivery was made to my grandfather's house which wholly satisfied his medicinal demands from that day until the date of his death many years later. I understand also that from that day on those who cared to look would have noticed that at the end of the day Dr. Bell–Irving usually walked home from the Club alone.

CHAPTER III

THE ROARING TWENTIES AND DIRTY THIRTIES

News of the signing of the Armistice which ended the Great War reached Vancouver very early on Monday, November 11th, 1918. Hours later, when people picked up their newspapers, word spread throughout the city. In the morning people left their work and began impromptu celebrations. By one in the afternoon some 25,000 people had gathered at the corner of Hastings and Granville Streets and, as the Vancouver "World" reported, "jangling klaxons shrieked, self-confident prim men and women hammered tin cans, blew horns and shouted in glee. . . . Confetti carpeted the sidewalks, the red paper of fire crackers fairly filled the gutters. . . ." That afternoon the celebrating crowds grew larger and there was a huge, hastily–organized parade with bands playing patriotic airs and people in cars went up one street and down the other, waving flags, tooting horns, and generally rejoicing that the war had finally ended.

It would be months before the veterans began to stream home. With a population of less than 450,000 at the outset of the war, British Columbia had contributed over 55,000 servicemen to the armed forces. More than 43,000 of these had served overseas and of this number, close to 20,000 had been killed or wounded. When the veterans did return in 1919, they would notice numerous changes. The premier of the province, Sir Richard McBride, had stepped down in 1915 and by the time the British Columbia battalions paraded through their local communities, "Honest John" Oliver and his Liberals were in power. Originally the war had caused considerable disruption in the province's economy but, with the increasing demands for British Columbia's metals, timber, salmon and other products, that had changed during the last two war years. Inflation had galloped ahead of wages and this was causing considerable labour unrest, a situation which became more volitile as discharged soldiers sought employment at a time when wartime orders were cancelled and industries returned to peacetime production. Although the soldiers had voted against prohibition, the new liquor laws were in force. British Columbia was dry, and one couldn't get a drink even in the new and imposing Hotel Vancouver at the corner of Georgia and Granville Streets which had opened in 1916. Veterans returning to Vancouver would notice that the city's fire department had become completely motorized and that traffic had increased so much that constables wearing white gloves and using white batons were at main intersections directing motor and horse–drawn vehicles. Traffic still moved on the left hand side of the road and would continue to do so for several more years. The old "News Advertiser" had disappeared. It had been bought by R. J. Cromie, a Vancouver Club member, and merged with the "Sun" to make the latter the largest daily west of Toronto with a circulation of 16,000. There were signs of change on the waterfront too. The Wallace Shipyards had built the first steel ocean–going vessel ever launched in Burrard Inlet and, wonder of wonders, in March 1919 the first commercial seaplane took off from the harbour carrying mail to Seattle. Things were changing, the pace was getting faster, and in the Vancouver Club life began to get a bit more lively as members returned from overseas to pick up the threads of their civilian lives.

In the decade following the war the most obvious change was the increase in membership. Total membership had decreased from 623 in 1914 to 541 in 1918. It jumped to 594 in 1919, passed the 600 mark in 1920, reached 681 in 1925 and was only two short of the 800 mark by

1930. The surge in membership was a boon to the finances of the club. Additional staff was hired and, of course, former staff members who had been in the services were given priority over other applicants. Only maintenance work had been done to the club for most of the war years but with more money available stocks of glassware and cutlery could be replenished, worn carpets replaced and furniture re-upholstered. The club definitely needed tidying up and made as attractive and homelike as possible.

One of the pleasant aspects of the club is not only the social life but the attraction of hosting and meeting some of the more interesting people in the province or in the country. This had been a tradition before the war and carries on to this day. Frequently a special dinner might be tendered to a member, sometimes to a senior politician or outstanding military commander or perhaps a distinguished guest from overseas. In mid-May 1919, for example, the club decided to have a dinner in honour of one of their own members, Major-General J. W. Stewart, recently returned from overseas. Later that year the former commander of the Canadian Corps, Lt.-Gen. Sir Arthur Currie was entertained at dinner. Six weeks later Admiral of the Fleet, Viscount Jellicoe of Scapa also accepted the club's invitation to dine.

An outstanding guest in 1919 was His Royal Highness, the Prince of Wales. It was Major-General Leckie who approached members of the General Committee with the suggestion that they should tender the invitation. When it was known he would be touring Canada, his presence was very much in demand by a variety of organizations. His schedule was already tight, but in August the club was informed he had accepted their invitation.

Confirmation that he was coming was received on August 25th, which left four weeks to make the final preparation. The club president, A. H. MacNeill, would have the ultimate responsibilty for the success of the dinner; the secretary-manager, H. R. Acton, would coordinate the staff's efforts and the chairmen of all the sub-committees would have to direct an unusual number of meetings to ensure that plans and preparations were completed on time.

The dining room ceiling was painted and arrangements were made to have the prince's motto "Ich Dien" displayed "with electrical illumination." Security precautions with the police had to be put in place, over $100 was spent on decorating the front of the club, half that amount used to obtain a canopy at the main entrance. Arrangements were made to have a red carpet leading from the curb to the main door of the club, and painters were directed to decorate the ladies reception room, hall, staircase and lavatory (the latter, presumably, for the private use of the royal party). An orchestra (Mr. Copley's) was hired for the occasion and it was to be tucked into the bay window area of the dining room. It was found that the prince's favourite flowers were sweet-peas. Fortunately they were still available locally and were to be the centerpiece of the table displays. Low palms were borrowed from Brown Brothers to be placed in the entrance hall. The chef and the head waiter both had extra help for the occasion and on the day of the dinner, September 22nd, members were requested to have their lunch elsewhere so that the dining room preparations would be completed in good time.

From the outset one of the difficult problems was who could attend. Four days after it was known the Prince of Wales would be coming, 175 members had made application for reservations. As with any occasion of this nature, it was a general rule that the first to apply would be the first to be granted. There would be no distinction respecting age, position, or any other attribute. All club members were equal in this respect. The Lieutenant-Governor was invited and there had to be fourteen reservations for the royal party. By September 8th there were 210 applications for table reservations from members alone. Originally the committee had thought it could handle 150 comfortably in the dining room. This was later increased to 200 and in the end 183 members and 17 guests attended the dinner.

It was, indeed, a magnificent affair. The staff, on whom so much depended, were at their best; the chef had performed wonders, the service was without fault, the speeches short and the Prince of Wales pleased. After dinner, when His Royal Highness left to attend a dance, everyone--members and staff--relaxed. They could feel quite proud of themselves.

In the next two decades the club hosted functions for a number of prominent visitors to Vancouver, including all of the Governors-General of Canada when they visited Vancouver. It had long been a tradition that the Governor-General and the senior members of his staff would be invited to become honorary members during their tenure of office and all accepted the invitation. They usually accepted the invitation to dinner and, in the case of the Earl of Bessborough, he was dined by the club both in 1932 and 1934. Sometimes the club was able to invite other special guests on the same occasion. In 1936, for example, Lord Tweedsmuir was dined by members and, at the same time, Admiral Sir Matthew R. Best and Captain M. de Merick of **H.M.S Appolo** who were visiting in port. Sir Edward Beatty, then president of the Canadian Pacific Railway and his party were in the city and they were invited, also.

Not all invitations were accepted. In 1936 the city was celebrating its Golden Jubilee. Sir Percy Vincent, the Lord Mayor of London, was coming to present the city with a replica of the City of London's mace so the club decided to dine him in August. As usual, however, the dinner would be for members only and invitations were not extended to anyone else. The city's mayor at the time was G. G. ("Gerry") McGeer. Under the assumption that the city's aldermen would be invited, McGeer, a club member himself, had gone along with the idea and since he more or less had 'control' over the activities of the Lord Mayor, everything seemed to be in order. When he found that the city's aldermen were not invited he recommended that the Lord Mayor accept an invitation to dine in New Westminster instead. The club's dinner was cancelled.

When it was announced that Their Majesties King George VI and Queen Elizabeth would be making a royal tour of Canada in 1939, the club wanted to hold a dinner in their honour. In November 1938, a letter was sent to Colonel H. S. Tobin. He was a club member, former commanding officer of the 29th Battalion ("Tobin's Tigers") but, more important, he was an A.D.C. to the monarch. Tobin made the necessary enquiries of the secretary of the Governor-General. Later, in a letter to the club secretary, Tobin wrote: "He tells me that he is being inundated with all kinds of invitations for Their Majesties to attend dinners, visit clubs, unveil statues, and hundreds of other things. . . ." A committee in Ottawa was given the task of sorting things out and the final approval of their suggestions would be made in England.

As it turned out, His Majesty was not able to accept the club's invitation. Nevertheless, the club was determined to join with other organizations in the city in putting up a display of flags, bunting and lights to welcome the royal couple and the best of several designs was selected and put in place.

The club itself was well situated to observe some of the ceremonies and processions. Their Majesties were due to arrive at the C.P.R. station at 10:30 a.m. on May 29th, 1939. They would then go by car along West Hastings past the club and then up Burrard Street, later returning via Granville. Members would have an excellent view of them proceeding up to Burrard. Moreover, Their Majesties would be leaving by ship for Victoria in the evening via the C.P.R. dock and returning two days later at the same dock to visit New Westminster. Since the club was one of the best viewing areas for these activities and since the demand was far greater than space, it was decided that May 29th would be a "Members Only" day at the club. As may be imagined every window was packed with members from the first to the fifth floor, and there would be many bar lockers opened and loyal toasts drunk.

* * * *

The dining room, where special dinners were presented with such elegance, was a main attraction for club members and it might be appropriate at this point to examine it a bit more closely, not only in the twenties and thirties, but even before the Great War. As we have seen, the club originated with a group of men who gathered to enjoy each other's company over a good meal. In the first club–house the meals were not only good but reasonably priced. In 1906, for example, there is a motion in the General Committee's Minute Book stating "that in addition to the a la carte system, members may make arrangements with the Steward to board at the following monthly rates:

Breakfast	*$12.50*
Lunch	*$12.50*
Dinner	*$17.50*

For three meals daily during the month -- $40.00.

At this time the club had neither its own chef nor its own cooks. Apparently the costs and payments connected with the dining room were handled separately. This system was in force for over a decade and a half. In 1907 there was a motion "that the Dining Room should no longer be farmed out but should be taken over and managed by the Club," but the motion was lost. A year later the matter came up again in committee when "a letter was read from the Steward, T. McAuliffe, in which he stated that he believed many of the members would be much more contented if the Dining Room accounts were taken over by the Club and that he, himself, considered it better in many respects." This time the committee agreed to the suggestion and, further, offered McAuliffe $110.00 per month to remain as Steward and take on the added responsibilities.

In the old club–house there was a main dining room and at least one private dining room. The latter could be used for lunch at a rental of $2.50 over and above the cost of food and wine, or $5.00 for dinner. Increasing membership led to an expansion of the dining room and hiring two additional waiters (wages for both--$960.00 per annum). It also resulted in a decision, in 1908, to establish a round table to seat twelve members. The round table was intended primarily for members coming in singly for lunch rather than accompanied by guests or fellow members. It served the dual purpose of making more efficient use of available space and at the same time giving members the opportunity of meeting each other socially and making new friends in the process. The wealth of experience and varied backgrounds of the members is a stimulus for conversation and it would be a very dull member indeed who would be bored by the table talk at lunchtime. The "round table" today is still thriving, even though the shape is changed and the number of tables doubled.

The price of meals was a continuing concern of the steward, the head waiter and the General Committee to say nothing of the members. This concern started in 1908 when the club became responsible directly for both the kitchen and dining room and this continues to the present day. If there are not enough members using the dining room, the loss is not only reflected there but in the bar as well. Even as early as 1919 there was mention of raising the minimum charges for luncheon. In August of that year, the club secretary made a survey of the members' menu selections for a week. He reported the following for lunches:

At 50 cents	*– 62 meals*	*– or 10.37%*
At 50–65 cents	*– 204 meals*	*– or 34.11%*
At 65 cents or over	*– 332 meals*	*– or 55.52%*

He went on to note that the average amount spent on meals was:

> *Breakfast – just over 60 cents*
> *Lunch – just over 60 cents*
> *Dinner – just over 90 cents*

In view of the small number of meals served at 50 cents, it was decided "not to raise the minimum charges at present." As a matter of interest, a similar survey was done in 1920, this time for the month of June. The average price paid was 65 cents for breakfast, 67 cents for lunch and $1.12 for dinner, or an overall average of 74 cents for 4939 meals served during the month.

Then, as now, there were far more members lunching in the club

If a club member was an active sportsman interested in shooting game, he could, if he wished, invite friends to dinner to enjoy the results of a successful shoot. It had been a custom for some time for members to bring to the club game they had acquired. It is interesting to note the club's Game Rules for 1929, which apparently lasted into the wartime years. The notice read:

> 1. *Game brought into the club by a member and sent to the Game Room by the hall porter must be entered into the Game Book kept for that purpose. . . . Tickets for each bird or piece of game, will be issued later and members will pay five cents for each ticket so issued to them.*
> 2. *When game is taken out of the Club, or ordered served within the Club, a ticket must be surrendered for each bird . . . and the removal entered into the Game Room Book. . . .*
> 3. *Orders for the service of game must be received before 11:00 a.m. for lunch or before 6:00 p.m. for dinner.*

Having friends in for a game dinner was one enjoyable way of dining, and one could always go to the bar for a nightcap--or perhaps to the card room or billiard room and have the drinks served there. A member on his own might do the same thing or perhaps retreat to the reading room or library. He could not relax and perhaps listen to his favourite radio programme because there were no radios in the club until the late 1930's. This led one member to enter the following in the Suggestion Book in October 1935:

> *Night life in Vancouver, destined to be the leading city of the Pacific Coast if not of Canada, is dead. Clubs are hard hit in these times. Members will not come in after dinner unless you offer them some attraction. New members will not join unless they can find something better than us old quakes getting around leaning on the bottle. They don't mind a sudden death but can't stand being bored to death.*

A few years later, in November 1939, another member expressed his opinion that one of the reasons why the club was not more popular

A formal presentation of Hunting Trophies by A.L. Hager, February 17, 1930.
(Club Archives)
Left to Right: E. Beetham, F.W. Peters, J.K. Macrae, F.W. Tiffin, K.J. Burns, R. Kerr Houlgate, A.L. Hager, F.M. Chaldecott, F.W. Rounsefell, G.N. Stacey, J.G. Woods, J.A. Macdonald. In foreground: A.H. MacNeill, J. Fyfe-Smith, George Kidd, J.P. Fell.

at night and the dining room finding it difficult to break even was ". . . simply because the cost of dining here is too high."

An idea of meal prices in the club in the 1930's is available from one or two old menus which are in the archives. This was the decade of the Great Depression but the samples are interesting nonetheless. On October 4th, 1935 a member could enjoy the following club dinner for one dollar: "Ox-tail Soup, Consomme; Filets of Sole, Boiled Salmon, Roast Guinea Fowl, Beef Tenderloin Steak; Potatoes, Beans; Deep Greengage Pie, Toasted Cheese; Coffee." Service in the bedrooms would cost 25 cents extra. If he wanted dinner a la carte, he could expect to pay a bit more as these sample prices suggest: Soups--15 cents; Fish--25 cents (or Fried Oysters and Bacon at 50 cents); Joints--between 50 and 55 cents; Cold Meats--the Melton Mowbray Pie was 45 cents; Salads--15 to 20 cents; Sweets--Deep Apple Pie was 15 cents; and Tea, Coffee, Milk, Postum or Hot Chocolate were all 10 cents each. Even in the early 1940's these prices had changed very little.

*   *   *   *

Prohibition had come into effect in 1917 and the immediate post-war years were the 'dry' years at the club. It was impossible to have wine with meals and even extremely difficult to have a drink except in one's own home. The law was aimed primarily at public bars and it had long been the contention of the Vancouver Club, as well as other clubs in the city, that their club should not be considered to be in the same category. Members looked upon the club as a home-away-from-home, and if individuals were permitted to consume liquor at home, why not at the club. There were instances when members would bring a bottle into the club and arrange to have it tucked away and quietly brought out at the appropriate moment. There were times, also, when a member might wish to bring in several bottles for a small party in the private dining room. Again, this was going beyond the law and, in July 1920, the General Committee warned one group "that under the regulations in the Prohibition Act liquors could not be served or consumed on the Club premises; and that employees were not allowed to serve or handle any liquor in the Club under pain of instant dismissal." Of course, there was nothing to prevent a waiter from bringing a member a glass, ice cubes and a mixer. Nevertheless, topping up the glass from a hip flask was not really club style.

Although one can assume that members, as individuals, probably wrote their government representatives about the liquor laws, a more organized effort was made on a national scale when a "Moderation Plebiscite" was sent to Ottawa urging certain changes in the Act. In October 1920, the club authorized the expenditure of $20 for a telegraph expressing the members' views on the subject. The demand for change was so widespread that the government actually moderated the Prohibition Act in 1921. It was music to the ears of the General Committee when the secretary "read the opinion of Davis and Co. to the effect that lockers for keeping members' liquors under the new Moderation Act would be legal."

This joyful news was acted upon with dispatch. An order for forty liquor lockers was given to a local cabinet maker. Each was to hold between four and five bottles, each had its own lock, and of course the cabinet of lockers had to be made in such a way that it would be compatible with the decor of the bar on the first floor where they would be located. The members were quick to rent the lockers, so much so that two months later the secretary was ordered to have another thirty-five installed. What the original rental fee was in 1921 is not known, but a committee ruling in 1925 stated that as of November that year, lockers were to be rented at two dollars per year, payable annually in advance. Moreover, the member was to pay a proportionate cost of installation. Lockers required for short periods--by guests staying in the club--would be charged fifty cents per month.

The number of liquor lockers increased steadily. One reason was that the rules laid down by the Prohibition Act remained in force for years, and if the club broke the rules, the concession it had gained might be cancelled. In August 1922 the club was "raided" by the police, and although no reason was given in the committee minutes, it seems someone must have reported the liquor law rules were being bent or broken. Five months later the secretary again reported the club had been "visited" by the "dry squad" a few minutes after 10:00 p.m. There were no complaints of liquor misdemeanors. In July 1923 there seems to have been yet another raid, and for some reason not recorded, the club complained to the mayor about it. Mayor Tisdall wrote to say "that none of his City Dry Squad had visited the Club." The secretary had interviewed the Deputy Attorney-General, officials in the Liquor Control Board, and Lt.-Col. McGugan, Chief Inspector of the Liquor Control Board, "none of whom had any record of such a visit." Obviously it was a fake raid, and who pulled it off was never discovered.

Meanwhile, during the 1920's, periodic notices were put up to keep straying members in line. In 1924 the General Committee laid down that no liquor should be kept behind the bar by anyone, and ordered that the bartenders "be instructed not to give a member's locker key to anyone without a written order from such member." Later that year the secretary "was instructed to put up a notice to the effect that no liquor, other than that bearing the Government seal, may be brought into the Club.'' Another rule in the Act stated that no liquor could be consumed in the club after 11:00 p.m., which apparently was resented and sometimes broken. This led the committee, in 1926, to resolve "that Members within the Club be politely notified at 10:55 p.m. that . . . no liquor may be consumed after 11:00 p.m.'' No matter how polite the waiter might have been, one cannot help but suspect that his announcement would have been accepted with the same joy as a British publican's ''Time, gentlemen, please'' cry to his customers.

Increasing membership in the club, together with a change in 1926, resulted in the General Committee making several suggestions respecting bar facilities at the club. The main bar was on the first floor, the site of the present Gun Room and recently refurbished bar beside it. To gain more room there was a suggestion to add a 75x30 foot room, made mainly of glass, which would be at the rear of the club and entered through the Reading Room. This proposal was unacceptable. As it was, one could take a drink from the bar and go through the Reading Room to the steps leading down to the small garden behind the club. The question was not raised again until January 1928 when the committee asked several club members, who were also architects, to discuss the question of alterations or additions to the building. Messrs. W. F. Gardiner, J. A. Benzie and J. Y. McCarter accepted the task and meanwhile temporary changes were made so that the western end of the Reading Room could be used as a bar annex.

During the Spring of 1928 the committee considered various suggestions proposed by the architects. The best idea, it seemed, was to move the bar from the first to the third floor. One of the largest rooms there was the Billiard Room, and from this room doors opened onto a balcony where there was a magnificent view of the harbour. There was a small bar and lounge next to the Billiard Room, and the club's architects decided this was the area to be enlarged. In June 1928, the General Committee gave printed notice of the proposed changes and costs. Since the new bar became one of the most popular rooms in the club for the next half century, the notice is given in some detail:

> *To the members of the Vancouver Club:*
> *Your committee, in consequence of the inadequate facilities in the lounge and reading room, has recently obtained professional advice with a view to the improvement of the service. . . . It has been unanimously decided to recommend that the bar be moved to the western portion of the billiard room, and that the billiard room balcony be permanently roofed and comfortably equipped and furnished as a lounge.*

>*The plan calls for a solid partition across the billiard room from the entrance doors to the centre balcony doors, thus ensuring quietness in the billiard room. A large portion of the north wall would be removed so that the bar and lounge would be one large L-shaped room. The suggested alterations would necessitate dispensing with three of the billiard tables, leaving three for the use of members.*
>
>*Building: The total cost of these changes is estimated at about $15,000 and would include, in the billiard room, 400 new lockers, new bar, plumbing, lighting fixtures, solid partition, redecorating and marbilized rubber flooring, and (on the balcony) plate-glass windows, storm windows, [and] lowering the present parapet so that the view would be uninterrupted; the whole room to be finished in either satin or mahogony.*

It was the committee's feeling that if the membership accepted the proposed changes, "the billiard room balcony would be converted into one of the most desirable rooms in the Club whereas under present conditions it is practically unused."

The suggested changes, submitted to a General Meeting of the membership, was accepted with only a few minor changes. Instead of taking away three of the six billiard tables, only two were withdrawn leaving four tables. The liquor lockers were moved into the new bar when it was finished in 1928 and the number of these increased over the years so that both walls of the shorter portion of the "new" bar and lounge are lined with them up to a height of six feet. Even after the Prohibition Act was withdrawn, a great many members found it convenient to have their own bottles available. On a busy day it saved time, it was somewhat less expensive than ordering liquor by the glass, and it also permitted a member to have on hand his particular brand which the club might not stock ordinarily.

There is one humorous story about another use of the liquor locker told by W. G. Leithead about his old friend and fellow member, J. Y. McCarter. Both were partners in the same architectural firm. "When I was young," he recalls,

>*. . . we were doing a lot of work for the Eastern banks . . . and 'J.Y.' used to entertain these people when they came out here. He was regarded as a gourmet and very knowledgeable about his wines. There was a regular routine. We would meet our guests around six o'clock and we always sat at the round table at the east end of the third floor bar. It didn't matter what anyone wanted to drink--they drank martinis mixed to 'J.Y.'s' formula. So one had a couple of jugs of martinis, then down to the dining room, not looking at menus or anything--he had organized the whole dinner with always very good wines.*
>
>*Then we would go up to the third floor bar and liqueurs.*

Again, people would sit down and they would be asked what they would like for a liqueur. Before anyone could really answer he would say: 'Before you name anything, I want to tell you what I have in my locker. I have a bottle of pre-war rye. I would suggest that we have that as a liqueur.'

I've watched people, very prominent Canadians, take the glass and sip and savour it and say 'They don't make it like that anymore.' They would really enjoy it. On special occasions it was 'Have another one!' These dinners I'm talking about went on for eight or nine years and that bottle of rye never went down! 'J. Y.' would just fill it up with some cheap rye and from there on it was the power of suggestion.

Obviously a man of such imagination and persuasive powers (his clan motto is 'Listen, O Listen!) would go far in the club. McCarter became its president in 1947.

During the 1920's and 1930's members had to be constantly reminded about the laws laid down in the Prohibition Act, even though it had been modified somewhat to allow liquor served in the club. Consumption of liquor was prohibited before ten in the morning and after eleven o'clock in the evening. On Sundays no liquor whatever could be served or consumed. Apparently there was some concern by the General Committee that even the posted notices might be ignored and the errant drinkers reported, and this resulted in a committee resolution in January 1929 ". . . that the Balcony blinds be down sharp at 11:00 p.m. on weekdays; that the East, West and North blinds be down all day Sundays and all blinds down and closed when the lights are on." It was going to be a long time before British Columbia's liquor laws would be relaxed and even as late as 1937 the Vancouver Club, along with other clubs in the city, were still trying to have the liquor laws amended so that clubs would have the power to serve liquor by the glass. Nevertheless, despite all the restrictions, at least one could have a drink at the club and that was something you could not get in a downtown restaurant or even in the opulent surroundings of the Hotel Vancouver at the time.

* * * *

The 1920's and 1930's were two radically different decades and some of the older members of the club must have experienced some difficulty in adjusting to the changes they brought. The 'twenties', of course, were the boom years, the so-called 'Roaring Twenties.' It is sometimes referred to as the 'Oil Age.' In 1918, for example, there were 275,000 cars and trucks in Canada; by 1928 there were over 1,000,000. Finding a place to park was getting to be a problem for the streets of downtown Vancouver were filled with Fords, Chevrolets, Pierce-Arrows, Maxwells, Durants and others. By 1928, the city found it necessary to install its first traffic lights at Hastings and Main. Outside the city the roads were still bad and a successful drive as far as Hope without a flat tyre was good for a topic of conversation. New packaged goods were appearing on the grocery shelves and by the end of the decade seven out of ten homes in Canada had electricity. The prices of wheat, lumber, pulp and paper and other primary products were climbing steadily. The C.N.R. and C.P.R. were spending hundreds of millions of dollars building branch lines and as the decade wore on, the automobile itself brought with it the demand for more paved roads, service stations and mechanics. With increased and cheaper means of family transportation, what were once outlying areas of Vancouver became more accessible. The Second Narrows bridge was built in 1925 and in the following year the Grouse Mountain Chalet was built after W. C. Shelly, a club member, built a road up the mountain. By 1930 work had started on the Burrard Bridge and with steadily improving roads and consequent amalgamations with neighbouring communities, Vancouver's population was nearing the 250,000 mark by the end of the decade.

The Roaring Twenties brought with it shorter skirts for women, jazz and rag-time music, the hip flask, talking pictures, neon lights, the electric stove and refrigerator and, wonder of wonders, the radio. The first radio broadcast went on the air in 1922 and by 1925, radio station CNRV could be heard regularly on Tuesday and Friday evenings. It was still an era, however, when one went to the cinema or to a variety show for family entertainment and of course on Sundays, stores, shops, theatres and just about everything else were shut down. On a warm Sunday afternoon Vancouver families would go for a drive or swarm to the beaches, but men were still forbidden by law to swim in a topless bathing suit. It was in 1927 that the Georgia Hotel opened and a year later construction began on a new Vancouver Hotel at the corner of Georgia and Burrard Streets. It was also in 1927 that the highest price was ever paid for a piece of real estate in downtown Vancouver when the Rogers Building was sold for $1,000,000. The buyer was "One-Arm" Sutton, another club member, whom we shall meet later.

The boom times of the 1920's had its impact on the club, particularly with respect to members. When the club house was built, it was anticipated that eventually it would serve 600 members. Initially resident membership was set at 400. In 1919, if one included Resident Life and Residents On Active Service, the 400 mark had been reached. During the early 1920's it was decided to increase the number of resident members. By the mid-Twenties it had reached 500 and late in 1929 the limit was increased to 550. Entrance fees had gone up also from an immediate post–war low of $100 to $300 by the latter part of the decade.

The reasons for the increases in both membership and fees were explained to the members at an extraordinary meeting in November 1929. In brief, in a letter to the members prior to the meeting, they were advised that "for some years [there has been] a steady increase in operating costs whilst revenue has not grown proportionately." Between 1924 and 1929 the committee pointed out that salaries and wages had gone up from about $64,000 to $79,000; the water rate had almost doubled; taxes had increased from $4,702 to $6,800 and repairs and renewals of china, glass and linen had doubled in cost in the five year period. Entrance fees were always an important source of money and unless the resident membership quota was increased that source would be reduced to filling vacancies caused by deaths among members. Aside from normal rising costs, the renovations made to create the third floor bar turned out to be more than expected—roughly $36,000. This meant getting a $17,000 mortgage which had to be paid on top of the building mortgage. These were persuasive arguments and the decision to raise resident membership to 550 was accepted. By the following year this category had reached 532 members, but from that year onward it began to go down. It would be fifteen long years before it reached that peak again.

The reason for declining membership, of course, was the decade–long Great Depression which started with the stock–market crash in the Autumn of 1929. The bull market, which had roared along for years, had a tremendous impact on every aspect of economic life in North America when stocks began to plunge. In Europe some nations found themselves on the verge of bankruptcy and in the early thirties Germany's desperate economic situation was one of the major causes leading to the rise of a new leader, Adolph Hitler. In Canada, the impact was devastating, made worse by drought on the prairies and stiff tariffs in the United States. Wheat fell from $1.60 a bushel in 1929 to 38 cents by the end of 1932, and when the drought came many prairie farmers saw their yield per acre reduced from 27 to 3 bushels.

In British Columbia, although spared the drought, the overseas demand for the province's primary resources declined. Unemployment continued to rise steadily. Relief gangs of unemployed men began to clear Point Grey and yet dozens of unemployed seeking work streamed into the city every day. By 1932, 34,000 people were on the city's relief rolls and two years later the provincial government, now led by Premier "Duff" Pattullo, raised the food relief rate for a family of five to $30 per month. Mass unemployment led to labour unrest and there were calls for a general strike. Construction came to almost a dead stop and for years the steel skelton of the unfinished

Vancouver waterfront, early 1930's, showing the clubhouse at lower right.
(City Archives)

Hotel Vancouver was a landmark of unfulfilled promise in the heart of the city.

There was a group of men in the Vancouver Club who were concerned about the impact of unemployment, and perhaps particularly about the plight of the unemployed veterans. A few days before Armistice Day, 1930 they addressed an open letter to the members of parliament and the business leaders of Canada through a press release. The letter, signed by thirty people, included such club members as Sir George Bury, H. B. Bell-Irving, K. G. Nairn, S. C. Sweeny, F. W. Rounsefell, N. R. Whittall, and H. S. J. Montizambert. They urged that the government "should mobilize immediately to prosecute a war against hunger and heart-rending despair, . . . against unemployment of the deserving." Canadians must realize that the country was in an economic depression which despite "the optimism of economists and capitalists, will last at least for six months more." They advocated recruiting, by voluntary means, a "peaceful army" of unemployed for a six month period. These volunteers would be given army pay and allowances, be subject to army regulations, and be boarded, fed and trained for peaceful endeavours in camps, and "used for works on the public demesne and not for private exploitation." The statement ended with the promise that "we are more than willing to bear our share of any necessary taxes" to help reduce the unemployment of men willing to work. The concept of "relief camps" under military direction was also being proposed by others in eastern Canada and the R. B. Bennett Conservative government in Ottawa took its first tentative steps in that direction in 1931.

The club's archives indicate that it did contribute to the unemployed in the city, but the records are very spotty. In November 1930, for example, it sent to the Great War Veterans Association a half ton of potatoes, five gallons of soup, two bags of bread and rolls and two dozen decks of playing cards. In March of the following year the club president, J. E. McMullen, reported to the annual meeting ". . . that the Club had donated to the Rest Billets of the Canadian Legion five gallons of soup and a quantity of bread and other food each day during the past four months." Even as late as 1939 money rather than food was being donated to the Ex-Servicemen's Billets, the Amputations Association and Shaughnessy Military Hospital.

Some of the present club members, reminiscing about their lives during the 1930's, give some idea of the difficult times in Vancouver. Stanley Horner was working for the B.C. Electric Co., collecting--or trying to collect --money for unpaid bills. He related the following:

> *On one occasion a woman in Shaughnessy in a big old home came to the door. I said my name is Horner and I have your account for collection. She slammed the door in my face and went*

and phoned Murrin, then president, and said your man tried to rape me. Of course the company was very supportive of the collectors they had and that [charge] died pretty quickly. Another time I went to collect from an Italian bootlegger on Main Street. The meters were in the basement. He let me down there but there were two Doberman dogs--guard dogs--and they almost tore the trousers off me. . . . I got out of there and it was a long time before he got any gas or power again.

Stuart Begg, whose father was also a club member, had started work in his father's automobile company in 1929. After four years in the parts department earning $12 a week he had become the senior parts man in 1933 and was making $21 a week. "For that," he recalled, "I worked six days a week with a half day off. Then about every fifth week I had to work all day Sunday."

Like Begg, John Rose was fortunate to have a job with his father's firm. After three years at the university he started out as an office boy in 1936 with Kirkland and Rose. "I was earning $35 a month," he said, "and at the end of six months they had to pay me the minimum wage which was $65 a month or fire me. Would you believe umpteen firms in town hired office boys for five and a half months and then let them go so they wouldn't have to pay that extra $30! It was standard practice."

Another member, Ralph Shaw, had taken two years of pre-medical studies at U.B.C. and hoped to go to McGill to complete his medical studies. Money was short, however, and he applied for a job with the H. R. MacMillan Export Company in 1930 at $90 a month. "I was delighted," he said, and with jobs so scarce he had reason to be.

Another club member, Douglas Maitland, was fortunate to get employment in his father's firm when he left school in 1932. He went to work as an office boy at $40 a month. "By 1935," he recalled, "it was down to $35 a month. At the same time, the fare on the Oak Street tramcar on which I travelled to work increased from six to seven cents. My mother used to make my lunch and continually advised me during the years that the price of bread was inching up a cent a loaf at the time. I paid $15 a month for board at home, so really I was going backward."

The unremitting financial difficulties being experienced by everyone in Vancouver as the depression dragged on had its impact on the Vancouver Club. From 1930 membership dropped steadily so that by 1935 there was a loss of seventy resident members and a loss of 119 in total members. Late in that year a special sub-committee was appointed "to make recommendations in connection with the serious operating loss" being experienced. It came to the conclusion that "the present membership is inadequate to continue the operations of the

Club on the present basis and some increase in membership is absolutely vital.'' It was suggested that members should consider names of men who might be proposed for membership. There were no names on the waiting list and the committee pointed out that this would be a good time for members to suggest suitable candidates.

Within the club, strict measures were taken to cut expenses and yet maintain good service. To increase or at least maintain the revenue from the bedrooms, their rental was reduced. Rooms with a bath, which in 1921 were renting at $50 per month or $2.50 daily were reduced to $40 and $2 respectively. The less expensive rooms were reduced proportionately so that a member or guest using a bedroom without a bath located on the side of the building would pay no more than $25 per month.

It was decided as early as 1932 to make some changes in the entrance fee. It had reached $400 in 1929 and normally a newly elected member was expected to pay the full sum on admittance. At an extraordinary meeting in August, an amendment to the constitution was passed whereby if a newly elected candidate wanted, and if the committee was satisfied as to his reasons, he could pay $150 on his election and $100 at each quarter until his fee was fully paid. To bring in more sons of members, their entrance fees were put at $200, or half the normal entrance fee, a practice which still continues. (Although this was meant primarily for sons whose father was then a member, it was extended in 1945 to sons whose father was a deceased member.)

Other cuts were made to reduce expenses. With great reluctance some of the staff had to be laid off and for several years all staff, from the secretary manager to the elevator operator, had their salary reduced proportionate to their pay. By 1937 all of the pay cuts had been restored, but by that time also the depression seemed to be easing slightly.

The various measures taken by the club during the decade resulted in its continued existence. As businesses failed or went bankrupt in the city there was an increased number of resignations. There were apparently some instances where a few members, wishing to remain in the club but unable to pay their annual dues, were supported in their membership by their more fortunate friends during a particularly hard year. The number of men who had their membership erased owing to their failure to pay outstanding accounts fluctuated in the depression. There were nine in this category during November and December, 1932. This resulted in the committee taking the unusual and almost desperate step for a few months in 1933 of allowing such a member to be reinstated when his bill had been paid up. Another step taken was to reduce the annual subscription to $20 for any resident member suffering financial difficulty who had held continuous membership in the club for at least thirty years, provided the General Committee voted unanimously on the matter. This, of course, would affect few members and it was laid down that there would never be more than ten in that category. Deaths, resignations and erasures were sometimes balanced by the election of new members, sometimes not, but from 1935 to the end of the decade, despite fluctuations, membership was sufficient to see the club through one of the most difficult economic eras Canada had experienced since its origin.

*   *   *   *

During the two decades under review many young men who joined the Vancouver Club were to become prominent in business, politics, the law and other areas of endeavour. Among the candidates elected in the 1920's, for example, were R. L. and R. M. Maitland, H. B. and Robert Bell-Irving. J.F. Malkin, Nelson Spencer, H. A. Wallace, K. E. Nairn, John Hart, Sherwood Lett, H. H. Stevens, Charles Woodward, L. J. Ladner, W. J. Van Dusen, Sir Stephen H.F. Lennard and Colin C. Ferrie, to mention only a few. In the 1930's, although fewer men joined, they continued to play an active role in the life of the city and the province. Among the accepted candidates in that decade were John R. Nicholson, J. Gardner Boultbee, Walter S. Owen, Arthur D. Biernes, Gerald G. McGeer, Dr. Leonard S. Klinck, John V. Clyne and others.

Some of the older members of the club remember those interwar years. The Honourable J. V. Clyne, for example, recalls that "the bar was quite well filled between five and seven in the afternoon. And in those days the club was open on Saturdays. I would always go down while I was on the Bench and go to the club for lunch on Saturdays."

Air Vice-Marshal Kenneth G. Nairn joined the club in 1922. Speaking of that era he said:

> Everyone knew one another. Billy and 'Puggy' Woodward used to be there, and all the timber people. They all gathered together. . . . It was always full because those were the days when the night boat from Victoria went back and forth and the people going to Victoria usually stayed for dinner at the Club (before catching the ferry) or the people who were over from Victoria stayed at the club. The top two floors of bedrooms were always full. The main dining room was always full at lunch and afterwards every table in the card room was fully occupied. . . . In the evening, at 5:00, there was usually a poker game going on . . . and a lot of people stayed down at the club for dinner, especially if the weather was bad.
>
> Of course there were no ladies in the club then except . . . in the ladies dining room. There were eight tables, I think, each for four people. . . . There were no elevators at the back and the ladies

would leave their coats down below in a little anteroom and walk up the stairs to the Blue Room where they could have their meal and that was all. Once a year they had a ball and that was a great affair.

In sports the club was well represented. . . . Original members and their sons formed a rowing club. In cricket we had old Fyfe Smith ... and we had quite a provincial team. At one time a British team came out and beat them. The eleven was made up mostly of members of the club and there was one staff member on the team also. In polo there were the Wallaces and Tammy Hamber . . . and several other good riders who used to play polo. They played with the Vancouver Polo Team. It was quite an event on Sunday afternoon. They used to drive out to Brighouse and play out there.

Then, of course, we had the old Jericho Golf Course. All the members used to play out there . . . and at the Shaughnessy Golf Course, and that's about all the golf there was. Capilano wasn't built then.

There were some interesting characters around. One very unfortunate thing occurred around 1925 or 1926. He was either drunk or under mental stress. He came into the club in mid-morning, went into the Reading Room and went beserk. All the chairs and things went out the window. We had a very fine old grandfather clock. He took that and threw it out the window. They finally got him out of the place.

Old Auley Morrison was a member, a well-known judge. He would talk everyone's head off. He would go and sit at the bar. In those days everyone had their own bottle. He would come and sit with you and drink out of your bottle as long as you would have him and tell all kinds of stories. He lived in an old house in the West End. About 3:00 one morning the phone rang. It woke him and he went downstairs to answer it. The person phoning said, 'Would you kindly get that dog of yours in the house. It's barking its head off out here annoying everybody.' Auley said: 'Who is this speaking please.' The fellow gave his name. Auley then said: 'I'm very sorry but I don't own a dog.' Auley waited several months and then, coming home very late from a party rang up the fellow around 3:00 a.m. and said: 'This is Auley Morrison speaking and I just phoned to find out if you found out who that dog belonged to yet.'

*   *   *   *

In the 1920's, Nairn continued,

It was more like an English club. If you were a new member you never spoke until you were spoken to. It was not a 'Hail, fellow, well met situation. People had to get to like you. While it was a typical western club in a lot of ways, there was a preponderance of British antecedents and one acted accordingly. There was an unwritten law that you more or less behaved yourself. Some older members did some things they shouldn't, . . . but they were forgiven. It took two or three years to get acclimatized and I found the club always most agreeable.

One funny thing I remember. Frequently at night some members left late. There was an old lady, a very decent old soul . . . who got to be known as 'Two Bit Annie.' She would stand out at the front door and it became a tradition that anyone leaving the club late would say goodnight to Annie and give her 25 cents. She would never say anything and she was there for a couple of years.

The Honourable A. Bruce Robertson joined the club as a young lawyer. His grandfather was a judge of the Supreme Court of British Columbia, his father (a club member) was appointed to that office in 1933 and later he achieved the same appointement. He was 29 years old when he became a member in 1933 and his memories of the club at that time are interesting. He describes it in part as follows:

In business and the professions there was a high proportion of Englishmen and . . . by 1933 it was diminishing but still very noticeable in the club. There was much more interest . . . in things that were going on in England than there is now. Frequently the discussions at lunch would be about events happening in the British House of Commons. A lot of people were interested in horse racing [which accounts for the club's sweepstakes today]. There was tremendous excitement about the yearly boat race between Oxford and Cambridge....

A lot of club members were veterans of the Boer War or Great War and many had held senior ranks. They continued to use their ranks in civilian life afterwards, and the club was filled with generals and colonels and so forth. . . .

When I joined the club the average age was considerably higher than it is now. One of the differences I note is that in those days many of your acquaintances you addressed by their surname. Nowadays almost everybody uses first names and it always sets me back on my heels when I'm introduced to somebody who is a third of my age and he says "Hi, Bruce."

Air Vice Marshal Leigh F. Stevenson joined the club as an Imperial Member in 1936 when he was posted to Vancouver to take command of No. 6 Flying Boat Squadron, RCAF. As an officer, he could be proposed and elected and did not have to pay an entrance fee. At the same time he could not hold any club office or cast a vote. Later, in 1945, he became a resident member and ultimately club president.

Stevenson remembers various aspects of the club and the people in it during the inter–war and wartime years. Recalling some of the incidents he said:

In the older days quite a few club members . . . would go there for a little male get–together, playing cards and have a drink. The wives would often wonder where they were and tele-phone the club and the steward at the desk, particularly Pyne, would always say: 'No, ma'am, he isn't here. He came in right after five o'clock and then he went out again.' Well, he hadn't gone out. He had gone upstairs. . . . So wives could never find husbands once they were in the club.

* * * *

(In the kitchen) they were great people for making great Mowbray pies and ham pies and things for members going away on their boats or on picnics. And the club used to have a cheese room. A big round of cheese would come in and they would be well–laced with whatever it takes to lace them. Club cheese really had some character. I remember one occasion (I think Jack Clyne and Tommy Davis were there) when I was going to join H. R. MacMillan on his yacht in Mexico. He sent me a wire to bring down a club cheese. By the time we got there I was glad to get that cheese off my hands and on MacMillan's yacht.

* * * *

It was really a low key club, nothing very effervescent about it. It has no objectives other than to provide a good home for the members. If it has an ambition, it's to prevent its name being mentioned in the press. It's not a 'doers' club . . . like the Rotary or Kiwanis [but the club is filled with doers].

* * * *

Certainly during the 1920's and '30's there were a great many members who were 'doers' in just about every realm of activity within the province. Possibly the one who garnered most publicity was a most unusual and adventurous businessman named "Major–General" Frank "One–Arm" Sutton. He came to Vancouver in 1927 and was accepted as a club member shortly thereafter. Born in England, he obtained an Oxford degree as a civil engineer. He entered the British Army during the Great War and took part in the Gallipoli fighting where he lost part of his arm when trying to throw back an enemy grenade which landed near him. After the war he led a restless life. He built bridges in South America, worked in the Texas oilfields, became involved in dredging for gold in Siberia, lost his shirt on that venture, but won the Shanghai Sweepstakes (worth $225,000 in 1925). He became involved in the civil war going on in China at the time and reportedly, for a while, was virtually war lord of the Chinese province of Szechuan.

When he arrived in Vancouver he was a wealthy man, although how much of the money he was to spend was his own, or whether he was investing for some of his Chinese acquaintances, is not known.

When a club committee checked on his background, it appeared satisfied that he was a gentleman with a rather aggressive entrepreneurial spirit.

Within a few months of his arrival, according to one newspaper report, "he had bought a home in Point Grey for $80,000 and was spending $15,000 on alterations. He had acquired Portland Island for $40,000 with the intention of developing it as a summer resort for an additional $200,000. He got Jonathon Rogers to sell [the Rogers Building] to him for $1,200,000. A week later he bought another downtown building for $400,000." In addition, the report went on, "he bought interests in mines, timber, cattle ranches, power sites and investigated railway possibilities in the northern part of the province." Once, while en route to Victoria, he jumped from the boat and swam to his newly purchased island rather than go the longer and more normal way. The C.P.R. boat stopped to the cries of "Man Overboard" and he was later fined for that escapade.

Sutton lost a vast amount of money during the Depression and returned to China to remake his fortune. When Japan declared war in 1941 he was put in an internment camp where his death was reported late in 1944. He wrote one volume of his memoirs and was said to be working on his second volume when interned. Without a doubt, he was one of the most colourful characters in the Vancouver Club during his brief membership in the late twenties.

A few months prior to Sutton's arrival in the city, the club lost one of its earliest members, Sir Charles Hibbert Tupper. Born in 1855, the second son of a former Canadian Prime Minister, he was called to the Nova Scotian bar after taking degrees at McGill and Harvard Universities. Active in poliics he became a member of parliament and later held several federal cabinet portfolios in the Conservative government. He was deeply involved in the Bering Sea arbitration over the sealing dispute between Canada and the United States and was knighted for his work as a Canadian member of the commission.

Sir Charles came to British Columbia in 1897, practised law first in Victoria and then in Vancouver. He became one of the outstanding members in his profession, a bencher of the British Columbia Law Society and a member of the executive council of the Canadian Bar Association. He remained interested in politics on both the provincial and federal level and despite his busy life was active in various other fields. He became president of the Children's Aid Society of Vancouver, vice-president for British Columbia of the Red Cross Society, and was involved in other charitable and patriotic organizations. Sir Charles served as president of the Vancouver Club during 1909 and 1910, and both his son and grandsons became members in later years.

Another well-known club member, Charles Woodward, was to

have his sons and grandsons carry on membership. Born in Ontario, the son of a farmer, he was given a modest sum by his father to start up on his own. He established a small store on Manitoulin Island on Lake Huron where he sold a general line of goods and bartered with Indians. After his store burnt down he came west in 1891 and started a small shop on the corner of Harris Street and Westminster Ave. Working from 7:30 a.m. to 7 p.m., the store prospered and he moved to a larger building on Main Street. By hard work and shrewd merchandising, Woodward's business grew until by 1904 he was able to establish an even larger department store on the corner of Abbott and Hastings Streets. Constant expansion in a growing city led this pioneer merchant to become one of the leading retailers in Vancouver. Although he joined few organizations, he was always a keen supporter of movements for improvement and progress of Vancouver for more than forty years until his death in 1937.

In the 1920's and '30's there were numerous club members whose businesses were expanding in the "Roaring Twenties" but who were struggling to keep from going under in the "Dirty Thirties". One could cite numerous examples, but William H. Malkin would be a reasonable choice. Born in England in 1868, he came to Canada when he was sixteen. After working on a farm and later as a store clerk in Saskatchewan, he came to Vancouver in 1895 when, he said, there was "nothing but stumps and water holes from Burrard to English Bay."

With his two brothers he bought a wagon and two horses and went into the grocery business on Water Street. Three years later he formed W. H. Malkin Co. Ltd. and his firm expanded as the city grew and the demand for his products increased. In 1902 he became president of the city's Board of Trade. His business expanded beyond the city and the province and although controlling his commercial empire took an increasing amount of time, he always maintained a keen interest in the city and its development. He was elected mayor of Vancouver in 1928, just after Point Grey and South Vancouver amalgamated with the city. In time he became a governor of the University of British Columbia, one of the founders of the Vancouver Art Gallery, vice-president of the Vancouver Symphony Society, president of the Vancouver Cancer Foundation, campaign chairman of the 1940 Community Chest, honorary lieutenant–colonel of the British Columbia Regiment, to mention only some of his activities. In 1934 he built the Malkin Bowl in Stanley Park and five years later donated six acres of land adjoining his home on Southwest Marine Drive as a public park.

Sutton, Woodward and Malkin are indicative of the variety of men and their interests who were members of the Vancouver Club in the inter–war years. There were many more, of course, and some will be mentioned later. Like so many of the older members they came from Great Britain or Eastern Canada and worked hard to achieve success in their various fields. It was in the inter-war period that more Vancouver-born members came into the club, some the sons of members but most from a variety of professions and businesses which, in some cases, had not even existed in earlier years. However, their numbers were comparitively small and the character of the club in the 1930's was little different from the 1920's. After the Second World War the age of the membership as a group was reduced, the numbers increased and the pace somewhat quickened.

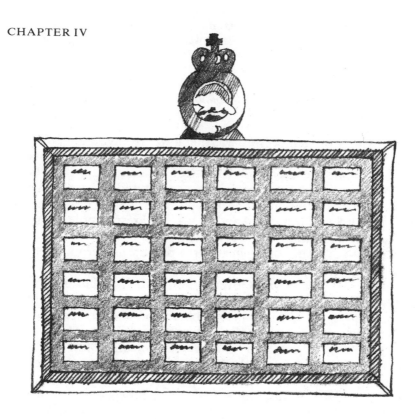

CHAPTER IV

THE QUALITY OF MEMBERSHIP

Although the number of resident members in the club declined in the 1930's, and there was a further reduction during the wartime years, no thought was given to weaken the criteria for membership.

From the beginning it was understood that the membership would be limited and that members should be compatible. There were no rules or regulations in the original constitution respecting who might be a member aside from the basic assumption that he would be a male. Nothing was said about age, race, religion, occupation, marital status or nationality. Since it was in the twenties and thirties where one sees the greatest mix between the earlier members and "new boys", it might be appropriate at this point to look at the membership and its composition.

The original constitution states:

Each Candidate for admission shall be proposed by one Member and seconded by another, by a proposal in writing, to be inserted in the book of Candidates, and signed by both mover and seconder; and shall be balloted for . . . after the lapse of two weeks from the time of such proposal. . . . No ballot shall be valid unless twenty members actually ballot; and one black ball in six shall exclude.

The essence of membership was that it was by invitation only and that the invitation was extended to the individual. There was never a class of corporate membership. The selection and election was done on a personal basis. The member's entrance fees and quarterly dues or even his normal expenses might be paid by his firm or corporation, but at that the individual was billed and he was held responsible.

The only exception to the rule mentioned above was when the club decided to offer honorary membership to the Governor-General and his staff during his term of office, and later the same privilege was extended to the Lieutenant-Governor of British Columbia. More recently, if a member of the club was appointed to the vice-regal post, he has been given an honorary life membership. One further group of men were almost automatically offered candidacy. These were "officers in Her Majesty's army and navy, or persons holding military and civil appointments under the Imperial Government, who may be stationed in Canada for an indefinite period. . . ." They were to be judged "eligible for election" as Privileged Members. This group was later tucked under the "Imperial Members" classification and, in time, their numbers were reduced to the senior officers in the three Canadian services stationed in British Columbia and the senior officer commanding the R.C.M.P. With the integration of the Canadian armed services, there is now only one senior officer and he is offered honorary membership.

For the ordinary resident, becoming a member traditionally has involved going through a number of stages for membership. An amendment to the constitution in 1907 laid down that all candidates for admission had to be "the full age of twenty-one years." In 1911 it was also ordered that the proposer and seconder should carry out a careful investigation of their candidate's social and business position, ensure that he has resided in Vancouver for twelve months and determine that he would be a desirable candidate.

The implications of being "desirable" are manifold, and an examination of the proposals for membership in the club's archives is revealing. Generally speaking the candidate is a friend of both the proposer and seconder or a business or professional acquaintance of long standing. Normally they would describe his present and past business or financial position, his membership in other clubs, his wartime record (this was particularly common in the 1920's), rank and decorations, his interest and involvement in community work, and round it off by the general statement that they felt he would make a suitable member. On one occasion, under "Occupation", the proposer merely put "Gentleman". Evidently that said it all. He was voted in.

The next stage in the procedure was to have the candidate accepted. If he was sufficiently well-known there would be little trouble. There would be other cases when, quietly, the membership committee might make enquiries. In the case of "One Arm" Sutton, for example, letters were sent to Hong Kong and elsewhere seeking further information about him. Normally this "screening" would be done closer to home. If something turned up which indicated a serious flaw in the candidate's character about which the proposer and seconder had no knowledge, they would be advised and the candidate's name withdrawn.

There were occasions when a candidate might be rejected. A candidate was not elected by a mere majority vote. If a member voted against (or "blackballed") him, the negative vote could cancel several of the positive votes. Originally it was one blackball in six, later in eight and still later in ten for exclusion. The purpose of blackballing was to ensure the candidate would be accepted by the largest number of members possible. The harmony of the membership was most important. At the same time one did not wish to embarrass a potential candidate, and thus it was always wise to withdraw his name if even a small number of the membership were thought to disapprove of him.

The system could be abused. Despite the fact that several of the club's founding members were Jews, after the Great War there were no Jewish candidates proposed for membership at the Vancouver Club (and at many other clubs across Canada for that matter) for several decades. This changed after the Second World War, but even then it was difficult for a while for a member wishing to propose a friend who was a Jew to let his name be put up for election in case of rejection.

There was one incident in 1927 which illustrates how blackballing could be abused. Some members, who were staunch supporters of one political party, decided to veto those candidates for membership who were from another political party. Their tactic worked, and when it became known a petition was presented to the General Committee requesting a special meeting to consider amending the constitution. The main speaker at the meeting was a very respected member, Campbell Sweeny. He was an honorary life president of the Vancouver

General Hospital, the Vancouver Rowing Club and the Vancouver Club. He was also honorary president of the Vancouver Cricket Association, an original member of the Jericho Country Club, a member of the Board of Governors of U.B.C. and an honorary life member of the Vancouver Board of Trade. When he spoke, members listened, and Sweeny proceeded to rap a few knuckles. He said in part:

> At the January [1927] ballot eight candidates were up for election, all proposed by Members of the Club in good standing and passed by the Committee as eligible under our Constitution and By-laws and four of them were rejected, why I cannot imagine. With a membership of over 500 ordinary and local members, leading men professionally, commercially and socially, our Club occupies an important position in the community and owes a duty to it as well as to itself, and it is a very serious matter that through the ill-considered and concerted action of a few of our members, indignity has been put upon fellow members, the proposers and seconders of the four candidates at the last election and great injury done to those fellow townsmen.
>
> I say this came about through concerted action because it is impossible to think that out of 147 ballots cast, . . . there could have been enough voters who each on his own initiative would so stigmatize his fellow members and his fellow townsmen against whom nothing derogatory to their personal integrity or social position can be advanced.
>
> I do not contend that every Member has not at all times the right to vote as he chooses, . . . but for Members to combine and under the protection of the secret ballot to accomplish a selfish end is surely contrary to all Club ethics.

Mr. Sweeny went on to note that in the period between 1909 and 1926 there was a total of 848 candidates of whom only 33 (or less than four per cent) were rejected.

It was obvious the system had been abused. As a result the membership approved the idea that the four rejected candidates be voted on again. Two were elected later that year, a third elected in 1929 and the fourth never. Two months after the special meeting the General Committee, appreciating the sensitivity of the task of members on the Membership Committee, resolved that the names of the latter "be not spread on the Minutes."

There was one other abuse of membership application which might be mentioned. Prior to 1963, as one former committee member put it, "There had been some juggling around whereby some so-called more important people were given priority over those who had waited for some time." After that date it became stated policy that potential members would be voted on strictly in accordance with their date of application.

Once a candidate had been accepted, he was given a copy of the club's Rules and Regulations. One of the first things he learned was that he was expected to pay his quarterly dues and club expenses promptly. Failure to do so would result in his name being "posted" on the notice board in the main lobby. This was considered a major embarrassment and generally resulted in prompt payment. However, a member might be on vacation, away on business or ill. He might also be forgetful. Whatever the cause, it was something to be avoided and arrangements were made whereby a member could have his club bill sent to his bank where it would be paid immediately. The friend of a posted member, seeing his name on the board, would often phone his friend so that he could attend to the matter immediately. A very good friend, knowing the member to be away or ill, might even pay the bill and collect from the member later. If posting didn't work, a polite but firm letter followed, and if that failed to bring a cheque by return mail, the ultimate weapon might be used--expulsion.

Although this was a rare occurrence it did and still does happen. A recent past president, reminiscing on discipline and posting, remembers incidents during his tenure:

> *We had several expulsions when I was president. One young man, whose father was quite well known and a very much admired citizen in the city, had a son. I don't know how old he was . . . but he was well recommended by two senior members of the Club. It was very difficult . . . for the General Committee not to accept him. Well, things went bad from the very beginning even while his father was still alive and a member. He had trouble paying his bills . . . and then his father died. Things got worse. It embarrassed his mother and in the end he was expelled. He should never have been a member to begin with. It was just bad screening.*

In 1971 the General Committee decided to abolish posting which took effect in September. The result was not favourable. The number of members who had not paid their bills within the fifteen days allowed began to rise significantly. In 1972 there were 56 names posted, by 1974 there were 69, 84 in 1975 and in 1986 there were 98. There was no doubt, the committee reported, that "the posting of names on the notice board was a great deterrent to non-payment or late payment of bills." Why was the posting system ended? Larry Dampier, who was on the committee at the time, gives this explanation:

> *What happened was that the names of delinquent members were posted, not on the main bulletin board where the guests could also see them but, rather, around the corner where, nor-*

mally, only members would see them. The point was not to embarass the member unnecessarily. On one occasion, to the amazement of some, and amusement of others, Mr. H.R. Mac-Millan was posted. Obviously, this was the result of a mix-up at his office; but, there it was, in accordance with the rules. This matter came before the General Committee and it was agreed that the Club should have a more business-like procedure. With a good deal of agonizing but with a lot of professional in-put from the members, a new programme of warning letters, follow-up notices and the use of bank-drafts, was introduced. Posting was eliminated, at least for some time; later, however, a modified form of posting was re introduced. In my view, no system can be completely satisfactory for all, in a private club.

Generally speaking there have been few occasions when a member has not honoured his debts promptly. Some have gone to exceptional lengths to do so, even when they found themselves unexpectedly short of funds. On one occasion, in 1923, a member found himself $177.65 in debt to the club. Evidently his financial circumstances forced him to resign but he wanted to honour his debt so he offered a large silver tray in payment. The club accepted it, had the inscription on it erased and held a raffle at $5.00 per ticket on the tray. Forty tickets were sold and the debt paid.

The club's rules and regulations grew as the years went by, and some were modified. In the early years, and even in the post-war era, the number of "strangers" (or visitors as they were later termed) a member could bring to the club was limited. Normally a member's guest entering the club would be taken to the "Strangers' Room," an area now occupied by the Secretary-Manager and his secretary. There he would wait until met by his host. The guest had to be accompanied at all times, and further, there were strict regulations respecting the number of times the same guest could be entertained in the club. Some of these rules have been relaxed, but rules of conduct in the club have never been modified.

One of the earliest entries in the Minute Book of the General Committee respecting conduct was in October 1901. A complaint was made respecting bad language used by two temporary members. The secretary was instructed to warn them that "should such a thing occur again [the Committee] would be compelled to place them on the black list and not allow them the privileges of the Club in future." Later that year another member was guilty of some infraction which, it seems, was taken as an insult to another member. The guilty member was suspended until he wrote a letter of apology to the victim and another to the general membership which would be posted. The member wrote the letter but the committee relented and did not post it. Nevertheless, a month's suspension was enforced.

Imposing discipline on members bending or breaking the rules required both firmness and tact. One did not want to curb individuality nor suppress mild eccentricity. However, sometimes the rod had to be displayed if not used. In 1916, for example, a complaint was received about a member respecting his "sleeping in various rooms while in a condition derogatory to the dignity of the Club." The culprit was warned "that should there be a further complaint, the matter would be dealt with in accordance with the provisions of the Constitution." A few years later a member was suspended for three months for entertaining to dinner a guest who "was out on bail on a charge of sedition." This was "contrary to the interests of the Club."

Sometimes the circumstances of an infraction of the rules were such that the offender was forgiven. In 1934, W. E. Burns was entertaining guests in the Ladies Dining Room. As he was leaving he spotted two dozen peonies in a bucket of water in the small coat room by the Ladies Entrance. They were a bit wilted and had been placed there for possible use the next day. For whatever reason he took them, leaving this note: "Pyne--Took the peonies--I could not resist. Please arrange so that I am responsible for their replacement. W. E. Burns." The night hall porter had to report the incident. Not only did the Committee forgive the crime, but honesty had its own reward-- Burns was not charged for the replacement.

One of the common infractions of club rules was members staying in the club well beyond closing time. Their names would be taken by the night porter as they left. Almost invariably they would be playing cards, particularly poker. Every means was used to warn them of the club's closing hour, (normally midnight) but it had little effect. They would be warned verbally ahead of time. Then the lights of the card room would be flashed on and off from the main switch a few minutes before the closing hour. Eventually the committee told the hall porter to switch off the lights completely in the card room. The players, intent on their game, would move to another room and carry on. Frequently they would play well into the morning. In October 1935, for example, the night porter, George Lawtry, signed out G. H. Worthington at 6:30 a.m., P. D. Gordon at 7:30 a.m. and when he was relieved at the desk at 8:00 a.m., he noted F. J. Mawdesley and James Hamilton were still playing! Others who enjoyed a good game of poker at this time were W.G. MacKenzie, H. B. MacDonald, G. Sweeny, Austin C. Taylor, Victor Spencer, W. B. Farris and B. S. Brown.

When rules were broken, punishment was meted out. Normally the committee gave the culprits a stern admonishment and levied a fine

September 20, 1962

" . . . If there's anything I can't stand it's a consumer telling a merchant
how to sell to a customer."

(the latter graduated to the hours the member remained in the club
beyond closing time) or even a short suspension. This would result in a
humble letter of apology, with the member paying the fine and swear-
ing it would never, never happen again. This stern resolution might
last one, even two months, until one or more of the keen poker players
would find themselves in a hot game, determined either to recoup his
losses or prolong his winning streak. Once again the hours would pass
and as they left familiar names would come up again on the agenda
under "discipline." Once again, depending on past similar misde-
meanours, fines would be imposed, suspensions allotted and written
apologies demanded. If nothing else, it was a minor source of revenue
for the club. There was a gentleman's agreement, of course, that one
would not try to bribe the night hall porter. He had to report the
miscreants. One who did not report eight members for some reason
was suspended from his job for a month.

It was rare when there were serious breaches of conduct, and
most of these seem to have occurred after the Second World War. On
an evening in July 1950, two middle–aged members in the dining room
got into a fight and blows were exchanged. One, whom the committee
judged struck the first blow, was suspended for 18 months. The other,
whose nickname indicated a hot temper at the best of times, was given

a two month suspension. On another occasion there was a nasty incident over a card game. Two of the four players were traditional rivals. During the game tension rose, names called, and a glass of liquor was thrown into the face of the rival player. This was an intolerable act and the punishment for this misconduct was a year's suspension.

One of the most serious offenses a member could commit was to sneak a woman into the club, particularly one who used to be termed a "soiled dove," a "princess of the pavement" or a "daughter of unhappiness." This could result in expulsion from the club in short order. Nevertheless, it was tried on several occasions. The last incident was committed not by a member, but by a guest of a member, who managed to get his willing female accomplice up to his bedroom with the intent of more than enjoying the view over the harbour with her. Her exit was noted and reported and his explanation was feeble. He left the next morning and when cleaning up his room, three pieces of irrefutable evidence of the evening's activity were discovered and brought to the secretary. The secretary showed them to the president, and both regarded the evidence with a mixture of anger, awe and envy. The member who invited the guest was terribly embarrassed but under the circumstances nothing could be done.

The new member in the club had a lot to learn whether he joined before or after the Second World War. If his father was a member (and the proportion of father and son members increased each decade) he paid only half the entrance fee and had probably dined at the club numerous times, probably more than the ordinary candidate. At that, his election was no more automatic than the ordinary candidate. But at least he would learn from his father some of the "do's and don'ts" in the club as well as the traditions. Although every member was equal, a number of the older members seemed "more equal" than others. Some liked to sit in a particular chair at "their" table in the dining room; others might have hung their hat on "their" hook in the cloakroom and a group of members might have sat at a certain table in the bar for the past twenty years and would resent a newcomer intruding. Dress, he would know, would be normally a lounge suit or jacket and slacks, the latter always with a shirt and tie and never, in the 1950's and later, with a turtle neck sweater. A club dinner meant wearing a dinner jacket; a more formal affair meant white tie and tails.

It took time to get to know the other members, particularly the older ones, and indeed it took time to become familiar with all the rooms in the club. It was not until 1946 that the committee decided to hold a new member's luncheon where the "new boys" could not only meet each other but when they could be shown all around the club and given a "fatherly" talking to by the president or a senior member of the committee. Later this was changed from a luncheon to a new members reception but the idea was the same--to familiarize the newcomers to the club and make them welcome.

One member, D. M. Clark, remembers his impression of the club when he came in after the war:

> *We new young crept very quietly around the club for a couple of years. It had always been a hallowed sanctuary and we were not about to step on people's toes if we could avoid it. In those days I didn't come into the club alone. I used to make sure I had some friend with me and we would come together. I soon got over that. It very quickly became a second home to me and it has been ever since.*

It might be noted, incidentally, that Clark had served as a field officer with the Seaforth Highlanders of Canada and commanded it after the war. His father, Brigadier J. A. Clark, had commanded the same unit in the Great War and had been a club member since 1915.

Clark's comments held true for many new members, especially in the mid-1940's period when the average age of the membership increased as the number of new and younger members was reduced during the war. Sometimes, however, the image of the older members as pillars of decorum and respectability could be modified in the eyes of the newcomers. Stuart Begg, for example, did not know he was a member of the club until he received a notice in the mail after his return from overseas. His father, a member for thirty years, had made the arrangements for him. As Begg stated later: "I took the notice into my dad and he grabbed it out of my hand and said, 'You're not supposed to know about this. You're a member of the club but don't ever go down there until I invite you.' This was his way of doing things. He did the same thing with my brother, Roy, who ended the war as a Group Captain in the RCAF."

When young Begg began to use the club as a member he witnessed an event which softened his image of at least one of the elderly, well-known members. This gentleman and his friends used to sit at a round table in the third floor bar. One day, Begg reports,

> *He, as usual, got a little bit filled and two of his friends, who were equally in the same state, helped him out, one on each arm. They got him on the elevator, went down to the main floor, took him into the cloakroom, got on his coat and hat, came out of the cloakroom to the south where there is a pillar. One friend walked on one side of the pillar and the other fellow on the other side and [their friend] walked smack into the pillar, hit his face and fell on his backside. I saw this happen.*

Another time the same elderly gentleman tripped on the rug in the hallway. The hall porters came to help him. There was one fellow trying to get his collar undone, thinking he was strangling. "Leave me alone," the older man cried, "if I'm going to die, the Vancouver Club is the place to be!"

The age gap between the new and older members has always existed and probably will continue. A newly elected lawyer who finds himself sitting across the round table in the dining room from a member who is a Judge of the Supreme Court is likely to wait for the older man to address him rather than vice versa. The honorable member, on the other hand, is quite likely wondering whether or not he has met the younger man, can't remember his name if he has, and would be pleased if the new member would introduce himself and save the embarrassment of admitting that they had met at a club function a few months ago. Sooner or later, however, the strangeness of new membership wears off, new friends are made, and in time the new member is beginning to think about sponsoring his own friends for membership.

Aside from his bill for his entrance fee, one of the first things a new member would be given was a booklet containing the club's by-laws, constitution and the list of members. No matter what decade he joined, he would do well to read it carefully. Assuming that he was elected immediately before or after the Second World War, and assuming he was neither the son of a member nor had belonged to any other club, there are a number of things which might have been of particular interest to him. One was the variety of memberships. Topping this list were honorary members, who paid neither the entrance fee nor the annual subscription. This was a very short list.

Resident members constituted the majority, but within this category, there were a few of the older men who had been members for thirty years and had their quarterly dues reduced to five dollars. In 1936, for example, there were to be no more than ten in this category at one time. In that year there were still some "Life Members" and "Original Members" in the club. Among the latter was Edward E. Rand who arrived in Vancouver a year before the city was incorporated. He was head of a large real estate firm; in fact he owned the oldest business conducted continuously under one name in Vancouver. He was 76 years old at the time and was to live to the ripe old age of 94 with 61 years of membership behind him. Another was W. F. Salsbury, then 89, an original member who, on his 90th birthday, was to be granted honorary membership by the club. There were others, of course, but the rarest were the Life Members-- those who, at the turn of the century, had signed over to the club six of their debentures from the Granville Club and had bought remission from certain fees.

The new member would find out that, if need be, he could become an absentee member. If, for business, health or any other reason he was going to be absent from the province for six or more months, he paid only a nominal quarterly fee. In the club he would also meet country members. These were men who resided outside a 25-mile radius and within a 300-mile radius of the club. These men paid only a $30 annual subscription and normally used the facilities of the club only when in the city on business or vacation. Imperial members, that is members of the armed forces or senior civil servants of the Imperial or Allied governments, were not subject to an entrance fee but did pay a monthly ten dollar subscription. Again there were few in this category and by the nature of their appointment, tended to rotate every few years.

Another type of membership was the "marine" member. This was open to ships' officers sailing on Royal Mail Steamers or any permanent line of ocean steamers established in Vancouver. They could be members without paying the entrance fee but had to pay an annual subscription of $24. Then there was the non-resident member who lived beyond a 300-mile radius of the club, paid an entrance fee but only a $10 annual subscription. There were the privileged members who were temporary residents in Vancouver, paid twenty per cent of the entrance fee and were able to obtain full resident status once they had paid the full fees on becoming permanent residents of the city. A supernumerary member could be any member who, by reason of disability through natural causes or war wounds, was unable to avail himself of all the privileges of the club. His annual subscription was $10 per annum. This was particularly beneficial to older, retired members who had been hit hard by the economic slump of the 1930's and who, owing to age, wanted to drop into the club occasionally rather than lose complete contact with it.

There was one more class of "members" one might meet at the club. An "introduced" member was a member of an affiliated club. In 1936, the Vancouver Club was affiliated with two overseas clubs (the Australian Club in Melbourne and the British Empire Club in London) and seven across Canada. By reciprocal arrangements, an introduced member could stay at the Vancouver Club for a limited time as could a Vancouver Club member visiting an affiliated club. They could not cash cheques, give I.O.U.'s or introduce guests. There were also introduced visitors and temporary members. The former was a guest of the member who lived beyond the 25-mile radius and could be put up at the club for two weeks; the latter was a candidate for resident membership outside the 25-mile radius.

The classes and categories of membership changed periodically or were modified as time went on. Basically the idea was that those who made most use of the club--the resident members--were expected to pay more for the privilege. The less frequent the club's facilities were used, whether owing to distance or disability, the more moderate the cost. It was a fair practise and continues to this day.

It has been noted earlier that during the 1930's the club's membership was aging. The new member would note the death of a member by his name listed on the bulletin board, and particularly, perhaps, by the position of the flag flying from the front of the building. The arrangement whereby the flag would be flown at half mast was first made in 1920, it being understood that knowledge of the member's death was "received prior to the funeral." Fifteen years later there was a refinement to this order. The new instructions were that the flag would be at half mast "from the time of death until sunset on the day of death, and then on the day of the funeral from morning until the conclusion of the service." This changed again in 1938 when a new General Committee resolved that the flag be flown at half mast "from the time of death of a member until the time of the burial service." This custom, to look ahead, was carried on for another four decades but was changed again in 1980. In May of that year a committee member, Larry Dampier, noted that although usually the flag would be at half mast for only one or two days following a member's death, there was a recent member whose memorial service was held ten days after his death. The ordinary member might have thought that there was something unusual going on. Dampier pointed out there had been several recent cases of this nature and felt the rules should be changed. H. Clark Bentall, then Chairman of the Membership Committee, proposed a compromise. The tradition would be continued, but for any one member the flag would be at half mast for a maximum of five days. His compromise suggestion was accepted and remains in force--at least at the time of writing.

In a book entitled *British Clubs* by Bernard Darwin, the author states:

> *A man may be perfectly fit to be a member of a club, in the sense that his character and his habits are above reproach, and yet he may be altogether without certain essential qualities. The clubable man ... does not merely get something out of the club but contributes something to it. He possesses more than the mere fitness which is after all but a negative virtue; the club will be, by however so little, the richer by his membership.*

There are a variety of ways a member may contribute to a club. On a personal level, of course, there is his bonhomie, his humour, his cheerfulness, his conversation and so on. One substantial way, of course, is his willingness to serve on the committees which not only govern but also help to shape the character of the club. The new member, whether he joined before or after the Second World War, would soon become aware of the committees' roles and the part they played in club life, and it might be well to examine this aspect of club governance at this point.

The club was run on basic democratic rules. All ordinary members had a vote, and generally the majority of votes cast determined the decision. There were two exceptions, both in the constitution. One was a blackball or negative vote cast against a candidate for membership which would cancel a number of positive votes. The second was a vote taken by the membership at a general meeting when a change in the constitution is involved. This required seventy-five per cent of votes cast for approval.

In the late 1930's there were five committees charged with the duties of looking after the club. The first and most important was the General Committee which consisted of the president, vice-president and seven members, a reduction of two members from the original constitution. There were also the House, Dining Room and Bar, Card Rooms and Billiards and Reading Room Committees. There have been modifications of this structure which will be mentioned later.

The General Committee was responsible for the general management of the club through the secretary. It controlled finances, fees, funds and club property; it dealt with complaints, made regulations, imposed discipline, arranged meetings, checked elections of candidates, and smaller matters. The House Committee looked after the building and the employees. Structural repairs and upkeep, the housekeepers' and hall porters' departments, heat, light and power--in general the maintenance of the building, its rooms and general upkeep also came under its control. The Dining Room and Bar Committee and the Card Rooms and Billiards Committee were concerned with those matters which their name suggests. Probably the fewest problems were faced by members of the Reading Room Committee which supervised the Reading Room, Silent Room, Library and services.

The General Committee was elected annually, a change from the earlier period when one-third of the committee was elected every three years in rotation. A member could serve for a number of years if elected and, during that time, he would expect to be appointed chairman of the other committees in rotation. In that way, he would become familiar with every facet of the operation of the club and might, ultimately, expect to be elected vice- president and then president. There was no "normal" time limit set on retaining the two top posts. For the first forty years of the club's existence presidential terms of office lasted from one to four years. It was not until 1965, on the suggestion of Thomas E. Ladner, that a one year term became normal for a period of twenty years.

Nomination for membership on the General Committee was a serious matter. A member could be proposed and his nomination seconded by friends. Strictly speaking, there was no "nominating committee," but by tradition the past presidents would meet and discuss not only the nominees for the committee, but for the senior positions of vice-president and president. There was also the question of which committee member might be stepping down. Attending the meetings of the main and sub-committees was one criteria which could not be overlooked. There might be a very competent and well-liked committee member who, for business reasons, found it impossible to attend the meeting as often as he might wish. Such a member might be asked to step down and make room for a nominee who had the time. Once the names were in, and the "nominating committee" tried to ensure there were more nominees than vacancies, the names were posted prior to ballotting. Ballots were cast in the club for many years but mail-in ballots were permitted after the war. Ultimately the decision of the membership would be made known and the new committeeman would start to learn his new duties and responsibilities.

To be elected to the committee was considered an honour, but it was no easy task. "The Committees and the Executive have always worked their hearts out," Past President Graham Dawson commented later. "It has been one of the remarkable things about the club—it has been well served by people who have volunteered to work." Another, reflecting on his years as a committee member and later president said: "The club, to my mind, had the finest committees you would ever find. They were prominent fellows and competent. There's no board of any company has a better board of directors than the club committee. They are members who own companies, are bank managers, chartered accountants, and so forth. They are hand picked, run the club and do it well." Another past president felt that the only criterion for committee membership was "to have a man who we think would make eventually a good president."

In brief, the calibre of membership on committees is unusually high and their powers great. Normally there are more candidates for election than there are vacancies to fill—but only a few. The General Committee itself is usually well attuned to the memberships' opinion and desires before imposing new regulations. As one member put it:

> *A basic philosophy of club life is that you elect a committee and give them pretty well free rein . . . to operate the club. If you don't like them you throw them out, but most of them are mature enough to know that you don't do anything in the club without*

the majority of people in favour of it. If you don't know whether
they are or not, you have a referendum . . . to test the water.

Although committee status is considered to be an honour, not everyone is willing to stand for election if approached. Committee work is time consuming. Not only are there the meetings themselves, but there is the need to be on hand for them. Some members' work involve a lot of travel and their presence in the city on specific dates is unpredictable. Others, busy with their firms or very involved in community work, international business meetings and so forth know they cannot give the time the work involves and decline nomination. Others who serve on the committee may leave after several years of good work. As one put it: "I served for six years and I thought if I go up to a vice-president, which they wanted me to do, then I would have to serve another year of that, then another year as president and then another year as immediate past president. So I would have another three years and I was terribly busy. So I got off, but I enjoyed the experience."

A past president summed up the club's governing body this way: "From my years on the committee I cannot think of any organization I've ever belonged to that runs more smoothly, despite the problems that crop up from time to time. It seems to me that the right decisions always have been reached at the right time and I think that testifies to the validity of the screening process for members of the committee."

* * * *

Assuming that the new member came into the club in the late 1930's and is still with the club for several decades, he would see some of the old traditions or customs of the club continue while others would be modified or dropped. One thing he would notice would be the tendency of some members to gamble, an inclination on which the General Committee kept a sharp eye. In its earlier days the club evidently had a reputation for this activity, so much so that in 1908 the secretary addressed a letter to the committee which read in part:

I would . . . earnestly urge you again to pass, if possible,
some severe measures respecting gambling and payment of gam-
bling debts contracted in the Club. Some rule regarding these
abuses should be deservedly popular and would, in time, remove
from the Club its worst feature as well as the stigma of deserved
disrepute which it has earned on this score.

Despite his suggestion, there was no change in the constitution or rules which laid down that "no game of hazard shall be played in the Club," limited the stakes of whist or other games, and further ordered that "all liabilities incurred in the card room or billiard room must be paid within forty-eight hours." The worst excesses and rule-bending in this respect appeared to be in the card room, particularly among the poker players. Large sums were known to exchange hands as the game continued into the night. One member, wishing to recoup, was seen to put his car keys on the table. His losing streak must have continued. Another member took them up. With some players even these would be small stakes, and stories of businesses being lost and won are part of the club lore.

At the bar it was quite common in the club, and in many other institutions as well, to toss a coin or roll dice to see who would pay for drinks. There were dice and a dice box at the club bar, but there grew up "an objectional practice of shaking the dice in various rooms." This was stamped on by the committee who ordered the dice and box must remain in the bar and nowhere else.

By far the most common and popular form of gambling the new member would notice were the various sweepstakes in the club which were popular in the 1920's and still continue. Normally they were based on horse-racing results, but in May 1924, for example, there had been one based on provincial election results in Vancouver constituencies. The Grand National, the Derby and the Cambridgeshire were favourites and others were added as time went on. A member would sign for one or more numbers on the list posted on the bulletin board and be charged a set fee. The horse would be drawn, the race run, and the first, second and third prizes distributed to the fortunate members. In time the winner of the first prize was expected to buy a drink for other members of the club but this resulted ultimately in the winner taking home very little of his gains.

In 1929 the committee decided "that five per cent be deducted from all Club Sweeps, the amount to be donated to Shaughnessy Hospital or other charity." A week after that decision the amount deducted from the Derby sweep was donated to the Fresh Air Fund. Later that year, when the Cambridgeshire was run, the deduction was split between the Western Association for the Blind and the patients at the Shaughnessy Military Hospital. By the early thirties the "Charities Account," as it was termed, was making payments to a wider variety of deserving groups which included the Canadian Legion, the Reverend A. Roddan Christmas Fund, Inspector Mortimer's Home for Unemployed Women, the "Sun" and the "Province" Christmas Funds, the Disabled Veterans, the Amputation Association, and others.

To look further down the road for a moment, in the post-war years the committee was taking ten per cent from the gross amount subscribed to the sweepstakes and diverted it to the staff retirement fund. At that time there was no regular pension scheme for the staff and although members, at Christmas time, were usually generous in subscribing to the fund, the number of staff retiring was making heavy inroads on the accumulated capital. This continued for many years.

By the early 1970's complaints about the size of one's sweepstake winnings compared to the cost of buying drinks at the third floor bar on the Monday following the race began to be heard. These, for a while, were ignored. Tradition is tradition, and a free drink is a free drink. However, as the price of drinks went up, the number of complaints increased. In April 1976, one of the committee members, Geoffrey Tullidge, brought the matter to the General Committee. The minutes describe the problem and the result:

> Mr. Tullidge pointed out that, for at least fifteen years, betting on the Club sweepstakes had been $5.00 per ticket. By tradition winners received 1st – 50%; 2nd – 30% and 3rd – 20% of the stakes. They also paid the same percentages of the bill for free drinks to all members present in the Club on the following Monday. As, over fifteen years, the price of drinks had risen astronomically, it had reached the stage where the winners were paying out one-third of their winnings for the free drinks. He recommended that either the betting ante be raised or that the period during which free drinks were dispensed be considerably curtailed. After discussion, it was agreed that one free drink per member present be limited to the period 12:00 noon to 1:00 p.m. the first working day following the race, and that the secretary speak to the Bar Three staff to ensure that this ruling is implemented.

Tradition and common sense were nicely merged. The ante, incidentally, was raised to ten dollars in May 1982. Tradition merges well with charity also.

There was yet another way a member could take an occasional gamble. In 1956 the club hired a bar steward who had considerable experience in the job with various city hotels. In time he began to sell lottery sweepstake tickets in Bar Three long before it was legal to do so. He did a brisk business but as his "customers" increased in number, the club secretary began to hear rumblings from the other bar stewards which he brought to the attention of the president. As the latter explained to the committee,

> . . . this bar steward was now spending more time on ticket selling, paying out, collecting and accounting, than on doing his proper job of taking and carrying out drink and food orders. In addition, the remainder of Bar Three staff have all complained, and are not prepared to do this bar steward's job while he makes extra money on tips from members and a share of any winning ticket, on top of his normal pay. As a result he has been ordered to desist from selling any more tickets. . . .

This posed something of a problem for the committee. All were agreed that, some members would wish to continue betting on the Irish Sweepstakes. At the same time, they agreed that "such continuance should not be at the cost of, or cause of, dissension among the Bar Three staff." The committee suggested, therefore, that the management should see whether a method could be worked out whereby House Rule 165 (no member shall give any money or gratuity to any of the employees of the club under any pretext whatsoever) would not be contravened but that a share of any winning ticket automatically go to the staff retirement fund.

It turned out to be a most acceptable compromise. At the next meeting in April 1980, the secretary reported the sale of lottery and sweepstake tickets had started again and "the bar steward in question has agreed to donate $100 a month to the staff fund as a prerequisite to his transacting business with members." Everyone seemed happy with this new arrangement, members and staff alike.

A member joining the club in the late 1930's would be told about an old custom, referred to as the ticket system, which he would see abandoned during the next fifteen years. Exactly when the club began to print its own money is not known, but apparently it was in use by the turn of the century. For whatever reason, small booklets of tickets, about the size and shape of a book of wartime ration coupons, were printed in different denominations of five, ten and possibly twenty-five cents. Each coupon or ticket bore the club's logo and the value of the ticket. A member could buy booklets from the hall porter and use these to pay for food, drink or other club services. There is a printed notice in the club's archives, unfortunately undated, which states: "Payment must be made by tickets for all charges under one dollar."

Other clubs used the same system, and since it was quite common for a member to belong to other clubs as well, a system was arranged whereby "club money" was acceptable elsewhere. The first recorded instance of this was in February 1905 when, at the suggestion of the Union Club of Victoria, the Vancouver Club agreed "to make their tickets interchangeable." A few years later the same arrangement was made with the Jericho Country Club. An interchangeable ticket agreement existed with the Shaughnessy Heights Golf Club but was cancelled in 1913 when the latter "changed its method of payment." During the 1920's the agreement spread to the Marine Drive Golf and Country Club, the Royal Vancouver Yacht Club and in 1930, the Point Grey Golf Club and the Capilano Golf Club in 1939.

Within the Vancouver Club the system continued in use during the Second World War. In March 1944, the General Committee "agreed that the Finance, House and Dining Room Committees should consider the question of charging all items to members' monthly accounts, thereby doing away with the present ticket system.'' Nothing was done on that occasion but in 1947 the Finance Committee was asked to investigate the desirability of replacing the ticket system by the use of signed chits. The latter, of course, had been in use for decades. The cost of food and drink in the club was increasing by this time. In 1941, for example, one could order a piece of pie and be charged 15 cents; now it was 20 cents. The same price change was noticeable in the cost of a bowl of soup. In brief it was becoming a bit more difficult to order a full lunch for less than a dollar. As a result the committee agreed that the use of tickets in the dining room should be discontinued, but that it would continue in force in the bar and hall porters' departments. It was not until late in 1953 that the ticket system was ended and the chit system took over completely. All unused tickets were asked to be returned. Members were refunded in cash or the value of the tickets credited to their account.

*   *   *   *

Before leaving our typical member who joined the club in the late 1930's, we might imagine ourselves to be with him for lunch and see some of his fellow members, both his own age and older, whom he would either know or recognize. First, let us look at his lunch order. He could have consomme (15 cents), six western oysters on the half shell (50 cents), grilled lamb chops (40 cents) with two vegetables (20 cents), hot apple pie a la mode (20 cents) and a pot of coffee (10 cents). That would be an unusually large lunch and the club dinner in the evening would cost less. However, our member is a hard-working man and is indulging himself.

At the next table he might see Walter Owen who was a recent member. A law graduate from U.B.C., he had been called to the bar in 1928, gained quick recognition as an up-and-coming lawyer and was presently serving as the Crown Prosecutor for the county of Vancouver. In time he was to become the president of the club and later the Lieutenant-Governor of British Columbia. A little further away might be Dr. Leonard S. Klinck, the president of the University of British Columbia. He was seen infrequently at lunch, mainly because of the distance between the club and the university. There were, in fact, few academic members of the club.

One member quickly recognized by everyone was W. G. Murrin. English by birth, and then in his early sixties, he had come to Vancouver before the Great War, joined the B. C. Electrical Railway Company and had risen to become president of that company as well as the B. C. Power Corporation. Aside from being on the board of directors of other firms, he was keenly interested in community affairs. He was past president of the Vancouver Little Theatre Association and the Vancouver Art Gallery, a director of the Vancouver Symphony and a member of the Institute of Electrical Engineers.

At another table on might see Ralph Campney. Born in Ontario, he entered Queen's University as a medical student in 1914 and had served in the war in Egypt and the Western Front. After recovering from wounds at Passchendaele, he joined the Royal Flying Corps and returned to Canada to study law. After a stint in Ottawa, he came to Vancouver, entered the legal profession, and at this time was chairman of the National Harbour Board. Later Campney was to be a successful Liberal candidate for Vancouver Centre and in 1951, the Minister of National Defence. Close by might be an elderly gentleman, aged 73 years, an original member of the club. This was Percy W. Evans. He had come to Vancouver in 1888. With his brother and cousin he had founded Evans, Coleman and Evans which had flourished over the years. He was also a director of the B.C. Telephone Company and in his younger days was among the founding members of what became the Vancouver Rowing Club.

There were a number of men having lunch who were pioneers of the city. J. W. McFarland, who joined the club in 1893, was among the first dealers in real estate in the city. He had come to Vancouver several years before the railway arrived, and his real estate business grew with the city. He was a charter member of the club as well as the Vancouver Board of Trade. Others would remember the city as it grew from a few sawmills and wooden shacks to its multi-storeyed steel and concrete buldings. There were older men in the dining room who were born before the telephone was invented, before the radio was ever thought of and before the automobile came into existence. There were younger men who, as boys, would remember when many of the streets in downtown Vancouver were covered with planks and when the civic slogan was

"In nineteen ten Vancouver then
Will have one hundred thousand men."

Times had changed, and the members of the club had much to do with the changes that took place. Our typical new club member of the late 1930's could converse with men who helped build the Canadian Pacific Railway, who were involved in developing the mineral resources of the province as branch railway lines developed and who were actively engaged in almost every profession and entrepreneurial endeavour one can imagine. Any member lunching at the round tables in the dining room was able, almost invariably, to join in an interesting conversation unless he was remarkably dull or shy--and there were few of those. In the late 1930's, without a doubt, there would be a great deal of talk about the situation both in Europe and China. Just as the dark clouds of the depression seemed to be lifting, there were warnings of another storm approaching. It seemed incredible that after only two decades of peace, rumours and predictions of war were being heard again. All too soon the storm was to break and, once more, Canada was involved in conflict for over six years.

CHAPTER V

THE WAR TIME YEARS

Although the 1930's was a harsh period for Vancouver and the nation in general, the city had experienced some progress. In the first years of that decade work had started on the construction of Burrard Bridge and in the summer of 1931 the Vancouver Airport and Seaplane Harbour was opened. A new newspaper, the Vancouver "News Herald" began publication and in 1937 the Canadian Broadcasting

MEMBERS

Lieut. D.P. Bell-Irving
Capt. H.M. Fleming
Lieut. C. Croker Fox
Lieut. F.L. Gwillim
Lieut. L.R. Hargreaves
Lieut-Col. W. Hart-McHarg

Lieut. J.G. Hay
Capt. John V.E. Isaac, D.S.O.
Lieut. J.K. Kennedy
Lieut. J.G. Kenworthy
Sergt. A.W. De Langsdorff

Lieut-Col. J.A. Macdonell, D.S.O.
Capt. C.M. Marpole
Major C.M. Merritt
Capt. D.M. Moore
Major J. McD. Mowat
Capt. George Sage

STAFF

Pte. S. Aylett — Pte. C.M. Ransom — Pte. T. Stead

Corporation opened its first radio station (CRVC) in the city. For several years the construction of the Lion's Gate Bridge had been underway and was opened for traffic late in 1938. Prior to this time there was only a comparatively small number of people living on the north side of the harbour but that was to change dramatically in the following decades. Another sign that the depression was lifting was the resumption of construction work on the new Vancouver Hotel. It had been built on land which the Vancouver Club had considered purchasing before deciding to build in its present location. When it opened its doors in May 1939 it was considered one of the finest hotels in Canada.

Although economic and financial worries were a constant problem for most people, there was no lack of interest in events both at home and abroad. To the south, President Hoover of the United States had approved the Smoot Hawley measure in 1930 which had raised tariffs and caused greater difficulties to Canadian exporters. Then, as now, news from the U.S.A. continued to intrigue Canadians. The arrest of "Scarface" Al Capone in 1931 was far more interesting than word about France building the Maginot Line or some wealthy German industrialists giving financial support to the Nazi Party. There was talk about developing television, but in the thirties in Canada more people were interested in listening to the radio. Favourite radio programmes frequently originated from south of the border. Jack Benny, Fred Allen, Amos 'n' Andy, Fibber McGee and Molly and later Bing Crosby and Bob Hope were enjoyed on both sides of the border, and their popularity could be matched in Canada only by "Hockey Night in Canada" when Foster Hewitt broadcast from the Maple Leaf Gardens in Toronto.

As the decade wore on, political leaders worked to bring an end to the economic crisis according to their own philosophy. In Germany, Hitler came to power in 1933 and, after building up his armed forces, began to demand that all Germans should live within the borders of the Reich, even if it meant extending the borders to encompass them. Stories began to circulate about German concentration camps and the stream of refugees from Nazi rule increased every year. The Italian dictator, Mussolini, ordered his troops into Ethopia in 1935 and the newly elected Canadian prime minister, Mackenzie King, ordered the Canadian representative at the League of Nations to vote against imposing sanctions on Italy. In the Orient, by the late 1930's, Japan was at war with China, and the newsfilms in the theatres were constantly showing wretched Chinese civilians running in terror from Japanese bombing attacks. These scenes were soon augmented by newscameramen filming Spanish civilians seeking shelter from bombs and shells when the Spanish Civil War started in 1936 just as the Ethiopian War ended.

News items which were followed with considerable interest in the club in 1936–37 were the press releases about King Edward VIII's relationship with Mrs. Wallis Simpson. What had been gossip and rumour turned out to have a solid basis and resulted in the monarch's abdication and the consequent coronation of King George VI in 1937. With the British government now under Neville Chamberlain, it was also the beginning of a period of appeasement.

Closer to home—and at this time Europe and its problems seemed far away—there were numerous changes one could observe. Automobiles now had four wheel brakes, more powerful engines and were becoming more streamlined in design. Radios with long and short wave bands were becoming common, and with a decent aerial one could listen directly to radio stations in Europe. Favourite dance tunes of the time included "Pennies from Heaven," "Stormy Weather," "Begin the Beguine" or "Harbour Lights," and in the late 1930's if one wanted to take one's girlfriend to a movie, the popular ones would be "Snow White and the Seven Dwarfs," "Pygmalion" with Leslie Howard or perhaps Alfred Hitchcock's "The Lady Vanishes."

Within the confines of the Vancouver Club there were no films shown, as one might expect, and there were no radios unless a live-in member had a small table model in his room. When the first radio stations in Vancouver began their operation in the early 1920's some members felt that the club should have a set. The idea was put to the General Meeting in 1923, and the minutes reveal that "a suggestion of a radio connection was unanimously voted against." There was no reason given. Perhaps it was felt to be too distracting. There were some things the committee felt the members would approve, however. In 1918 a member had offered to supply the club with daily stock quotations, presumably by installing a ticker tape. He was given permission to do so "but without any exclusive privileges in connection therewith." Election returns were followed with keen interest, and it was not uncommon for the club to have a C.P.R. telegraph terminal and operator in the building during a national election day. In the 1926 federal election, for example, the club could enjoy this service for only thirty dollars.

It may have been the increasing tension in international affairs in the late 1930's that led the club to reconsider its stand on radios. In the summer of 1938 both the Canadian Westinghouse Company and the B.C. Electric Railway Co. offered to lend the club a radio "on special occasions." The club did get one and a small radio was placed in the large card room on two occasions. The first was a broadcast speech by

Neville Chamberlain and the second, two days later, was a speech by Adolph Hitler. Sixty members attended to hear the British prime minister's talk, only forty were there to hear the German Chancellor. In August 1939 the performance was repeated on the occasion of a speech by Viscount Halifax and Premier Daladier of France. No member was present to hear Halifax, and only one came to hear Daladier.

With the outbreak of the Second World War, and more particularly with the German blitzkreig successes in the Spring of 1940, the demand for news reports grew. In May 1940 a member complained that the club's radio was too old and too weak. He added: "I think this club can afford to supply its members with a modern radio, particularly under modern war conditions." The committee agreed. A new radio was purchased and instructions given that it should be placed in the small reading room and left there. There was also to be a notice on the radio noting that "it is for the purpose ONLY of allowing members to listen to broadcasts of interest generally to members." With the radio firmly accepted, the committee also ended a tradition of almost fifty years. Henceforth, it ruled "no telegraph service would be necessary for the federal election day."

When the Second World War broke out in September 1939 there was little of the excitement that had greeted similar news in 1914. When the Germans marched into Poland it seemed almost to be the culmination of a succession of aggressive moves Hitler had made ever since he had gained power. Canada was not the only country to be caught unprepared, but the combination of the economic stress caused by the depression coupled with the failure of the federal government to appreciate the dangers presented by a well-armed Germany resulted in the Canadian armed forces being unable to offer any significant assistance to the war effort for months if not years.

There were numerous Great War veterans among the club's members and during the inter-war period there was a firm connection between these members and military or service-connected organizations. After the Great War, for example, a Canadian Corps of Commissionaires was formed to help provide veterans with remunerative employment. In Vancouver, the British Columbia Corps of Commissionaires was formed in 1927, with many club members serving as trustees of the unit from that time even to the present. Among the first to offer employment to the new corps was W. C. Woodward, while other club members who served as trustees in the early years included J. P. Fell, J. S. Tait, Victor Odlum and W. G. Murrin. During the thirties, Major J. G Fordham made available a vacant warehouse building in the present "Gastown" area to provide needy veterans with shelter. Other club members serving as corps trustees found the necessary equipment, furniture and food supplies to keep the shelter running. In the inter-war years, as British Columbia Corps of Commissionaires grew, other club members who contributed their time and energy to the corps included such members as Barney Johnson, Cornelius Burke, D. M. Johnson, A. D. Bell-Irving, Leigh Stevenson, A. W. (Nick) Carter, Alf Watts, Gordon Bell-Irving, Cecil Merritt, Don Clark, H. P. Bell-Irving, James Stewart, Theo Du Moulin, Don Spankie, Tom Brown and Arthur Lungley.

There were numerous club members during the inter-war years who took a more direct interest in maintaining some degree of Canada's defence potential by supporting various city reserve regiments. Only a few can be mentioned here. One was Brigadier-General J. A. Clark. He had commanded The Seaforth Highlanders of Canada during the Great War with great distinction and during the remainder of his life remained deeply involved in the well-being and efficiency of his regiment. Together with other club members such as J. Fyfe Smith, Austin C. Taylor, J. H. Roaf, E. W. Hamber, W. H. Malkin and Lt.-Col. R. M. Blair, Clark was instrumental in getting the federal government to build the Seaforth Armoury in 1935-36. To pry $240,000 from Ottawa to purchase the land and construct the building was a feat in itself in the midst of the depression, but all during the pre-war years Brigadier-General Clark put his heart and soul into supporting the regiment. He was to become honorary colonel of the Seaforths in 1957. The three previous honorary colonels--Major-General J. W. Stewart, the Honorable E. W. Hamber and Colonel H. R. MacMillan--were all members of the club as was the architect who designed the armoury, J. Y. McCarter.

Another regiment which had close connections with the Vancouver Club was the British Columbia Regiment (Duke of Connaught's Own). Several club members had been instrumental in its formation and others (including the club's secretary-manager, B. M. Humble) had fought with it in the Great War. In the lean, inter-war years W. W. Foster and H. F. G. Letson--both club members--had commanded the unit in the 1920's. The regiment was supported in various ways by another club member, Clarence Wallace, who later was appointed its Honorary Colonel, and yet another member, H. E. Molson, commanded "The Dukes" at the outbreak of the Second World War.

These are only two of several reserve army units in Vancouver which struggled to maintain some degree of military efficiency during two decades of public indifference and government apathy towards all things military. With the outbreak of war, a great effort was made to manufacture the arms and recruit and train the men and women who volunteered to serve in the armed forces. It seemed to need actual danger to bring the needs of the navy, army, and air force to the attention of the public, and it is to the credit of a number of Vancouver Club members that they worked in the lean years to assist the reserve forces when their need was greatest.

As mentioned earlier, it would seem that the average age of the club membership increased, particularly during the decade of the depression. This was owing primarily to the lack of new and younger members joining the club and, naturally, the aging of those who remained. As a result there was no great exodus of members leaving to join the armed forces. During the Great War there were as many as ninety listed as active service members in one year. In the Second World War the highest number of active service members in any one year was 21, and that was in 1940. In 1941 and 1942, there were 15, eleven in 1943, ten in 1944 and only five in 1945. Fortunately, none of these members were killed in action, which accounts for the absence of a memorial plaque to Second World War veterans in the lobby of the club. A number of these members made a major contribution during their wartime service and a brief mention of just a few of them would be appropriate.

Sherwood Lett had joined the club in 1929. He served overseas with the Irish Fusiliers of Canada in the Great War, winning the Military Cross at Amiens. After graduation from U.B.C. he attended Oxford University as a Rhodes Scholar. He joined a Vancouver law firm in 1925 and maintained an active interest in the militia in the inter-war years. He joined the active forces when war was declared and, as a brigadier, he led the 4th Canadian Infantry Brigade in the Dieppe Raid in 1942. In this action he was wounded and awarded the Distinguished Service Order. He assisted in the planning for the American–Canadian attack against the Japanese in the Aleutian Islands and in 1944 was again in command of a brigade in the Normandy Campaign. Here he was wounded again and his active military career ended. After the war he served as chancellor of the University of British Columbia from 1951 to 1957. He was appointed chief of the Canadian delegation on the International Supervisory Commission of the cease fire in Indo–China. He was appointed Chief Justice of the B.C. Supreme Court in 1955 and, eight years later, he became Chief Justice of the Appeal Court. When he died in 1964, tributes to him poured in from all over the country, but perhaps the words of Prime Minister Lester Pearson summed up his life best when he wrote: "I know of no Canadian who has served his country in war and peace with greater distinction and more unselfishly."

Another member, a veteran of both the Boer War and Great War, offered his services once more when war broke out in 1939 also. Victor W. Odlum, a journalist and businessman, had grown up in

Vancouver. After a distinguished war service, and aside from his business interests, he became vice-chairman of the Board of Governors of the Canadian Broadcasting Corporation, served on the National Research Council, and was elected a member of the Legislative Assembly in the mid-1920's. Major-General Odlum was appointed commander of the 2nd Canadian Infantry Division in 1940, a position he held for almost two years.

Major-General John P. Mackenzie was 55 years of age when the Second World War broke out. Another veteran, he had won both British and French awards as an officer in the Great War, and had been general manager of Hamilton Bridge (Western) Co. in Vancouver. He went overseas in command of the engineers of the 2nd Canadian Division. Promoted to brigadier, he was later sent back to Canada to become the Quartermaster General for the Canadian Army from 1942 to 1943 and then Inspector General for Western Canada until he retired from the army in 1944. He returned to civil life and became general manager of Western Bridge and Steel Fabricators Ltd. in Vancouver until the mid-1950's. Mackenzie, at that time, lived at the Vancouver Club and was one of the three or four members who died in the club.

One more member should be mentioned. Kenneth Nairn had joined the Lord Strathcona's Horse during the Great War before transferring to the Royal Flying Corps. He served as a pilot in the 105th Squadron during the Great War and in the inter-war period he was with the firm of Price Waterhouse. A professional accountant, he volunteered his services again in 1939 and within an exceptionally short period he was promoted to the rank of air vice-marshal in charge of accounts and finance at Air Force Headquarters in Ottawa during the period from 1941-1944. Nairn had joined the club in 1922, and enjoyed sixty-six years of membership before his recent death.

In the early years of the war the experience and expertise of various other club members was called on by the armed forces. Some of those who joined the "active service member" classification included A. T. MacLean, Victor A. MacLean, Richard Walkem, C. C. Ferrie, H. E. Molson, A. D. Bell Irving, H. F. G. Letson, R. T. Colquhoun and F. J. Mawdesley. Some of the staff left to join the services also. Probably the best known was H. T. Skelley, the doorman. He had been a regimental sergeant-major and during the war he became a commissioned officer.

At the beginning of the Second World War the Vancouver Club took steps reminiscent of similar actions taken in 1914. One of the first resolutions adopted by the General Committee in October 1939 was to reactivate "war absentee" membership for those on active service with annual dues reduced to $10. Employees joining the forces were granted leave of absence without pay with the guarantee that their seniority and present position would be maintained for them. The committee also granted temporary membership (without dues) to senior officers during the period of the war, and it agreed that all officers, not normally resident in Vancouver, could be introduced as visitors or as guests.

In November 1940, the club opened its doors a bit wider. Those granted temporary membership were allowed to maintain their status even if later they became permanent residents of Vancouver owing to the exigencies of the service. Moreover, any regular member who was serving overseas with the forces was exempt regular membership dues. In 1942 the doors opened even wider. In July the committee decided that officers, of field rank and above, in the three services could use the club with no monthly dues. They were not allowed to bring in guests, they could not cash cheques without approval, and they had to purchase club tickets with cash to pay for food and drink. There is no record to show how many senior officers took advantage of this offer, but it is apparent a fair number did. Despite the decline of resident members during the war, the club seemed to be busier than ever. Navy, army and air force officers using the dining room might account for part of the increasing number of meals served, but the tremendous economic activity generated by the war swept away the black clouds of the depression and members could afford to spend more money.

In the Spring of 1944, even before the Allies had invaded mainland Europe, the General Committee made a major decision. Looking ahead to the victorious end of the war, the committee

> . . . resolved that anyone who had volunteered for General Service, and who shall have served full time in any of His Majesty's Forces in Canada or abroad, or in the United States Forces in Canada or abroad, between September 1939 and whenever hostilities ended, need pay only a $200 entrance fee. This special rate to remain until 200 such Resident Members, being ex–Servicemen, shall have been elected, or until three years after the war is officially over, whichever will occur first.

A rider to the resolution stated that all such ex–Servicemen's entrance fees were to be reserved specifically for refurnishing the club and not to be used to pay off the club's mortgage.

Although it would be true to say that the war affected everyone in the club, for the most part it had only a minor impact on the club itself. There were some of the staff who left for higher paying jobs in war industries, particularly after the Spring of 1940 when the Germans overwhelmed France and Canada began to realize that it must contribute more to the war effort. When Japan entered the war, there was an immediate demand in British Columbia that Canadians of Japanese descent should be moved from the coastal region, and this meant the club lost its Japanese bellboys and had to find replacements for them. As the Japanese overran the Far Eastern colonies and dependencies of Great Britain, France and the Netherlands, there was fear by some of an attack on the Pacific Coast, and as early as December 1941 the secretary–manager, B. C. Binks, was instructed "to take the best temporary measures possible" respecting air raid precautions.

One new feature added to the club's routine was a scheme for promoting the sale of War Savings Certificates. The General Committee decided that

> . . . a draw be held each month from November to February inclusive. The list to be posted on November 1st with entries at $2.50 each for any number desired. List to close on the 6th day of each month. A club dinner to be served at $1.00 per cover on the date of the drawing to be arranged. War certificates to be purchased and apportioned to the three winners in the following ratio: 1st prize--60%; 2nd prize-- 30%; 3rd prize--10%.

This form of sweepstake started in November 1940 and continued until July 1946. These "war savings drawings" resulted in $21,584.00 worth of certificates being distributed to the winners.

It was not until 1942 that the club began to feel the pinch of wartime restrictions, and at that it was nothing in comparison to its affiliated clubs in London which had been subjected to bombing and severe rationing since the Autumn of 1940. In Canada, however, the government was slowly but surely widening its control over the national economy. Rationing of a variety of items was already in force and was to increase in scope. The victories of the Japanese reduced the supply of rubber and the re-capping of old tyres became commonplace. Gasoline was rationed and the production of new automobiles for civilian use stopped as factories were converted to the sole production of military needs. It became difficult to obtain building materials of almost any kind owing to wartime demands and priorities, and skilled labour was at a premium. Something of this is reflected in the operation of the club. The Annual Report for 1942 read in part:

> The third year of the war has brought many changes. Food rationing and controls of various kinds have made it increasingly difficult to obtain certain supplies, provisions and so on. The situation is such that it is quite often beyond the control and power of the catering department to maintain the old standards. During the year, too, the turnover of employees has been quite heavy, with the result that the services are not as good as desired. It is nevertheless gratifying to know, notwithstanding these difficulties, that the volume of dining room and other departmental businesses has increased measurably.

Probably the average household felt the impact of food rationing when it came in May 1942 more than did the club. Sugar was rationed at half a pound per person per week, and it was estimated that rationing of tea and coffee would mean the householder would be able to buy from one-half to three quarters of her normal purchase. Rationing did put a curb on the chef's exuberance, perhaps, but even as late as May 1943, there was only mild concern expressed by C. A. Cotterell, then club president, when he told the committee "that further rationing of some commodities may make it necessary to curtail private parties and to limit the choice of menus." Fortunately a dinner menu for the club exists for the same day the president made his comments (May 21st, 1943). It is reproduced below in full so the reader will be able to judge rationing in the club in wartime.

DINNER
Friday, May 21st, 1943

Spring Onions, 10¢   Mixed Olives, 15¢   Celery, 15¢
Tuna Snacks, 15¢   Oysters on Half Shell, 60¢

SOUPS
Cream of Tiki Toheroas, 15¢
Consomme, 15¢

FISH
Salmon Trout, Meunier, 30–50¢
Grilled Whole Sole, 25–45¢

ENTREE
Veal and Ham Cutlets with Green Peas, 45¢

JOINTS
Chicken under Glass, Eugenie, 65¢ (Mushrooms and Asparagus Tips)
Roast Shoulder of Pork, Savoury Dressing, Apple Sauce, 50¢

COLD MEATS
Pressed Ox Tongue and Potato Salad, 45¢

Melton Mowbray Pie, 55¢   Head Cheese, 40¢
Club Baked Ham, 55¢   Club Brawn, 40¢
Steak and Kidney Pie, 45¢   Roast Pork, 50¢

VEGETABLES
Garden Peas, 25¢   Boiled Onions, 10¢
New Beans, 25¢   Hashed Browned Potatoes, 05¢
Spinach, 10¢   Steamed New Potatoes, 10¢

SALADS
Russian Salad, 45¢   Combination, 35¢
Pear and Cottage Cheese, 20¢   Sliced Tomatoes, 20¢
Avocado (½), 20¢   Lettuce, 20¢

SAVOURY
Creamed Haddie on Toast, 15¢

SWEETS

Pumpkin Pie, 15¢   Strawberry Ice Cream, 15¢
Jelly Omelette, 20¢   Stewed Figs, 15¢
Apple Pie, 15¢   Baked Apple, 15¢
Table Dates, 20¢   Mint Parfait, 20¢
                    Sliced Bananas and Cream, 20¢

CHEESE
                Philadelphia Cream Cheese and Jelly, 20¢
Imperial, 20¢   Old Ontario, 15¢   Cheshire, 15¢
Edam, 25¢   Roquefort, 25¢
Tea, 10¢   Coffee, 10¢   Hot Chocolate, 15¢
Bottled Buttermilk, 05¢   Bottled Milk, 10¢   Cocoa, 10¢

MINIMUM 75¢
BUTTER AND SUGAR SERVED ONLY ON REQUEST

The war also brought changes in the liquor laws. Several years after prohibition was enforced during the First World War, the Vancouver Club, as well as other private clubs in the province, had obtained permission for the members to keep liquor in lockers. By law each locker had to have a lock and key and each had to be identified. As we have seen, this was the only legal way in which liquor could be served in the club. Periodically the number of lockers was increased. On the completion of the third floor bar in 1928 about fifty of the old lockers from the first floor bar were given to the Officers Mess of the Seaforth Highlanders of Canada and new lockers (built at a cost of about $12.00 per unit) were constructed to match the panelling of the enlarged bar. Some members had more than one locker, but then some were thirstier than others.

Although the system worked, it was a bit awkward, especially for non resident members. One could not buy a glass of wine with dinner nor get a drink from the bar without having one's own bottle. As early as 1937 the Vancouver Club joined with other clubs to try to get the provincial liquor laws amended to allow clubs the power to serve liquor by the glass, but it was not until 1940 that such permission was given. This was done by what was called the "pool system." Under the new regulation, members could pool their purchases using a club pool permit. "No club shall sell any liquor from the said pool," the regulation stated, "but may make a reasonable charge for such service."

The Liquor Control Board was determined to keep a tight grasp on how liquor by the glass could be dispensed. Another section of this regulation stated:

> *Members or guests of the Club shall not participate in the pool until they have contributed to same. Any member or guest desiring to join and participate in the pool shall make a contribu-*

tion thereto. Such contribution shall be evidenced by a script-book issued to such member or guest. Script-books must be issued containing script of the value of $2 and $5 or $10. . . . The script-books shall be numbered serially and shall be issued in regular order according to their serial numbers. . . . The person issuing [script books] shall write upon the cover the name and Individual Liquor Permit number of the member or guest to whom the script is issued, also the date of issue, and shall make a record thereof.

Other paragraphs of regulations followed. It was not an easy system to manage and when liquor was rationed in 1943 there was a period when it almost foundered. The use of club lockers continued and, in the post- war era, well over 150 new lockers were added. The pool system continued until 1953 when the last of the pool tickets were redeemed and all liquor purchases were made using chits. Liquor rationing, of course, ended shortly after the war, but it was some time before the fine wines from Europe and elsewhere were readily available in the club's wine-cellars.

By 1943 the war had reached a turning point. In North Africa British and American forces had swept German and Italian forces from the continent and in the summer Canadian troops were part of the Allied invasion of Sicily and Italy. Massive Russian attacks against the German armies on the Eastern Front resulted in the relief of Stalingrad and a general advance along a battlefront which stretched thousands of miles. In the Far East, General MacArthur was thrusting his way toward the Philippines. Allied bombers were pounding Germany unmercifully and on the high seas the unrelenting struggle against enemy submarines began to pay handsome results.

In 1944 the news from the war fronts related one victory after another. For Canadians, with close to 1,000,000 men and women in the three services, probably the most exciting news was the opening of the "Second Front" with the Allied landings in Normandy and later the thrust north into Belgium and Holland. Canada's navy had expanded to include some 500 naval vessels and the air force had grown tremendously with Canadian squadrons serving in almost every theatre of war. In Western Canada, which early in 1943 had almost 60,000 troops ready to counter any Japanese attack, army units were withdrawn or reduced as the danger lessened. In Vancouver itself, the city was never so busy nor so crowded. By the end of the year there were close to 7,000 positions which could not be filled owing to the labour shortage. The province's shipyards were launching a ship every week. The production of timber, minerals, food and almost everything else was at a maximum, but strict government controls over wages and scarce commodities kept inflation well under control.

Victory over the Axis Powers came in May 1945. It was welcome but not unexpected. A week prior to the official announcement, the General Committee decided that when the official announcement was made, "the ordinary activities of the Club be carried on as is done on Armistice Day," but on V-E Day (Victory in Europe Day) itself, the members would not be allowed to introduce local guests "for any reason whatsoever." Apparently there was no special club celebration of V-E Day, rather each member rejoiced at the news in his own fashion. For some, who had sons killed in action, the celebration would be mixed with a sense of loss but for everyone there would be the relief that their sons would soon be returning home.

During this period the club elected to honorary membership two men who had played an outstanding role in wartime. The first was Lt.-Col. C. C. I. Merritt and the second was Major-General B. M. Hoffmeister.

Merritt was born in Vancouver in 1908. His grandfather, Sir Charles Hibbert Tupper, was president of the Vancouver Club in 1909 and 1910 and his father had been a member also until he was killed in action during the Great War. Merritt, after graduating from the Royal Military College, returned to study law in Vancouver and eventually became a senior member in Bull, Housser and Tupper. While an articled student he became a commissioned officer in the Seaforth Highlanders of Canada. He went overseas in 1939 and was promoted to command the South Saskatchewan Regiment a unit which, a short time later, was selected to take part in the Dieppe Raid.

For Lt.-Col. Merritt it was a day he would never forget. From the time his regiment landed on the beaches until the last shot was fired he was in the thick of battle, leading and encouraging his men and exhibiting "matchless gallantry and inspiring leadership." For his action this day he was awarded the Victoria Cross, the highest decoration the monarch can bestow on any soldier. He was captured at Dieppe and remained a prisoner of war until hostilities ended. As a gesture of its admiration the Vancouver Club made him an Honorary Life Member in October 1942.

One might say that what Merritt achieved in battle, Hoffmeister achieved in war. Hoffmeister was also a militia officer with the Seaforths and was given command of the regiment late in 1942. He took the unit into battle in Sicily in July 1943 and was awarded the Distinguished Service Order for his leadership. Promoted to command a brigade a few months later, he was awarded a second D.S.O. for his leadership during the battle for Ortona. Promoted again to the rank of major-general to command the 5th Canadian Armoured Division, he won a third D.S.O. for his role in smashing through the Gustav and Hitler Lines and was also made a Commander of the

British Empire. Later, for his superb handling of his division during the liberation of the Netherlands, he was made a Commander of the Bath. He was awarded various foreign decorations for his war service and, many years later, he was made an Officer of the Order of Canada.

Although he had fought long and hard in Europe, Hoffmeister volunteered to command the division being organized in Canada in 1945 to fight the Japanese. He held this appointment until the atomic bomb brought peace to the Pacific later that year. He was made an Honorary Life Member of the club in July 1945. After the war, Hoffmeister held senior executive positions in the H. R. Macmillan Export Co. and ultimately became President and then Chairman of Macmillan and Bloedel. In 1958 he was appointed the B. C. Agent-General in London and later President of the Council of Forest Industries of British Columbia.

During the war, resident membership had shrunk from 476 in 1938 to a low of 424 in 1942. Some sixty new members joined in 1943–44, and with victory in May 1945 the resident membership bounced to 581. Five years later it had reached its constitutional level of 700, while overall membership in the 1938–1950 period had increased from 695 to 937. Well over 100 of the new resident members were veterans, and it might be appropriate at this point to give a thumbnail sketch of the military service of some of them. This war-time experience serves as a quiet bond among many club members even though their post–war activities in the business, commercial and other fields are widely divergent. As young men they shared a common cause; as older men the memories linger on.

H. W. ("Spud") Akhurst was 26 years old when the war broke out. His father had been a club member since 1907. He enlisted in the navy in 1942, was commissioned and was serving in *H.M.C.S. Alberni* during the assault on Normandy. In August 1944, while patrolling against U–Boats in the English Channel, his ship was hit by a torpedo and sank so quickly there was no time to release the ship's boats and floats. Only 31 members of the crew survived. Among them was not only Akhurst but another club member, I. H. Bell. "Spud" joined the club in 1947 and Ian Bell joined in 1955. After the war, Akhurst worked in his father's firm, Akhurst Machinery Ltd. He took over control of the company and expanded its operation until it had branches from the Pacific to the Atlantic with world wide imports from all the major industrial countries.

Tom Brown was 27 years old when the war broke out. Born in Vancouver, he graduated from U.B.C. and attended Oxford University as a Rhodes Scholar. He was Adjutant of the Irish Fusiliers in 1939 but saw action in Europe with the Essex Scottish Regiment. He was severely wounded in the face during the crossing of the Seine River in August 1944 when commanding the battalion. After numerous operations he returned home, joined the club (his father was a member) in 1946, and with his father resumed his work as a stockbroker with Odlum, Brown. As the firm increased its business, Brown became a major shareholder and ultimately Chairman of the Board.

Among the numerous Bell-Irvings who served in the navy, army and air force during the war, one who joined the club in the immediate post-war era was H. P. ("Budge") Bell-Irving. He went overseas with the Seaforths in 1939, took part in the Sicily and Italy campaigns, commanded the regiment in October, 1944 and in May, 1945 led his battalion into Amsterdam to free that city from five years of enemy occupation. He returned to Canada as a brigadier, joined the club (his father and grandfather were members) in 1946 and later established the Bell-Irving Realty Ltd. Keenly interested in a variety of organizations, he was to become President of the Vancouver Board of Trade and later he was appointed Lieutenant-Governor of British Columbia.

Three post-war members who shared common dangers during the war were Cornelius Burke, Thomas Ladner and Douglas Maitland. They had first met as students at the Shawnigan Lake School for Boys. All three decided to join the navy and after brief training in Canada, they received their first serious naval instruction in England. Within a short time they were in action. Ladner's ship was torpedoed off Iceland late in 1940. He was rescued from the oil-covered sea just in time. Maitland, who had transferred to motor gun boats in 1942, had two of his boats put out of action by mines and another by enemy aircraft, was lucky to return to base each time. By 1942 all three were serving in motor gun boats with the Royal Navy and in 1943 they were transferred to the Mediterranean where they were involved in the invasion of Sicily and Italy. By this time each was in command of a motor gun boat, making hit and run raids on the Italian coast. As senior, Maitland was given command of the 56 Flotilla, and the three of them shared exciting actions in the Mediterranean and Adriatic ranging from attacking enemy ships to landing agents on the enemy-held coasts. By the end of the war Maitland and Ladner had been awarded the Distinguished Service Cross and Bar, and Burke the same decoration with two bars, in recognition of their action. Dubbed "The Three Musketeers" by the press, the three officers returned to Vancouver and, by 1947 were among the veterans who joined the Vancouver Club.

These six examples of immediate post-war club members could be multiplied over twenty times. All faced the same problems of getting re established in civil life, finding a home, raising a family and renewing old friendships. They were to bring a breath of fresh air into the life of the Vancouver Club which had just passed its 50th anniversary. The second half century would see numerous changes, but club traditions were to be carried on.

CHAPTER VI

WINDS OF CHANGE

In the decade following the Second World War, the premises of the Vancouver Club resembled the home of a gentleman living in what used to be termed "reduced circumstances." The carpets were wearing thin, much of the furniture needed re-upholstering, the animal heads hanging in the lobby were looking increasingly forlorn as their fur gathered more dust. The plumbing was beginning to act peculiarly as aging pipes and drains accumulated more rust. The club needed more income if it was not only to maintain something of the old standards, but to attract new members as well.

There was no doubt that there had to be an increase in charges to members. At the turn of the century the entrance fee was $50 and quarterly dues $12. By the beginning of the First World War the entrance fee had jumped to $300 and the annual dues to $100, the latter payable quarterly. This increase coincided with the building of the new clubhouse. At the crest of the boom years, in the Spring of 1929, the entrance fee for resident membership was increased to $400. Although some thought had been given to halving this fee in the depths of the depression, the proposal was turned down, although sons of members (and in 1945 sons of deceased members) were given the privilege of membership for half the ordinary resident's fee.

During the war there were some fee increases owing to losses the club was experiencing. There was a $25 increase in dues for Non-Resident and Provincial members to $50 and $75 per annum respectively. In 1943 meal prices were increased by $7\frac{1}{2}$ per cent, corkage on a bottle of liquor was raised from 60 cents to a dollar, and the price of a drink went up ten cents.

These were modest increases and on reflection it is remarkable that for a period of almost two decades, fees, dues and prices remained fairly stable. Part of this was due to the decade-long depression and part due to the government control on wages and prices during six years of war. One must also give credit to the club presidents and men on the General Committee who volunteered so much of their time then, as now, to the well-being of the club.

By 1948 the combination of need to refurbish the club and the increase in the membership waiting list resulted in the first of a series of additional dues and fees. The upkeep of the building, the cost of service, equipment and of furnishings was at a record high level. The need to renew rugs, drapes, china and cutlery was all too evident. As a result the annual dues of $100, set in 1914, were raised to $150. (There had been several assessments of $5--for the Staff Retirement fund, for example--so that the member was actually paying $125 before the raise). The entrance fee for resident members went from $400 to $500, and the fees for other categories of members were increased proportionately.

The club's entrance fee remained stable for a decade but in 1959 it was raised again to $750. In the late 1960's, as inflation increased slowly, it was apparent that another raise was necessary, even though annual dues had edged upward in the interim. In proposing this measure at the 1966 annual general meeting, the committee presented the membership with the following comparison of its charges compared with other clubs.

	Entrance Fee	Annual Dues
Vancouver Club	$ 750	$225
University Club (Vancouver)	750	180
Terminal City Club (Vancouver)	1000	230

Toronto Club	1000	300
Manitoba Club	500	240
Union Club (Victoria)	500	168
St. James's Club (Montreal)	750	400

Once again the fees were increased and by the end of the decade there was a hefty jump when the entrance fee reached $1500.

These were not the only costs which went up. During the decade of the depression, a member could get a bedroom with bath for $40 a month or $2 per day. If he was willing to put up with a room on the side of the building, and trot down the hall to use the bath or toilet, he could have it for $25 per month or $1.50 per day. The rates for the same rooms was increased in 1943 to $50 and $30 respectively per month. In 1947 the monthly rate for the same two rooms jumped to $60 and $40 and by the mid–sixties the price was increased by about 25 per cent. By 1972 a front bedroom with bath was $60 per month or $5.50 daily, but guests of members were required to pay an extra dollar a day and not permitted to take advantage of the monthly rate. These prices were reasonable compared to the better downtown hotels in Vancouver, and the increases were modest. The rooms were small, there were no radios or television sets and they lacked certain amenities hotels provided. Nevertheless the beds were comfortable, there were numerous amenities of the club and the meals were everything one could wish for.

In the dining room the increase in prices was a bit slower but nevertheless steady. Ever since the club took over control of its own kitchen staff in 1908, the revenue provided by the dining room was carefully watched. A nice balance between staff and diners had to be maintained. In 1933, for example, when membership was slipping and the number of meals served decreased, the committee permitted members to introduce "citizens" for lunch. In 1941, when membership slipped again, the committee ruled that as a means of increasing revenue in the dining room and bar, "that local residents be permitted to come [as guests] to the Club for luncheon more than the one day a month at present allowed. . . ."

Another step taken to increase the volume of meals served, though not the price, was to allow mixed dinner parties in the main dining room. In April 1944 the Dining Room Committee recommended that the then Ladies Dining Room (commonly known as the Blue Room) should be refurnished as a lounge. The matter was put to a vote, and 277 members were in favour of the change while 41 were against it. The new rule was to come in force after the new lounge was redecorated and furnished, but due to the difficulty getting appropriate furniture owing to wartime shortages, the ladies had to wait until the latter part of the year before they could enjoy dining with their husbands in the main dining room.

In the immediate post–war years membership increased dramatically, so much so that once again the old restrictions on introducing local citizens for lunch were reimposed. At the same time there was a great deal of expensive work going on upgrading the kitchen. The equipment was some thirty years old and there was considerable renovation in progress. Food costs and wages were rising, and as a consequence it was decided to increase the price of lunches by 10 per cent and dinners by 25 per cent effective September 1948.

Prices, of course, are relative. When the club put on its first smorgasbord dinner in January 1949, the cost per person was $2.50, and considering the magnificent presentation of cold and hot dishes, to say nothing of the desserts, it is no wonder that it has remained a popular affair even to this day. Nevertheless, on a more modest scale, and keeping in mind that one could have a club dinner for one dollar during the war, a decade later the prices of the sandwich menu must have caused some of the older members to reflect on "the good old days." The following are from a sandwich menu dated 1955:

Chicken and Lettuce	*.75*	*Roast Prime Ribs of Beef*	*.75*
Baked Ham	*.75*	*Jellied Ox Tongue*	*.70*
Corned Beef	*.65*	*Sockeye Salmon (canned)*	*.70*
Portuguese Sardines	*.75*	*Shrimp, Lettuce & Mayonnaise*	
			.80
Crab, Lettuce & Mayonnaise			
	.75	*Club Sandwich*	*1.00*
Clubhouse Sandwich	*1.25*	*Sirloin Steak Sandwich*	*1.35*
Tenderloin Steak Sandwich			
	1.50	*Hamburger*	*.75*
Denver Sandwich	*.70*	*Toasted Cheese*	*.65*

Increased prices in the dining room were matched by those in the bar and for the rental of bar lockers. In 1929 the club bought an additional twenty lockers at a cost of $11.35 per locker. Owing to the demand by new members after the war, more than 70 new lockers were built and installed at an approximate cost of $20 each in 1961. When 30 more lockers were ordered in 1969, the unit cost had increased by 30 per cent. In the same year locker rentals went from $18 to $24 per year owing to the labour in servicing them. In terms of space, over the long term there is probably no single part of the club that has earned so much revenue as the liquor lockers. Perhaps that is as it should be, considering the amount of quiet pleasure contained in so small an area.

The rise in entrance fees, dues and other costs did not reduce the number of men interested in becoming members of the club. When the war began in 1939 there were about 500 resident members. This dipped to a low of 421 in July 1942, not including 15 on active service. In May 1945 when the war in Europe ended, resident membership was 513. A year later the number had increased to 606 and by the Autumn of 1947 the number had reached 662. Of the 149 new members since the end of the war, 123 were ex–servicemen.

Part of the reason for this influx of veterans was the club's decision to reduce the entrance fee by half for veterans. This meant a $200 saving. Moreover, if the veteran happened to be the son of a member, he was required to pay only half the remaining fee--or $100. At the Annual Meeting in 1944, a resolution had passed stating that the club should consist of 550 resident members and 200 resident ex–servicemen, in addition to the other classes of members. In March 1947, however, the number of ex–servicemen allowed to join at the reduced rates was lowered to 150 "since the ordinary membership had filled up during the past year. . . ."

By the end of 1948 resident membership was very close to 700 and total membership nearly 1000. In the annual report of 1950, the president was able to report a situation which the club had not experienced for decades. Not only was there a large waiting list (79 applicatant awaiting admission) but this number represented 29 more than the previous year. Only 27 resident members were admitted during that year which meant that a new applicant might expect to wait for nearly three years before he could become a member.

This was an encouraging situation for the club, but rather frustrating for those wanting to join. It got worse as the years went on. In September 1952, when the entrance fees increased from $500 to $750, it was also agreed that resident membership should be limited to 750 plus other categories, but even this slight increase did little to relieve the pressure of those wishing to join, By 1954, for example, there were almost 200 on the waiting list and four years later there were 249.

There had been some fears that raising resident membership to 750 would put an undue strain on the staff, facilities and conveniences of the club. An analysis of the problem was made and it was found that the additional numbers were manageable, especially as the staff had increased to 77. "These findings," according to Ralph D. Baker, the club's president in 1954–55, "are perhaps pertinent to the matter of the long list of applicants now awaiting admission to the Club. . . . The bottom of the waiting list is at present about five years for admission. This is discouraging to many otherwise qualified and desirable applicants and prospective applicants and is especially distasteful to sons of long–time members and to their fathers."

All during the remainder of the 1950s there were approximately

250 applicants on the waiting list, with between 50 to a high of 70 applications being received each year. The openings remained fairly constant as members died, resigned, moved to other cities, and so forth. One member, remembers his impatience at the time. He had joined the Terminal City Club and every time he walked past the Vancouver Club and saw the club flag at half mast, he would think of it in terms of his being one step closer to admission. (He was admitted eventually in 1961 and later became president).

The tremendous log–jam was, if not broken, at least relieved in May 1961 when the General Committee decided to use its discretion in absorbing 100 new members within a twelve–month period, at the rate of not less than five per month. "If for any reason the increase in Club facilities are cancelled, the income of new members [will] be halted until resident membership reverts back to 750." This decision had an immediate impact. By 1962 the number of waiting applicants went down to 181, then to 96 in 1965 and by 1971, when resident membership was increased to 900, the waiting list had decreased to 47. By August 1978, the waiting list had dropped below ten, the first time this had occurred in three decades. By the 1980s, clubs in Canada and elsewhere were beginning to "go a–courting."

If hundreds of men are willing to wait years to join the club, it is only natural to ask why. What did they perceive to be the attractions of the club and why did they decide to accept the invitation to apply. This question was posed to several dozen members and their answers are interesting. "I got into the club . . . in 1946," Tom Brown said. Since his father was a member and Brown was a veteran, he paid only $100. "I had a lot of friends who were members of the club," he added, and he decided to join "because it seemed a good thing to do."

Robert J. Orr became a member in the late 1960s. After serving in Italy and North–West Europe as a company and battalion commander, he had returned to Canada and worked as a senior executive officer with several automobile companies. He decided to leave business and to come to Vancouver to study law. He is probably the only member who, on his application, has "student" listed as his occupation. As a businessman, Orr had visited Vancouver and had been a guest at the club numerous times. His reasons for joining are best expressed by his own words:

> *I liked the atmosphere of the club. It seemed to offer a place that you could go where there were gentlemen. It didn't seem to be a salesman's club [where] half the people were there to see what they could get out of it. It seemed to be a gentleman's club where you can go at lunch time and not worry about what you say and you can have some stimulating conversations. I found I was right and I think it's a great club.*

As with many others, William Leithead first came to the club as a guest. An architect with McCarter and Nairn, he was proposed by J. Y. McCarter. He welcomed the idea. "Before I was a member," he said, "I was here very often for dinner with clients of the firm and I always enjoyed it, both the atmosphere and the members. [After I joined] I can truthfully say that some of the happiest hours of my life have been spent in the club."

"Larry" Dampier, after returning from overseas, had worked for Lever Brothers and became marketing vice-president in the U.S.A. before coming to Vancouver in 1956 to become vice-president of Sun Publishing Company. His friend, Don Cromie, who owned the Vancouver "Sun" and was a club member, suggested that Dampier should join. It took five years before his name reached the top of the waiting list, but meanwhile he had corporate membership in the Terminal City Club. He recalled later:

> *There was no way you could advance on that waiting list beyond the proper order. [By the time I joined] I had been a guest as frequently as you were allowed. . . . By the time I became a member I did know the members fairly well and it was a great delight to me when I finally made it. . . . I think the membership process of the Vancouver Club is excellent. . . . It is thorough and . . . if you make it into the Vancouver Club you have passed some of the fairly rigid tests that it takes to get into a first class club.*

Theodore Du Moulin left his law practice to join the artillery during the war. On his return to Vancouver he was unable to take advantage of the veteran's entrance fee but he did manage to join in 1956. His reasons for joining were obvious. "I just liked the idea," he said. "My brother was a member . . . and our firm [Russell and Du Moulin] was just across the road at 850 West Hastings, which was very handy for lunch. Also, I knew quite a few members of the Club."

A. A. ("Tim") Hugman had been a $10-a-week bank clerk in Montreal when he joined the army and ended up commanding a squadron of tanks in Italy and Holland. His post-war employment eventually led to an offer from MacMillan-Bloedel which brought him to Vancouver. Eventually he became President and General Manager of Export Sales Company. He joined the club in 1957 after a two-year wait. A corporate member of the Terminal City Club, Hugman was pleased to join the Vancouver Club. As he stated later:

> *I think there is an enormous air of dignity in this club and the membership, when I joined, was composed of senior important people in practically all aspects of society. I guess that is perhaps the main reason [why I joined] plus the fact that I had developed a number of friends in the two-year waiting period who were*

members. I have always regarded it as a great privilege to be in the
club, meeting any number of people who have since become great
friends. . . .

The reasons why men joined the club, and the above members
are used only as random examples, were quite varied, but in essence it
was for good fellowship, an amiable atmosphere, excellent cuisine and
the chance to relax in a place which to many was a home away from
home.

As in the pre-war years, most of the new members had their
business in downtown Vancouver. The busiest time for the club would
be between 11:30 a.m. and 2:30 p.m. when the dining room would be
so full that there would be two sittings necessary to accommodate
those wishing to have lunch, even though some members might be
having theirs in the third floor lunch room or perhaps having a
sandwich and a drink in the bar. There were many in the city, however,
who might have been welcomed as members but, owing to the location
of their firm or office, would have found it inconvenient to make full
use of the club, especially at lunch time. There were only one or two
club members from the universities, for example, and in the case of
U.B.C., not only would it take considerable time to drive to the club
and find a parking space, but there was a comfortable faculty club on
the campus which suited most of the academics. In brief, the appeal of
the club continued to be to those who could make the fullest use of its
facilities.

The new members joining in the post-war era would have met, in
time, some very interesting older gentlemen in the club, many of
whom had played a considerable role in the development of the city,
and in some cases, the province. One of these was Sir George Bury.
Born in 1866, he started work as a junior railway clerk after teaching
himself shorthand. For a short time he substituted for the secretary of
the president of the Canadian Pacific Railway, Lord Shaughnessy,
and later was promoted to become temporary secretary for William
Van Horne, then general manager of the C.P.R. He impressed both,
and it is claimed he brought the "new" typewriter into general office
use by the company. He learned the railway business by travelling with
Van Horne, and at a very early age was given some difficult tasks.
"When the superintendent of the sleeping and dining car department
was shot by a disgruntled porter," a newspaper account relates, "Sir
George was put in charge. A brass ruler rapped over porters' heads
helped the 21-year-old superintendent to keep them in check." In
1890 he was made superintendent of the wild and unruly North Bay
Division. He grew a beard to help disguise his age (24 years), but for
his superiors his drive and energy, not his age, were the determining
factor in his promotion to other large and difficult positions on the

C.P.R.'s track. By 1907 he was general manager of the western lines and the great five-mile tunnel through Rogers Pass was built under his supervision.

By 1914 Bury was vice-president in charge of the company's entire operating system. While overseas in 1916 inspecting the work of the C.P.R. construction battalion in France, he was approached by the British government to go to Russia with Lord Milner. Russia's huge military and industrial potential was under-utilized owing to its poor transportation system. Bury was one of the most highly regarded transportation experts in North America so he went with the British commission to Russia early in 1917. He met the Czar who formed such a good impression of him that every day he sent Bury a bottle of champagne for lunch!

Bury was in Petrograd in 1917 when the revolution started. He took photographs of the mob scenes and early clashes and in his report on Russia's railway difficulties, also advised the British prime minister of the impending collapse of Russia. Bury was knighted for his work in 1917, returned to Canada and resumed his work. In 1918, when Lord Shaughnessy retired, Bury expected to step into his shoes. When he was informed Edward Beatty was selected, the story is told that he stomped out of the office and slammed the glass plated door so hard that the glass broke. Another story relates that the glass didn't break so Bury broke it with his cane. The C.P.R. gave him a very generous pension, and in his later years he used to rejoice that he was costing the C.P.R. far more than the firm anticipated! He lived until 1958 when he died in his 92nd year.

Sir George had a habit of sitting at a round table in the corner in the third floor bar which had an excellent view over the C.P.R. railway and docks. In time a circle of his friends used to sit there with him--H. S. Kirkland, Robert McKeen, B. W. Greer, A. G. Larson, J. Y. McCarter and one or two others. Sir George used to arrive promptly at 11:30 a.m., go to "his" table for a drink and have several more with his friends. They formed a merry and convivial group. On March 6th, 1945, which was his birthday, a ship called the *Greenhill Park* blew up while at the C.P.R. dock. As one member tells the story: "When the big explosion took place, Sir George and three of his friends were sitting at the table. It shattered all the windows of the club. Everyone ducked, but not old Sir George. It was his birthday and he had had a few and thought it was some sort of celebration his friends had arranged."

Bury, recalls another member, "would regale everybody with stories of the past and was always highly entertaining and quite opinionated, but every one thought he was wonderful and loved him dearly." Sir George was always impeccable in his dress, and usually ordered his shirts, ties, and so forth from his London tailors. His taste was sometimes a bit unusual. If wearing a striped shirt he had the stripes on his cuffs and sometimes his collar run parallel to the stripes on his shirt. A pearl tie-pin in his tie and a boutonniere in his lapel were as much a part of him as his cane and bowler hat.

One day another member, a consultant architect, was with some painters who were about to redecorate the third floor snack room when along came Sir George, somewhat unsteadily. "What are you doing?" he asked Ned Pratt. "Painting the ceiling." "It's the wrong colour." And he asked, "Where are you mixing?" "In there." Sir George went in to talk to the painter and said, "Put some yellow in there," pointing to one can with his cane and then another, he remained for some time before leaving. "Anyway," Pratt relates, "he got the colour all mixed up and said, 'Now, there's the right colour, put that on.' The guy goes up and puts a big splotch on. Bury said, 'That's the way it should be,' and off he goes. It was exactly the same colour as in the room next door!"

There is no doubt that Sir George dominated "his" table in the bar, and no one would think of sitting there without his invitation, with the exception of "the regulars." It became such a tradition that his long time friend, J. Y. McCarter, arranged to have a small brass plate placed on the table which read "Sir George Bury. This is his place." It was a nice touch which amused Bury. The inscription apparently was based on the words appearing on the label of Old Parr whiskey--very appropriately so. It is also appropriate that when the club decided in 1951 to have a large plaque hung outside the entrance to the third floor bar listing the names of club members who reached their 90th year, Bury's name topped the list.

Another well-known club member and past-president was W. C. Woodward. He was a young boy when his father came to Vancouver to establish what was to become a thriving business enterprise--Woodward's stores. Educated in Vancouver, he left school when he was 16 years old to work as a $15 a month junior bank clerk. After serving in various branches, he was posted to Havana, Cuba at his own request. After six years with the bank he left to start a brokerage business in Havana. "I went broke just about as fast as it could be done," he said later.

Woodward returned to Vancouver to work in the department store and, at the outbreak of the Great War, served overseas as an artillery officer. After the war he became Honorary Colonel of the 15th Field Regiment, R.C.A., and maintained an interest in the militia during the rest of his life. He became president of Woodward's in 1937, the same year he started his three-year term as president of the Vancouver Club. During the Second World War he was a "dollar-a-

January 19, 1967

"You know how they escalate . . . next thing you know it's the marines and B52s . . . "

year" man in Ottawa assisting C. D. Howe, the Minister of Munitions and Supply. Late in 1940, when returning from Britain, the ship Howe and Woodward had taken was torpedoed but both were rescued. Returning to his business in 1941, Woodward was appointed Lieutenant-Governor of British Columbia, a post he held until the end of the war.

As Woodward's expanded its outlets to include Victoria, Edmonton and elsewhere, "Billy" Woodward's business interests widened also. When he died in 1957, he was vice-president of Neon Products of Western Canada and a director of the Royal Bank of Canada, MacMillan and Bloedel Ltd. and the Union Steamships Ltd. He was also a former president of the Vancouver Board of Trade, a life Governor of the Vancouver General Hospital and a life member of the Canadian Club, a founder of the Vancouver Little Theatre Association, and was a strong supporter of the works of the Salvation Army. But aside from his business and community interests, Woodward was a very respected and well liked club member.

His brother, P. A. ("Puggy") Woodward was also a member of the club. As a young man he had helped to build his father's department store in 1903. He, too, entered his father's business after the Great War and in 1919 he was largely responsible for starting Canada's first self-service food store, the forerunner of the groceteria. Dubbed an "eccentric genius" by one newspaper- man, he was one of the best merchandisers in the city. What their father had started the two brothers expanded into thirteen retail outlets in Alberta and British Columbia. As a club member "Puggy" was involved in various escapades which are well remembered. He retired in 1958 and for the next decade devoted his full time to his charities. When he died in 1968 he had given about $5,000,000 to the University of British Columbia, the Royal Jubilee Hospital and to a variety of other institutions in the province.

H. R. MacMillan was 34 years old when he joined the club in 1919. Born and educated in Ontario, he achieved a master's degree in forestry from Yale in 1908. After a two-year battle with tuberculosis he worked for the federal and then the provincial government becoming British Columbia's Chief Forester in 1912. During the Great War he was appointed a federal Timber Trade Commissioner looking for new timber and lumber markets. After the war he formed the H. R. MacMillan Export Co. to sell British Columbia forest products on the world market, a business which previously had been in American hands.

His business flourished, and in the mid–thirties he added shipping and manufacturing to his business. During the Second World War he was another of the club's "dollar–a–year" men and was president of Wartime Merchant Shipping. In 1951 his company merged with Bloedel, Stewart and Welsh to form MacMillan and Bloedel, Ltd., the largest firm of its kind in British Columbia selling lumber, timber, pulp and paper and associated products around the world. During the course of his career, MacMillan was made a Member of the British Empire for his wartime work and in 1971 was invested as a Companion of the Order of Canada, the nation's highest civilian award. He received several honorary doctorate degrees and was also Honorary Colonel of the Seaforth Highlanders of Canada.

There have been at least six biographies or autobiographies written about club members but so far none has been written about H. R. MacMillan. His name is synonomous with the growth and development of the forest industry in B.C. in the 20th century. He was a wealthy man, possibly in his time the richest member of the club. At the same time probably no person in the province gave so many millions of dollars to the universities, churches and to the people of the province as "H. R."

As a club man he tended to be reserved. One member remembers him as "a very rugged, hardworking, brilliant pioneer-type of industrialist [with] a great force of character." Others remember him as "dynamic," "forceful" and "all business." The Honorable J. V. Clyne, whom MacMillan lured from the bench to become chairman and chief executive officer of MacMillan-Bloedel, saw him as a tremendous force in the economy of the province. There were other sides to him other than his business interests. He was an ardent reader and fisherman and enjoyed hunting and the outdoors. He could, on occasion, display a keen sense of humour beneath a gruff exterior. He was a greatly respected club member and a good and generous friend to those who got to know him well.

One more well-known gentleman whom new post-war members might have met was Victor Spencer. Born in Victoria in 1882, and a veteran of both the Boer War and the Great War, he worked in his father's pioneer department stores in Victoria and Vancouver and in time saw it develop into a chain of nine stores throughout British Columbia. One of his major interests was ranching which he took up seriously after the Great War. He bought Earlscourt ranch near Lytton which specialized in pure bred Hereford stock, and later purchased three other ranches in the Kamloops area. In time, and in partnership with the Honorable Frank Ross, he acquired the 650,000 acre Douglas Lake ranch, one of the largest in the British Commonwealth.

"Colonel" Spencer, as his staff used to call him, had far ranging business interests and was a pioneer in several. He started a tobacco growing business on Sumas prairie, he encouraged apiarists and helped start the province's thriving honey production and he was one of the principal figures in developing the Pioneer Gold Mine. Pioneer combined with Bralorne to become an extremely successful mining company. His other business ventures are too numerous to mention, but no matter how involved he was as an entrepreneur he remained an affable and friendly member. He was an enthusiastic supporter of amateur sport and, among other things, he bought the shells in which the Vancouver Rowing Club-U.B.C. team trained for and won the 1956 Olympics. He was a man who usually worked behind the scenes to help a variety of groups ranging from ex-servicemen's organizations and the 4-H movement to educational activities. As one person commented on hearing of his death early in 1960: "He was a wonderful person, kindly, warm-hearted and generous." He was also a good club member for slightly over 40 years.

These are only a few of the senior members in the club in the post Second World War years. More than one present-day member supports the opinion of a recent ex-president when he said: "I think they were far more interesting people than we are today.'' Possibly a future member might reflect the same thought when examining the careers of the new members coming in during the 1940's and 1950's. Certainly the senior members at the time were an adventurous group in many ways. There was still an overlap among the then seniors with the pioneers of the province, but in comparative terms, there was still lots of room for development in a province and in a city which were still growing.

*   *   *   *

In the immediate post-war years, as we have seen, there was almost a flood of new members into the club. This almost created a generation gap which, inevitably, was going to have an impact on the governance of the club and bring with it some slow but subtle changes which, in the long run, were to meet the general approval of all.

A small indication of this turned up late in 1945. In October the General Committee received a letter containing a proposal for the purchase of the lot adjoining the club property on its west side. The committee decided ''it was not in a position to consider the matter . . .'' but the matter came up again in December when it was reported ''that there appeared to be a feeling amongst the membership at large in favour of the proposal.'' The president therefore agreed to approach the representative of the owner to obtain an option to purchase.

The idea was not a new one. As early as March, 1923 the club had the opportunity to buy 50 feet of the lot adjoining the western border of the club at $400 per foot. It was unaminously turned down at the annual general meeting. A year later, at a similar meeting, the suggestion was made that the incoming committee should see what could be done about buying a portion of the property. The wheels ground very slowly, but in 1925 it was reported that the lot, 73 feet long, could be had for $480 per foot or about $35,000. The club secretary was instructed to present a counter-offer of $30,000 for the full lot, or $480 per foot for only 23 feet. Considering the fact that the lot was as deep as the club's property, the counter-offer was turned down by the owner.

In 1926, with the Canadian economy booming along, the club was asked by Bell-Irving, Creery and Co., Ltd. if it wished to buy the lot for $51,500 but this was turned down also. Nevertheless at the annual meeting two months later, a notice of motion (by Victor Spencer and N. R. Whittall) proposed that the 73-foot lot should be bought and an addition to the club built to provide further accommodation for increasing membership. In addition the new lot could accommodate squash-racquet and badminton courts, a gymnasium, a swimming pool and a Turkish bath. The proposal failed to pass.

Twenty years later, when the subject came up again, the scene had changed. James Richardson and Sons, Ltd. owned the lot. They had bought most of it with the intention of erecting a two-storey building, but the building would have a frontage of only 50 feet. Between it and the club would be a strip of land about 20 feet which ran for about 130 feet where it entered a space about 75 by 55 feet adjoining the C.P.R. property. The price requested in 1946 for this hatchet-shaped land was $30,000. The General Committee was in favour of the idea, feeling that the club ". . . should take advantage of this offer in order to secure for itself the necessary light, preservation of view and to provide for possible future requirements of space." An extraordinary meeting was held and the ballot count was 60 yeas, 32 nays. Since a 75 per cent majority was needed to pass a resolution of this kind, the club once again missed an excellent opportunity. Several members who were there suggested that the older members tended to vote against the motion, but perhaps one could also blame the younger members for not turning out in force. Nine "pro" votes would have swung the weight in favour.

****

Under normal circumstances, the vice-president succeeds the president of the club. There are exceptions, of course. He might be transferred by his firm to another city, he might become seriously ill, he might be elected to a political office or his own affairs might be such that he knows he cannot devote the time demanded of the president to oversee club business. Normally, too, there is only one person whose name is put up as a candidate for president. In 1948, however, there was a change in this normal procedure and as a result the previous year's vice-president was not elected and Walter Owen was. In the same year the Secretary-Manager, B. C. Binks, was replaced by Arthur J. Brown. The two events were not unrelated. It would seem that a number of members, perhaps especially the newer ones, began to feel that the club was being run by a small number of older but influential men and were determined to break the pattern by exercising their rights under the constitution. Putting Owen up for election as president and then voting him in is looked upon by many as a much needed change. The release of Mr. Binks from office came about as a result of his refusal to carry out an order by Owen because Bink's felt the older members would not agree with it. Such a challenge to presidential authority could not be permitted, and Binks was quickly on his way.

The slow transfer of power from the older members to the new took place smoothly and without rancour during the 1940s and '50s. The greatest changes in the club in the post-war decades were the

A quiet, comfortable corner of the Reading Room.

renovations that went on in the post–war decades. The last major change had been when the third floor bar had been expanded. Much had to be done, and with mortgages available at three and a half per cent, the club decided to borrow and renovate.

One of the first things done was to buy new carpets for the two Reading Rooms. (At this time there was a Small Reading Room next to the present Gun Room.) New carpets were also bought for the Large Card Room, the Ladies Lounge and the entrance and stairways leading to it. The Ladies Lounge itself was redecorated and some of the furniture in it re-covered. The elevators and dumb-waiters were checked and repaired. In the basement, the two cold rooms were reconstructed and new refrigeration equipment installed and the main kitchen received a major restructuring with new equipment. The latter was about thirty years old and was scrapped.

In the basement the club's heating plant had deteriorated to a serious degree and consequently was using not only excess oil but the club had received warnings from the city's smoke inspector. Putting in a new automatic oil furnace would not only cut the fuel bill by about

25 per cent, but it would eliminate the necessity of employing two of the three engineers on staff. This combined saving, it was felt, would pay for the cost of the new furnace within four to five years.

There were changes on the first floor as well. When the new secretary–manager arrived in 1948 there were still animal heads hung on the walls of the main lobby. These were removed to a storage room in the basement, a room already containing old trunks, golf bags, and so forth left by members years ago. Brown's office was a tiny room tucked behind the main office where the catering manager is now located, and the catering manager's office was in the basement. This situation was to be changed, especially since in 1947 the construction of the James Richardson's new office building next door cut off most of the light and air on the west side of the club. It was decided to use what had been the Strangers Room, renamed the Visitors Room, for the secretary–manager's office. This was a room on the immediate left of the main entrance to the club. Henceforth visitors could wait for their hosts in the main lobby, and henceforth, too, the secretary–manager would be able to look out the window and have some badly needed space. The main office was to be in several rooms built above the tradesmen's entrance, connected by a stairway to the first floor.

One small change was made in the men's cloakroom which might be mentioned in passing. The scales had weighed innumerable members since the early twenties, possibly even before, but in 1948 Arthur Brown managed to obtain a three–seat shoe–shine stand which had been used for years by two Italian brothers in downtown Vancouver. The stand was refurnished and reupholstered, Leo Gemma was hired as a part–time shoe–shine boy and, as Brown reports, some of the younger members used to think it the height of self–indulgence to have a shoe–shine while having a drink. Gemma was an expert, and he also did an excellent job on two–tone shoes, so much so that some members would bring down their wives' shoes for him to polish. He also produced some first–rate home–made wine, and this sidelight apparently supplemented his income. A shoe–shine, incidentally, cost 20 cents and at the time could be paid for in cash, by ticket ("club money") or by charge.

In addition to the renovations mentioned above, the House Committee noted that the drapes in the dining room had deteriorated beyond repair and much of the club's furniture needed fixing and reupholstering. There was much to be done, but by 1948 a good start had been made.

With the secretary and the clerical staff moved to their new offices, it was felt that the vacant space, together with a small addition from a nearby cloakroom, could be made into a small but attractive private dining room. Work on this began in 1949 and was completed by May, 1950. It had a Chinese decor and was called the "Ming Room". It could seat 18 members comfortably and was advertised as being available "for luncheons, staff cocktail parties and dinners." It served a very useful function until additional and larger private dining rooms were created on the upper floors. The cost of renovating and furnishing the Ming Room, incidentally, was estimated at $4,000. To the surprise, wonder and delight of the committee, the actual cost came to only $3,620. This precedent remains almost unique in the club's history.

The success of the changes to the first floor of the club house, together with the increasing membership, led to a series of almost breathtaking suggestions by the House Committee in 1951. It suggested, in brief, that some of the bedrooms should be eliminated, the lounge on the second floor should be enlarged by taking in the Blue Room, the third floor bar should be enlarged by absorbing the billiard room and providing an additional snack bar, moving the billiard room to the front of the fourth floor, leaving that floor with four bedrooms and a poker room. Finally a new Blue Room was suggested which would be divisable by folding doors into three private dining rooms.

A major restructuring of this nature had to be considered with some care. By the time it reached the annual general meeting in March, 1952 the general proposal had become more specific. The third floor bar, when extended, would be able to seat 150 rather than 100 people. The billiard room on the fourth floor would have an oyster and salad bar next to it which could be used as a dining room when the main dining room was reserved. On the fifth floor only three bedrooms would be kept, the same as the fourth floor. Additional dining room accommodations would fill the remaining floor space. A new passenger elevator was now included in the scheme, and the second floor lounge, enlarged by taking in Blue Room space, would allow 80 rather than 30 persons to be seated where they could enjoy coffee after lunch and so hasten the process of clearing the tables on busy days.

The proposals had some merit, and some of the ideas were to be used a few years later. As a major project, however, it was unacceptable to the members. In 1954 a more moderate proposal was submitted, on request, from an architectural firm which envisaged a cocktail lounge on the roof above the billiard room and, by filling in the court on the west side and developing the accommodation on the east side additional room for lounges, a men's private dining room and a new elevator. The total cost, including furnishings, was estimated at about $700,000. The report was received and tabled, and for the next five years there were no major changes in the club.

There was one room which never existed in the club but which was discussed by members for almost twenty-five years. This might be a good time to dwell on a question that first arose in the General Committee when, in May 1960, it was mentioned that a number of members had expressed the need for a steam and conditioning room in the club. Deeply involved in other, more pressing, matters the committee took no action. Two years later R. M. Hungerford was authorized to make further enquiries and he reported there seemed to be a fair amount of interest in the idea. Several months later, Hungerford and Robert Keay drafted a questionnaire which was sent to all members. The response showed 251 in favour and 145 against the proposal. In the next year, C. E. Pratt presented drawings and an estimate of costs, which came to between $25,000 and $30,000. It was authorized at an extraordinary meeting in January 1964, but the authorization provided that the committee have discretionary powers.

By 1967 nothing had been done. In its June meeting the General Committee "resolved that in view of the relatively small demand for this service and because of the several spas which have become available in the city since 1964, [we] do not exercise the authority conferred upon it. . . ."

Sixteen years later, at the annual general meeting, the matter came up again. It was pointed out by the Honorable George Van Roggen that the members of the Terminal City Club enjoyed a Jacuzzi, showers, changing room, swimming pool, exercise bicycles, weight lifting apparatus, a treadmill and a masseur. The committee once more took it under consideration and it was felt, in order to have substantial headroom, the old boiler room in the basement would have to be used. It would cost about $10,000 to get rid of the furnace and boilers and ten times that amount to renovate the room. Once again the committee felt that the wise course would be to poll the members. A questionnaire was sent to members in the July 1983 newsletter, and the bottom line asked the key question: "Would you be prepared to pay $30 per month for the use of these facilities?"

The results were interesting. Out of 1020 in-town members and 203 out-of-town members, 130 had filled in and returned the questionnaire while others sent in comments. Only eight per cent of the total membership favoured the idea and were willing to pay the extra $30 per month. A further 46 members were in favour but not prepared to pay the extra amount. Thirty were undecided and, although not asked in the questionnaire, 187 members stated, some vehemently, that they did not think the club should have any form of health club at all. One member was heard to remark that he "did not want the smell of soggy jock-straps wafting up to the entrance hall of the club" when he came in to dine.

There was another room in the club--the library--which might be examined briefly. For many years, there was no record of how many books were in it for many yaers, and not until 1926 was there much mention of it in the minutes of the General Committee or even the suggestion book. In that year a sum of $100 was granted by the committee for the purchase of books, but this annual grant was drastically cut during the depression of the 1930's. Members could borrow anything but reference books and since there were a fair number of live-in residents, one can assume there was a modest but steady turnover of reading material. It was not until 1959 that A. D. Bell-Irving, a committee member, suggested that an effort should be made to arouse more interest in the library and it was agreed it should be brought up-to-date and a survey made of its use. Two professional librarians called in to examine the club's holdings recommended that the club maintain its reference books, but dispense with its books of fiction since it would cost too much to catalogue them. The use of the library had dropped drastically since the club now had radios and was on the verge of getting a television set.

Although the club bought a television set in 1960, it was another thirteen years before much was done about the library. It was decided to move it from the first to the third floor in the Silent Room, a small room adjacent to the Card Room, and a place to which one could retire for a quiet snooze or perhaps write a letter. The club had about 1,000 volumes, most of which were purchased in the inter-war era. The books were catalogued and cross-indexed and a survey of the membership was conducted to obtain an opinion about the need to start a club lending library. Of 426 replies, 69 members were in favour, 345 were against and 12 had mixed feelings.

With about 80 per cent of the members against the proposal, once again advice from a professional librarian was sought. Ultimately it was decided to sell some (with members having first choice), give some to the public library and the University of British Columbia, and retain those which might interest the members and for which there was shelf room. General reference books would be held but up-dated.

In the long run, the library was gradually reduced and with the major changes in the club following amalgamation, the club's books are now neatly shelved in the Gun Room or the Reading Room. The increase in membership has not brought with it a demand for more books, but probably the greatest blow to the library usage came with the end of permanent live-in members and the dwindling of the number of bedrooms for guests.

*   *   *   *

The changes which took place inside the club in the 15- to 20-year period after the war were modest. In the city and the province it was an era of great change and tremendous economic activity. In the heart of the city the demolition of the old Hotel Vancouver in 1949 marked the first step in the restructuring and rebuilding of the downtown core, a process which would continue for another four decades. There was a building boom which seemed unending. The suburbs were being filled but the demand was constant. The post-war "baby boom" resulted in a call for more schools and, ultimately, more colleges and universities. In 1952, when the "new" Social Credit party came to power in the province, there followed a period of tremendous construction of highways, bridges and dams which further stimulated the economy. The old city streetcars were being phased out and replaced by buses, and downtown traffic was becoming so congested that by 1957 the one-way street system in the city's core was introduced. Television, which first reached the city from Seattle in 1948, soon began to challenge radio as the most popular form of home entertainment and travel by swift jet-engined aircraft began to carry more and more passengers who, in earlier days, would go by train or ocean liner.

By the mid-fifties Vancouver's population was nearing 400,000 and with new automobiles again available after the wartime shortage, North and West Vancouver started to grow rapidly. The volume of trade through the port of Vancouver increased each year and club members, with their magnificent view of over the harbour, could note the growing number of merchant ships coming and going under the Lion's Gate bridge.

Along with this tremendous economic growth and change, however, there were many disturbing events taking place in the world which, in some instances, seemed to threaten the prosperity of the nation and, in others, certainly altered long-held concepts of global affairs. In Europe the "Cold War" had started in the immediate post-war years and when Russia exploded its first nuclear bomb in 1949, Europe was more solidly divided with the formation of two armed camps—NATO and the Warsaw Pact. Nuclear warfare became a possibility and, for the first time, Canada saw itself as a potential participant in a nuclear exchange between two superpowers.

On a wider scale, the old empires were in the process of dissolution. The Belgian, French and British empires were slowly granting independence to former colonies and dependencies, sometimes peacefully but sometimes with reluctance and bloodshed. Dozens of new states, independent for the first time, were emerging in Africa and the Far East. Japan was beginning to make a tremendous recovery, which would astound the world in the 1960s and '70s, while Germany, even though divided, was in the process of an economic recovery which no one would have believed possible in the late 1940s. The Middle East, owing to its importance as an oil-producing area, began to exercise its collective strength as the main supplier of essential fuel to an increasingly industrialized world. The firing by the Soviet Union of an earth satellite into orbit in October 1957 — "Sputnik I" — seemed to symbolize, in a way, the changes that were in process in the decade and a half after the end of the war and there seemed to be no end in sight. Some of the older members might grumble that "the world was going to Hell in a basket," others would take it in their stride and keep up with the pace while retaining the old standards they valued.

CHAPTER VII

ENTERTAINING IN THE CLUB

By the 1960's and 1970's, those serving on the controlling body of the Vancouver Club--the General Committee--were mostly members who had joined the club in the post-war years. Like their predecessors, they were faced with a number of challenges which changing times and social mores imposed on the club and its traditions. They also had to deal with an aging building. The Xerox machine, computers, word processors, communication by satellite, transportation by jet-aircraft, robot machinery, automatic sensors and a variety of inventions too numerous to mention were changing business and the life of businessmen. The leisurely two-hour lunches began to fade and the demand for space for private dining rooms began to rise. The opening of new hotels and restaurants, most of them with liquor licences and a good selection of wine, made it necessary that the club look carefully at its own dining room and entertainment policy. The increase in wages meant the club had to improve salaries, pensions and health benefits for its staff. A hard decision had to be made whether or not to continue having permanent residents in the club and, for economic reasons, the reduction of the staff had to be considered. Elevator boys were replaced by an automatic elevator, the boiler engineers gave way to steam heating and bellboys were no longer hired. Some of these changes were in process in the 1940's and continued in the following decades.

Perhaps one of the most obvious results of the increase in both the speed and volume of travel by jet aircraft was on the number of the club's affiliation agreements. Looking backward for a moment, the earliest mention of a form of affiliation was made in 1905 when, at the suggestion of the Union Club of Victoria, the Vancouver Club agreed "to make their tickets interchangeable." A similar agreement was made in 1909 with the Jericho Country Club and later with the Shaughnessy Heights Golf Club. In the 1920's the "exchange of tickets" agreement was extended to include the Marine Drive Golf and Country Club, the Royal Vancouver Yacht Club and the Point Grey Golf Club. The last arrangement of this type was made in 1939 with the Capilano Golf Club. Each of these clubs had its own "club money," books of tickets or coupons each bearing a certain value and used within the clubs. Since members frequently held membership in several clubs, it was a convenience--more or less like today's credit cards--to use this "money" in any club where dual or triple membership existed.

Club affiliation carried far more implications than an exchange of tickets. It involved accepting a member from another club and giving him the rights and privileges within the clubhouse as would be mutually agreed upon. Generally it meant the ability to stay at or perhaps visit a gentleman's club in another city and enjoy the conveniences and amenities of that club as one would at home. Affiliation offers were by no means automatic and sometimes they were made with clubs having mixed membership. An affiliation might be arranged with Club "Y" in expectation of members' visits, but if members from both clubs rarely used the opportunity, the affiliation might be dropped by mutual agreement. In a word, affiliations were not permanent but were negotiable and based on mutual interest and cooperative responsibility.

The question of affiliation first arose in the Vancouver Club in 1910, but not until May 1911 was the Secretary instructed to write "to the leading clubs in Canada, Seattle and Portland respecting affiliation . . . and asking on what terms could such be arranged." About two weeks later a reply was received from the Arlington Club in Portland saying it was opposed. Perhaps other replies were not encouraging either for in the August 1911 minutes of the General Committee a curt entry noted that the entire subject was dropped.

Actually the club's constitution made no provision for affiliation, but one can appreciate how miffed the committee must have felt at the time.

Perhaps this original rebuff accounted for the enthusiastic response the club gave to an enquiry late in 1912 from the British Empire Club in London "asking if arrangements of a reciprocal nature could be made as between members of that and this club." The committee was so delighted that "the secretary was instructed to write that [although] there is no authority for such an arrangement in our Constitution, the Committee unanimously accepts your invitation on behalf of the Club to take effect at once, and will ask the Club at the next annual meeting to endorse their action." Almost half a century earlier an American naval officer during the Civil War had given the famous order: "Damn the Torpedoes! go ahead . . . full speed!" The committee must have felt the same way but at the Annual General Meeting they passed safely through the minefield when a new clause (18a) was added to the constitution which allowed a member of the British Empire Club to be a Temporary Honorary Member of the Vancouver Club for one month without payment, and for five additional months at $10 a month.

With the ice broken, a second affiliation was made with another London club, the Isthmian, in June, 1913 and by 1916 the list had grown to include the St. James's Club (Montreal), the Toronto Club, the Garrison Club (Quebec) the Hamilton Club, the Rideau Club (Ottawa), the City Club (Halifax) and the Constitutional Club (London). During the 1920's and 1930's, several additional affiliations were arranged--the Junior Athenaeum and Cocoa Tree Club in London and the Edmonton Club. In the late 1930's, affiliations were made with clubs in Australia and New Zealand.

After the war the list began to expand. More London clubs agreed to affiliation and in 1965 the first affiliation with an American club--the Outrigger Canoe Club in Hawaii--was established. During the 1970's the network spread eastward in Canada to the Union Club in Saint John, New Brunswick and westward across the Pacific to the Hong Kong Club. By the 1980's there were affiliations with clubs in Scotland, South Africa and Sweden. In number, affiliated clubs had grown from a mere handful to three or four dozen, an indication of the tremendous amount of travel, both for business and pleasure, in which club members were involved with the advent of what is sometimes called the jet age.

The nearest club with which the Vancouver Club is affiliated is the Union Club of Victoria. For several decades it was not uncommon for the two clubs to exchange tickets, since many men were members, in one category or another, of both clubs. It was convenient for them to take the ferry to the other city, stay the night at the club (both were only a few blocks from the docks), conduct their business and then return. There was an interruption in this agreement and, in the post-war era, when airplane travel between the two cities became more frequent and night travel by air common, the pattern was changed. For this and other reasons, there was no affiliation between the two clubs for many years. During the 1970's, Vancouver Club members were extended the privilege of using the Union Club's facilities, even though only 77 Vancouver Club members also had membership in the Union Club. This unofficial one-way affiliation was changed in 1979, when full-scale affiliation was restored, quite appropriately on the 100th anniversary of the Union Club. By mutual consent, it is the only affiliation that does not require introductory cards.

*   *   *   *

The growth of Vancouver brought with it a considerable expansion of entertainment facilities ranging from first-rate ballrooms to theatres. Added to this, of course, was the increasing popularity of television programs which could be seen at home and an ever-increasing number of social, educational, sports and other events which were attractive especially to the younger members. Dwindling attendance at club functions began to concern the committee and in the post-war decades there were constant efforts to improve and sometimes change social events at the club.

One function that was carried on was "members' night." On that evening the club was closed to ladies and only out-of-town guests could be included to dinner, followed by cards or billiards. Another popular tradition was the New Year's Eve parties and supper dances held at the club. In the late 1940's, incidentally, these cost $15 per person, but increased to $20 in the 1950's. The New Year's Eve parties, however, began to lose favour. Parking was always a problem, reservations were usually limited to a hundred couples, "drinking-and-driving" enforcement was becoming more efficient and numerous other options for celebrating the New Year were becoming available. In 1953, a proposed New Year's Eve Ball was cancelled owing to poor response to the invitation. In the 1960's the situation did not improve and as a result in 1969 the committee decided not to have a New Year's Eve party because of general disinterest in the affair over the past three years.

Spring Balls, however, became more popular. These, of course, were formal affairs with members and their guests in white ties and tails and the ladies in evening attire. In 1971, when the first one was held, 300 people attended but by the middle of the decade attendance had dropped to 212 persons, and of that number 68 were guests. To

For PLATE information see page 161.

PLATE 1   The Entry Hall

PLATE 2   The U.B.C. Room

PLATE 3   The Blue Room

PLATE 4   Snow Geese Over Fraser Delta
                            by Hugh Monahan
                          Presented by Fred Auger
                                41 x 29

                          Eagle Pass at Revelstoke
                            by E.J. Hughes
                  Presented by Friends of George Cunningham
                                46 x 36

PLATE 5   Horseshoe Bay & Howe Sound
                            By W.P. Weston
                  Presented by Friends of George Cunningham
                                46 x 42

                          The Crooked Staircase
                            by Emily Carr
                        Presented by H.R. MacMillan
                                33 x 50

PLATE 6   The Billard Room

PLATE 7   Dining Room

PLATE 8   World War Veterans   Left to Right

FRONT ROW: R.A. (Gus) Lyons, A.M. (Buster) Brown, C.A. Bird, Hon. Clarence Wallace, Hon. N.A.M. MacKenzie, J.Y. McCarter, R.W. Neil, Harold C. Grant, George S. Clark, Donald R. MacLaren, Alfred W. Carter.
CENTRE ROW: M. Gordon Brodie, Hon. J.O. Wilson, Colin C. Ferrie, A.F. McAlpine, W.H. Raikes, L.F. Stevenson, H.J. Bird, Hon. A.E. Lord, N.C.K. Wills, Carl I. Hall, C.S. Thicke, Sir Stephen H.F. Lennard.
BACK ROW: Robert H. Hedley, W. Alex Eastwood, George F.V. Hudson, John R. Horne-Payne, Wilfrid J. Borrie, F.D. Mathers, Allan C.L. Kelly.
SITTING ON FLOOR: R.J.G. Richards.

Vancouver Club Picture Collection

Over the years, a varied assortment of pictures have decorated the walls of many rooms in The Vancouver Club including photographs, lithographs, sketches and political cartoons while others, particularly those relating to British Columbia's varied political climates, have mysteriously disappeared.

Beginning in 1968, an effort was made to develop a collection of paintings by local and western artists, of scenes reflecting the unique character of the Pacific Coast. Plate 4 & 5 are examples of this growing collection. Some were gifts by members and others purchased by the club.

GOURME

Wines

CHAMPAGNE

LANSON PERE & FILS

BLACK LABEL JEROBOAM

FRUIDMER

VIN BLANC DE BLANC

MONZILLON ~ LOIRE ATLANTIC

CHATEAU LOLAN

MEDOC 1966

SAUTERNES

LA TOUR BLANCHE

IER CRU CLASSE 1969

"Pour vivre heureux et vieux,
N'écoute pas ton médecin,
Fait comme lui, boit
du bon vin."
. . . Voltaire

INNER

Menu

FOIE GRAS DE STRASSBOURG

A beautiful blend of fresh goose liver, truffles and seasonings imported for this occasion from Strassbourg. If you measure quality by cost, the quality of this foie gras is very high — costing over twenty dollars for a tiny four-ounce tin.

POTAGE LADY CURZON

Turtle soup with a difference — a tantalizing liaison of egg yolk and thick cream with a dusting of curry powder added for flavoring and color. The potage was slipped under the broiler just before serving to give a delicate golden topping.

HOMARD THERMIDOR

According to gourmet cook Julia Child, this dish was created on January 24, 1894, at Chez Maire, a Paris restaurant on Les Grands Boulevards, to celebrate the opening of Victorien Sardou's play, Thermidor. It is composed of cooked lobster, flown in fresh from Halifax yesterday, combined with butter, minced shallots, seasonings, brandy and mushrooms, in a rich cream sauce, the whole baked in the lobster shell, and served tonight in special "lobster-folded" napkins.

SORBET AU CITRON

Tangy lime sherbet prepared in the Vancouver Club's kitchen, a traditional part of a gourmet dinner. This course will refresh your palate for the rich entree to follow.

LE CANARD DU LAC BROME MARCO POLO

Truly a gourmet delight, created for tonight's dinner by Heinrich Fischer. The duck was boned, then marinated in a sauce of a little water, white wine, soy sauce, fresh ginger, minced shallots, garlic and brown sugar for forty-eight hours. After marinating, the duck was roasted in its own marinade to give you the richly browned meat you are enjoying this evening.

RIZ SAUVAGE

Purely Canadian, the nutty-flavored wild rice (actually a hand-picked grain, not a true rice) was imported from Keewatin, Ontario, though it was gathered in Shoal Lake, Manitoba.

PECHE ET AIRELLE

The peaches were first marinated in Canadian rye whisky before being filled with tangy whole berry cranberry sauce.

SOUFFLE GRAND MARNIER

Every gourmet dinner should have such a finale, and every chef should be allowed one "secret" recipe, so the recipe for tonight's dessert will remain a secret.

attract more people, the committee decided that for 1978 the Spring Ball could be a black or white tie affair. Members were to be permitted to bring more guests and the charge was set at $60 per couple. Despite these changes, the Spring Ball did not last beyond the 1970's. In May 1980 the minutes of the General Committee record its fate:

> The chairman advised those present that the Dining Room Committee has done some research on the poor attendance at the Ball. This year only 139 paying members and guests had attended, compared with 196 at the 1978 Spring Ball. There was a resulting loss of $1,609 on the evening. This was a great disappointment as, apart from attendance, the Ball had been an outstanding success. The poor attendance seemed to indicate that it was not a popular function. The Dining Room Committee recommended that, before another Ball was held, a survey be taken--possibly through the medium of the Club newsletter; and that the possibility of inviting members' sons and daughters (18 years of of age or more) to attend with the parents be investigated.

The results were not encouraging and the idea was dropped. One cannot say that after almost ninety years an old tradition was ended, for even the New Year's Eve Ball was not carried on every year without fail. Nevertheless in earlier years it was an event which was looked upon as one of the social highlights of Vancouver, an elaborate and gala affair which was talked about for weeks afterward. However, times change and the Vancouver Club had to take the new trends into account.

One popular affair in the post-war years was the "football buffet." When the city started having evening football games, and since many members attended the games, the club arranged to take its members to the games by bus. Cocktails were served at five and a buffet, or the regular dinner menu, would be available at six. The last bus would leave the club at 7:45 p.m. and after the game it would bring the members back where they could pick up their cars at the Metro Parking Lot at the corner of Hastings and Hornby Streets and go home, or return to the club for a nightcap. Having a chartered bus saved a lot of time and grief trying to park near the game itself, and by arranging to buy a block of good seats, those attending were saved the time waiting in a line-up to buy tickets.

One event which was and is always popular with members and their families was the Christmas buffet. The kitchen staff made a major effort to create a presentation of sumptuous dishes which were a variety of delights. Part of the enjoyment of the gourmet offerings was the table decorations-carved figures in ice, beautifully decorated cakes and pastries, Christmas scenes in tallow, a traditional boar's head displayed in medieval style and many other original pieces baked, shaped, carved or created to give an eye-catching appeal to a beautiful buffet.

With the increase in membership, by 1970 the Christmas buffet was held for four days before Christmas. The first and second floors were opened to ladies (similar to the New Year's Eve Ball) and the Lobby Lounge Bar was open to them as well to ease the pressure on the Blue Room staff. By 1976 the Christmas Buffet had been extended to seven days and the chairman of the Dining Room Committee, Geoffrey H. Tullidge, reported that all seven days were sold out by noon on the first day of booking. A total of 1,373 members and guests had attended the dinner buffets and another 398 persons had attended the two luncheon buffets. At that, there was a long waiting list which, at its peak, totalled 413. By 1979 the Christmas buffet was extended to nine days, partly to accommodate the demand and partly to reduce the somewhat crowded seating in the dining room. Four years later it was agreed that two of the evenings should be called Family Nights to which children aged 15 years or more could be invited. It was a nice touch and in a way the wheel had almost come a full circle when one reads of the Children's Party the club used to host at the turn of the century.

One traditional entertainment which continued in the club almost from its beginning was the "Tom and Jerry" Party held at the end of the year. A "Tom and Jerry" was the name of a mixed drink based on rum and, according to some of the older members, the party used to be held on New Year's Day. A number of members were officers in the local militia units who would attend regimental levées at officers' messes and then return to the club to greet each other. In time what started as a habit was changed into a tradition which included all club members meeting and greeting each other at the end of the year rather than on New Year's Day, when many would be in a fragile condition from the previous evening's celebrations. After the Second World War the club president began to invite the incumbent lieutenant-governor and, since many of them were also club members, these parties were frequently enhanced by his presence in a very informal atmosphere. Most of the senior members attend every year and it is a traditional time for good fellowship.

During the 1970's the entertainment offered at the club had become fairly routine. The "Tom and Jerry" Party, the Spring Ball, the Annual Club Dinner, the Club Bridge Night, the Snooker and Slosh Tournament, one or more Gourmet Dinners, the Christmas Buffet Dinner and a Wine Tasting Party and Buffet Dinner. During the 1980's, in order to attract more members to use club facilities, several additional entertainment events were added and almost all have proven popular.

GRACEFUL DANCING GIRLS molded of translucent paraffin beautify a downtown club's Christmas buffet centrepiece. Marcel Chaleil, patissier, left, puts on final touches while Chef Ivan Wheatley admires the artistry.   *(Pacific Press Library)*

Early in 1986 the club decided to have a Father and Sons Dinner Night. It was advertised in the club newsletter as "an excellent opportunity for the male members of the family to have a stag night at the club." The son had to be 15 years old, but the family part was extended to include grandfathers, grandsons, uncles, nephews and even male in-laws. This was so successful that 190 sat down to dinner and of the 76 on the waiting list, over 40 were still trying to get in at the last moment. The following year it was repeated event and in 1988 it was made into a two-evening affair to accommodate the demand.

Another entertainment idea which was very much enjoyed was the Dinner Theatre. This started early in 1985. It was decided to have a reception, followed by a dinner with wines and liqueurs, after which there would be a live theatre performance. The first presentation was a comedy, "Chapter Two," put on by a Calgary theatre company. Comments from members were "overwhelmingly positive," and moreover the club made a profit! Later in the same year the club tried the same thing again, and Robert Brodie was able to report "that 22 and 23 October were two of the most successful evenings ever held at the Vancouver Club." Both nights were a sell-out and there were 60 members and their guests on the waiting list unable to get a reservation. Once again it was a comedy--"Marriage Anyone"--and "was full of laughs from beginning to end." This was a "first" for the club and it would appear by its success to be a forerunner of more theatre nights to come.

Another suggestion for entertaining the members was also put forward in the 1980's. It was felt that the club should have a dinner where both the food, decor and entertainment of various nations would be stressed--a sort of "ethnic night". The first of these was the British Dinner Night in February 1985. The British Consul General, Stanley Stephenson and his wife were the hosts and helped in a variety of ways to make the evening a success. Naturally kitchen and bar staffs offered British fare and drink appropriate to the evening. There was even a Beefeater at the door to set the tone of the entertainment and, of course, appropriate music during dinner itself. Once again the event was very well received and, again, profitable. Other similar national dinner nights followed, all with the enthusiastic support of the various consuls-general and consuls in the city. For them it was an excellent opportunity in a pleasant way to promote the interests of their country and, for the club, it provided an interesting and enjoyable evening for members and guests.

Group entertaining in the club takes various forms, including one or more members, with the permission of the committee, taking over the entire dining room for some special occasion. The Sir Winston Churchill Society of Vancouver, for example, has used the club several times. The Vancouver branch was established in 1979, and several club members belong to it. The society sponsors high-school debates on various aspects of Churchill's career and helps raise money to provide fellowships for university graduates to attend Churchill College in Cambridge. Each year it holds a formal banquet which is addressed by a distinguished speaker who knew Churchill personally. A group or society of this nature, and one that can guarantee 150 or more diners, makes a welcome addition to dining room revenues.

Another example is the Sir John A. Macdonald Society. This group was established in Canada's centennial year by several club members--David Graham, Michael Francis, Jonathan Parker and others who felt that Canada's first prime minister should receive greater attention and recognition in a convivial atmosphere. The society has used the club's dining room for its annual dinner several times. On one occasion the society commissioned a life-size statue of Sir John, had it shipped from Italy, managed to get the heavy crate up the elevator and finally placed in the centre of the dining room. It was unveiled by Robert Stanfield during dinner, a gourmet affair which went on until well after midnight. Sir John, a noted tippler, must have been pleased at the praise showered on him, at the amount of liquor consumed, and at the pipes and drums of the band brought in for the occasion. In any event at the end of the banquet nobody was in a condition to remove the 400-pound statue so Sir John remained where he was for another day, beaming on Conservative and Liberal members alike as they had luncheon. The statue now stands outside the city hall in Victoria, but the society gave the club a smaller version of it which is located in the Reading Room.

In these two examples, and others could be mentioned, entertainment at the club was for members and many guests. On occasion a group of members would organize their own entertainment in the club although on a much smaller scale. One example was the Witanagemot Society, formed in 1955 for the purpose of gourmet dining. The name is derived from the Old English-- "witena," meaning "wise men" and "gemot" or "meeting". Historically it described the old Anglo-Saxon national council or parliament, but for those who either formed or later joined it, it was a time to dine with close friends once a year and enjoy a gourmet luncheon which started at noon and went on for hours, frequently well into the evening.

The society started when a group of members were sitting in the club one Friday. They were a mixture of businessmen, lawyers and professionals. They had been working hard, sometimes during the evenings, and the pressure was beginning to tell. They decided then to take the afternoon off and, for once, enjoy the club and its facilities to the full and relax. They were old friends, most of them veterans, and

The luncheon carvery table, attended by Vern Zugesik, in the main dining room.

from this evolved the idea of an annual luncheon which was planned with great care with Chef Ivan Wheatley. At first the luncheon was held in the Ming Room, then the Blue Room. The "wise men" numbered between ten and twenty and included, among others, Tom Ladner, Ralph Shaw, Douglas Maitland, Peter Evans, Cornelius Burke, Fred Auger, "Spud" Akhurst, William Hurford, Laurence and Richard Cutler, Harry Housser and Howard Jones. "Corny" Burke describes some of the fun they had:

> *I was known as the Common Clerk for years and I was responsible for sort of organizing these annual lunches. They were simply monumental. . . . We were all in great shape in those days and could tackle these great lunches [which] would last until about six o'clock. There would be eight or nine courses, with wines.*
>
> *We would single out somebody each year to honour. I remember when Tom Ladner produced his sixth child . . . so we had Ned Pratt design a chastity belt for him. It was made out of*

old armour and we made charts showing this chastity belt had been discovered in the desert near where the Dead Sea scrolls were found. We got Ladner into this chastity belt and "lost" the keys to the locks on either side of it....

And when Ralph Shaw became president of MacMillan-Bloedel, we gave him a crystal ball on a large mahogony base to help him peer into the future and that was good for an hour's speech from Shaw. We had a wonderful time.

It was the sort of group which could emerge within the club. They made their own entertainment more or less as occurs in a wardroom or officers mess. Songs were sung with more gusto than talent, with sea shanties always included and two old English ballads "Cock Robin" and "Green Grow the Rushes" becoming almost traditional. Light-hearted banter, humorous speeches and some buffonery filled the time between imaginative and sometimes exotic dishes from the kitchen, the whole proceeding presided over by a Grand Druid. The Witanagemot continued their annual meeting for almost twenty years. The members aged, waist-lines expanded and, for some, the six-hour luncheon began to lose its appeal. The wisemen's ranks started to thin also, but for those who were members, the very name Witanagemot brings back pleasant memories of good food and good fellowship.

There was another group which started to meet in the club during the Second World War and, although the original members have died and the reason for the meetings have changed, a group of members have carried on the tradition for over forty years. During the war several members who were involved in shipping and related concerns began to meet in a private bedroom where they would have their lunch served to them. Prominent among them were Andrew Graham, Ernest Riddle, Frederick Glendenning, F. C. ("Tat") Garde, Walter Owen and others. There are no records of these luncheon meetings, but basically the purpose was to find a spot where they could enjoy the club and, particularly, discuss shipping and transportation business in private. Wartime security measures regarding the shipping of war material across oceans infested with enemy submarines made it essential that their conversation should be private. There was no objection to the group dining privately, and indeed, there was nothing in the club constitution which forbade it.

After the war they continued to lunch in what was sometimes referred to as the Shipping Room or Room 15, which referred to the number of the room rather than the number of men who were part of the group. Actually, those using Room 15 (now Room 5) is limited owing to the restriction of space in the room where they have lunch. Also, rather than having business luncheons, what has evolved, is a group of members who are old friends, who enjoy lunching together in a very convivial atmosphere. Now a two-room suite, Room 5 is rented from the club and all extra services paid for by those members.

*   *   *   *

Entertainment in the club, aside from friendly games in the Billiard or Card Rooms, has always depended heavily on the ability of the chef and his staff and on the service provided in the main and private dining rooms. Before the 1939–1945 war, the club was open seven days a week and all of its facilities were available to the members. Considering the number of live-in members this was almost a necessity. During the war, however, certain changes were ordered in order to effect more economy. During the Summer of 1941 the dining rooms were closed on Sundays and the bar hours were restricted to between 10:00 a.m. and noon. To increase revenue during a period when resident membership was down, two measures were enacted in the same year. First, there was to be a minimum charge of 50 cents for breakfast and lunch and 75 cents for dinner. Second, the committee decided that guests be "permitted to come to the Club for luncheon more than one day per month at present allowed. . . ."

The end of the war, together with the rapid increase in members, completely changed the situation. At noon the dining room was full and the committee asked the members to exercise restraint in bringing local residents to lunch and suggested using the dinner hour instead. This did not work so the committee decided to bring back the old by-law that a local resident could be brought to the club for lunch only once in any given month.

There was another problem. The dining room was losing money. The cost of food and wages was increasing steadily. To counter this, a blanket increase of 10 per cent on luncheon prices and 25 per cent on dinners was ordered late in 1948, the first of a series of increases which would continue during the following decades. To attract more members to use the dining room, the first smorgasbord dinner was introduced in January 1949, a feature which became very popular and continues as buffet dinners to the present day.

The dining room itself was redecorated in 1957, the woodwork cleaned in 1962. Once again the lovely graining and shade of the Austrian oak of the walls and columns in the dining room appeared as it used to be when Maples of London first constructed it before shipping it to Vancouver. Another improvement came two years later when the club received from England a supply of china with the club crest on it. The war had prevented a replenishment of crested china and, out of necessity, a proportion of it did not carry the beaver crest whether that animal was looking right or left. Crested glasses and stemware arrived shortly thereafter.

A number of the members also belonged to the Pennask Lake Fishing and Game Club. In some manner, now unknown, the used Vancouver Club crested china appeared at the Pennask Club.

Another improvement in the dining room was the decision to do away with the strip carpeting which lay between the tables. In 1962 the committee paid $11,000 for a new carpet which would cover the entire floor. (It would be replaced in 1976 for $23,100).

Perhaps one of the major changes in the dining room came in 1962 when John Newcliffe was hired as chief steward. He had been working in Montreal but had received his professional training in Switzerland. He faced a problem, among others, of an ageing staff trying to serve an increasing number of members. Moreover, new hotels and restaurants were luring away some of the experienced men for higher wages and there were complaints about slow service. Newcliffe accepted the challenge with zest. He brought a breath of fresh if cool air into the way the kitchen and dining room operated, improved the service, worked with the chef to offer more varied menus, and was instrumental in improving wages. He suggested that dining room prices were quite out of line. As late as 1965, for example, he informed T. E. Ladner, then club president, that a cup of coffee, then ten cents, should be twenty cents and tea should go from 15 to 25 cents. Owing to the large turnover in the dining room staff he persuaded the committee to break with tradition and employ female staff; the wine cellar was restocked, a new inventory control system established and steps were taken to make the buffet dinner more attractive in presentation. To save money, the main kitchen and dining room were closed on Saturday during the summer months of 1967, a custom which became permanent in 1970. By 1969, when patronage of the football buffet and bus service event began to fall off, arrangements were made to have an earlier dinner not only when the Lions were playing a game in the evening, but also on those weekdays when the opera or symphony were performing.

There were further improvements in the 1970's. For many years chefs and chief stewards never knew how many would be sitting down to the ordinary club dinner. There was no reservation system which would allow the staff to plan, prepare and serve the evening meal in a manner which would combine high standards and economy. This began to change in 1972 when members were asked to make reservations. To have on hand a staff ready to serve twenty tables when only five are occupied is bad enough, but it is worse when there is only sufficient staff to serve five tables when out of the blue a flood of members and guests arrive. There were bound to be complaints and a more strict reservation system was the only answer. The committee agreed, passed a motion putting the new rule into effect, but the members tended to ignore the instructions to the extent that in 1975 up to 75 per cent of the evening diners had no reservations.

The dinner dance had become quite popular by the 1970's. As long as the dining room had only three strip carpets running between the tables it was a comparatively easy task to clear the floor for dancing. When the new dining room rug covering the entire floor was laid, clearing the floor became major problem. As a result a portable dance floor, roughly 20 x 24 feet, was bought in 1976. It cost a little over $3,000 but when the labour of moving tables and chairs, rolling up the carpet and then reversing the operation is considered, the floor probably paid for itself within the year.

Dancing, of course, means music. Normally at a buffet dinner or similar function the club hired a pianist but for a dance a quartet or perhaps a six-piece band would be engaged for the evening. In 1985 Hubert Chapman, who was responsible for spicing up the club's entertainment programme in the 1980's, suggested that the club hire the Moonglow Ballroom Orchestra. It was a ten-piece orchestra under the baton of 68-year-old Walt Horrobin. It played the "golden oldies" in Glen Miller style and was as far removed from the "hard rock" and screaming singers enjoyed by many young people of the time as one could hope to find. It was a big success and led to a repetition of the event, although later with a smaller orchestra, at subsequent buffet dinners.

There are times when club members will accept changes and times when they will not. Since 1967 Frank Shurben had been engaged as the pianist in the dining room for special dinners. Early in 1977 the committee agreed to a suggestion that a high-fidelity public address system should be installed in the dining room and "appropriate" taped music played over the system for the enjoyment of members and their guests. This, as the saying goes, went over like a lead balloon. After a month's trial it was reported that

> ... *some twenty-five members had raised objections for one or several of the following reasons: 1) the loss of prestige and tradi tion in no longer having a live musician; 2) an outright objection to taped music in a dining room of such elegance, decor and atmosphere which does not befit the dignity of the club; 3) requests can no longer be played and 4) a sense of loyalty to Frank Shurben who has played at the club for some ten years.*

The committee, wisely, decided to compromise. The pianist continued to play until he retired in 1982, when he was replaced by another. The "hi-fi" system was retained and has given good service when guest speakers are invited.

Despite the changes and improvements made in the dining room in the 1970's, by the 1980's attendance was beginning to slip badly. It was certainly no fault of the kitchen staff. In March 1987, for example, three of the club's staff participated in a culinary art show held at a local hotel. As result the head chef, Ivan Wheatly, won one gold and one silver medal, the sous chef, Ferdinand Reinstadler, won three bronze medals and the garde manger, Hiroshi Yoshinaga, won a bronze.

One way of having the members make greater use of the dining room was to institute a monthly food minimum charge. A committee member, Robert G. Rogers, reported that the Shaughnessy Golf and Country Club had instituted such a system in 1976. It had proved most successful in improving evening attendance at that club. It was one of several ways, he suggested, of keeping club dues down (they had reached $530 by this time) and could even be instrumental in combatting the recent large increases in the cost of food. Actually that suggestion had been discussed a year earlier and at the time had been turned down. However, the committee did decide to send a circular to the members suggesting that they should make more use of the dining room in the evening on ordinary nights and hinted strongly that if patronage of it continued to lag, a minimum monthly food charge might be introduced.

Despite the circular and later notices in the club newsletter extolling the virtues of the food and service, over the next several years

The Annual Christmas Buffet in festive array, in the main dining room.

the dining room continued to lose money. Special dinners were well attended and so were the buffet dances, but on the average far too few were enjoying the excellent cuisine provided in the evening. In July 1983, for example, David L. Helliwell, chairman of the Finance Committee, reported that in that month alone there was a deficit of $9,509 in the dining room and the situation was not improving. The projected yearly deficit was causing concern and something had to be done.

When William G. Leithead became president in 1984 he asked his vice president, George W. Hungerford, to head a special food and beverage task force to do a statistical analysis of the main dining room, to undertake a full study of prices charged, mark-ups, a comparison with local restaurant prices, and then make a commentary regarding the ambience of the club's main dining room compared to other dining facilities. This done, the task force was to make recommendations how the attendance and economics of the main dining room in the evening might be improved. As sub-committee members, Hungerford had Philip Owen, Hubert Chapman, David Helliwell, John Pitts, William Leithead and past-president Sydney Welsh. It was a strong committee and it needed to come up with proper answers. As Hungerford said later:

> . . . *we were down to averages of about twenty-four diners a night. But some nights you would go in there and there would be only one table of diners. It was becoming quite a depressing sight. It was also depressing for the kitchen staff and the waiters who were all standing by. They're geared up to serve up to a a hundred people but few were turning up.*

One of the first things the task force decided to do was to send a questionnaire to all members. It was a carefully crafted document designed both to inform the members of the situation, the various alternatives available, the need to change in some directions, and asking opinions from the members regarding everything from menus to lady guests.

The response was remarkably good. Over 70 per cent of the members replied indicating their preferences on what attracted them most--and least-- respecting the dining room and entertainment. By July 1984, all the answers were tabulated and the task force made the following recommendations which were approved by the General Committee. First, the age limit for guests of members was lowered from 18 to 15 years. Second, the ladies' entrance was to be renamed the "evening entrance" and from six in the evening onward it was to be used by all members and their guests. Although 42 per cent of the members responding indicated they were content to keep the men and ladies entrances, there was a sufficient number who indicated that the idea "posed a very real problem for spouse or guest," and some indicated that it was a very real problem indeed. The solution was a compromise, of course, but despite some grumbling it was accepted. Third, dancing to live music at the Thursday evening buffet was to be given a trial starting in September. Fourth, a special bulletin advising members of coming social events would be mailed to members at appropriate times. (Perhaps the intent here was to ensure the member's wife might see the notice and express an interest in it). Finally, the task force suggested that in view of the continuing low attendance, the Finance Committee should examine the idea of a quarterly or semi-annual evening meal charge just in case.

It was realized that "a lot of flak might be received from senior members" respecting the recommendations. On the other hand, in many cases it was the ladies who frequently chose the venue for dinner with guests and there was a significant number who regarded a separate ladies entrance with distaste. Moreover, it was reported that July 1984 was the worst for dinner attendance in twelve years. In that

The third floor bar, facing the harbour. Sir George Bury's "place" was in the far corner by the window.

month alone the club had to shoulder a loss of $30,453. Thus, while the recommendations were accepted and enforced, and while Hubert Chapman pushed the idea of "consular" or national dinners, theatre dinners, "big band" music and the like, attendance began to improve but not quickly enough to stave off several measures it was hoped might be avoided.

One of the reasons for the slow recovery was that the recommendations were put into effect in mid-summer, a traditionally lax time in the club for dining-in and entertainment. By the end of August the chairman of the Finance Committee was projecting a dining room loss for the fiscal year of 1984 of $140,000. To cover this, he suggested various solutions. One was to increase membership from 925 to 950. This would bring in $100,000 in entrance fees. Another was to start a semi-annual minimum meal charge of about $204 per annum for resident and diplomatic members, covering all evening food consumption in the club. He also suggested a graded dues increase. The first two ideas were presented at a Special General Meeting in September and received a surprising unanimous agreement.

It was a good move, but not quite good enough. The dining room attendance improved but this time changing habits among members, gradual as they were over the years, had increased the deficits of the 3rd Floor Bar, Billiard Room and Card Room. Fewer members were drinking liquor and those who did were drinking much less. The Billiard Room had not made a penny of profit for decades. The Card Room used to be full, and of course there was a steady call for drinks and sandwiches from the players. Moreover, although authority was given to admit another 25 members, the number of resident members remained at 930. What was happening was that an increasing number of resident members were able to transfer to life members, a situation which allowed them freedom from paying annual dues owing to their long membership in the club. In 1984 there had been 20 transfers, then 24 in 1985 and a projected 33 in 1986. Life members have all the rights and privileges of ordinary members but, naturally, their dues were missed. Added to that was the fact that the era of the long waiting list to enter the club was gone while a situation was nearing when members would be asked to suggest potential candidates for nomination.

The new president who had to resolve the problem was George Hungerford. He was young (41 years old) for the position but his family had a long association with the club. His great grandfather, William Farrell, had been a pioneer Vancouver businessman and a member of the club in 1896. His grandfather was a member and his father, R. M. Hungerford, had been president of the club in 1966. It was the only time there had been a father and son who both held the same office and both active members. Hungerford, a lawyer, was also the first club president to be the recipient of an Olympic Games gold medal (1964) and had been made an Officer of the Order of Canada the year before he was elected club president.

Hungerford called another Special General Meeting in September 1985. He' outlined the situation as it existed, quoted statistics, gave projections of a very unsatisfactory financial situation which would emerge without a change, and requested authority to increase the minimum evening food charge to $360 per year. With over 75 per cent voting in favour, the motion passed. When it came into effect the results were obvious. Patronage of the dining room increased, the deficit went down and, as the club newsletter reported, there was "a great boost in the morale of our catering staff."

A second questionnaire was sent out in November. It asked a simple question: "Are you in favour of allowing ladies to be guests of members in the Main Dining Room at luncheon?" In the covering letter the president explained that the committee had considered the concept of a Ladies Dining Room, but from the point of view of finances and service, it would be better if the Main Dining Room was made available. The results showed that the members were not quite ready to break with that tradition. Lady guests for dinner had been approved over forty years earlier. The vote in 1985 was close, but a 75 per cent approval was obviously not possible. Changes were in the offing, however, and in another four years the hair on the beaver in the club's crest would stand straight up at the new proposals being considered.

*   *   *   *

The Dining Room has been the focal point of club entertainment for decades. In the postwar period the membership has frequently given a club dinner for some visiting dignitary or, at times, for one or more of their own members. It would be tedious to mention them all, but there are some which stand out in the memory of many of the present members.

One of the earliest special dinners was for His Excellency, Field Marshal the Right Honorable Viscount Alexander of Tunis, recently appointed Governor–General of Canada. This was the first time members were permitted to attend wearing a dinner jacket rather than white tie and tails, probably owing to the fact that there were a large number of veterans in the club who would not have had the time, nor possibly the money, to buy formal dress since the war had ended. In the following year, 1947, Mr.Justice C.H.Locke was honoured at dinner on the occasion of his appointment to the Bench of the Supreme Court of Canada.

During the 1950's there were several club dinners for members. Late in 1950 the Honorable Clarence Wallace was honoured on his appointment as Lieutenant-Governor of British Columbia. He was born the year after the club was founded, became a member in 1921, and had become president of the Burrard Dry Dock Co. in 1929. He was a driving force in the huge shipbuilding program in Vancover during the Second World War and was on the board of directors of several other large firms. He was also the first provincial lieutenant-governor born in the province.

Early in 1951 two other members were honoured: H. R. Mac-Millan on his appointment as a Canadian representative on the Defence Production Board of NATO, and Sherwood Lett on his election as Chancellor of the University of British Columbia. Major-General Victor W. Odlum was tendered a dinner on his return to Vancouver which marked the end on his appointment as Canada's ambassador to Turkey. One special dinner which everyone enjoyed must have been the one held in June 1959 when, at long last, the club mortgage was burned.

A guest who attracted great interest was Field Marshal Viscount Montgomery of Alamein. His brother was a member of the club and his nephew, John D. Montgomery, is a present member. For Montgomery's visit, the dining room was packed with 225 members with an overflow in the Blue Room. His visit on May 6th, 1960, was within two days of the fifteenth anniversary of V-E Day, and with so many veterans in the club, all were anxious to hear his opinion on the world strategic balance at that time.

It was the club's custom to invite a newly appointed Governor-General to dinner on the occasion of his first visit to Vancouver. This was done when it was known that His Excellency Major-General Georges P. Vanier would be arriving in the summer of 1965. The invitation was sent and the reply accepting it was received, but with the reply was the understanding that Madame Vanier would accompany her husband.

Thomas Ladner was president of the club at the time and the General Committee gave him the responsibility of making the necessary arrangements for the head table. Madame Vanier and her lady-in-waiting would be there, but what other ladies should be invited? With great consideration, Ladner made his selection. His own wife was not invited; rather he asked Major-General the Honorable and Mrs. George R. Pearkes, the serving lieutenant-governor, and two former lieutenant-governors and their wives, the Honorable and Mrs. Clarence Wallace and the Honorable and Mrs. Frank Ross. The latter gentlemen were both club members and Major-General George Pearkes had been an Imperial Member in the 1920's.

The whole affair went off beautifully. R. T. DuMoulin, who was there at the time, recalled

> *The Governor-General made quite a speech and threw in a few French words but 99 per cent was in English. Tommy, as president of the club, got up and spoke almost entirely in French. I never knew he could speak it! The Governor-General and Madame Vanier were just delighted and the members of the club, even though they couldn't understand it all, were bloody proud of it too.*

It happens that Ladner's mother was a French lady and she made sure her children spoke French.

During the 1970's there were numerous special dinners. One, in 1973, was given in honour of the life members of the club and in 1976 it was proposed that past-president J. Y. McCarter should be honoured when he reached his ninetieth birthday in September. This good idea was made better when the club expanded the concept to include all other nonagenarian members. There were not many, but those who were invited included W. S. Lane, C. S. Thicke, A. D. Anderson, E. F. Carter, L. J. Ladner and D. L. Gillespie. Two somewhat similar dinners in 1977 and 1978 were thoroughly enjoyed. The first was termed the "Comrade in Arms" dinner for members who were veterans. The second, in 1978, was for veterans of the Great War. It was sixty years since that war ended but there was a remarkable turnout nevertheless. The club president, D. Michael M. Goldie, wrote each member before the dinner asking him what he was doing on the exact day of the dinner sixty years previously and used their accounts with great effect in introducing them. He appointed three Second World War veterans (the Honorable J. L. Nicol, Brigadier D. M. Clark and Air Vice-Marshal L. F. Stevenson) to speak particularly for the naval, army and air force veterans. It was an outstanding success. Some eighty members either wrote or talked to the club president or to the club secretary, John Chutter, expressing their delight. It was also reported in the committee minutes: "The last members (including some of the veterans!) left the club at 6:15 a.m." Now that was a dinner!

In the 1980's there were several dinners which stood out. There was one for Brigadier the Honorable H. P. Bell-Irving and another for the Honorable R. G. Rogers. Both were members, and both were guests of the club honoring their appointment as Lieutenant-Governor of British Columbia. It was during Rogers' term of office that the club decided to grant honorary life membership to lieutenant-governors who had been appointed, while members of the club, to the vice-regal post. Formerly the lieutenant-governor was offered honorary membership only while in office. This extended honour, at the time of writing, is unique to these two men as past lieutenant-governors, although four others, for other reasons, hold honorary life memberships.

*   *   *   *

Probably the best entertainment in the club is generated by the members themselves when they begin to swap stories or relate humorous incidents relating to other members. To know the members and the nature of the club makes the story more enjoyable, but not to know either can result in only a polite smile and quizzical look on the face of those unfamiliar with the person or place. Some club jokes probably had their origin long before the Vancouver Club was formed. An example might be this one: "Club member to club president: 'Would it be permissible if I brought my mistress to dinner at the club?' Club president: 'Certainly, old boy, provided she is the wife of another member!'"

Sometimes club humour is expressed in quiet wit. In 1974, J. Norman Hyland, then in middle age, produced a letter from Leon Ladner. Ladner, a distinguished lawyer and one of the senior partners in the law firm of Ladner Downs, came from a pioneering British Columbian family. He had reached his ninetieth birthday and was informed that his name had been placed on a board with the names of other 90-year-old members. Ladner wrote in reply: "Dear Norman, Many thanks for your letter of November 29th--an important day for me. I am delighted to be honored with a brass plaque. I hope to live long enough to see your name on one."

The minutes of the General Committee rarely contains items of a humourous nature, but there is an item in the March 31st, 1980, minutes which has amusing features about it. Evidently in August 1979, the committee heard about a paragraph in *TV Guide* referring to a Vancouver Club in the Hotel Toronto in Toronto. The secretary wrote to the manager of the hotel asking him for details about it. The manager, incidentally, was Steve Halliday, a native of Vancouver and now a club member. No reply was received until February 1980 when the manager replied that the club had opened the previous month. When the reply was received, the minutes noted that "the crest on the letter paper is similar to our crest except that the beaver becomes a duck and is surmounted by an umbrella instead of the royal crown, and the inscription inside the circle reads 'The Vancouver Clube' instead of Vancouver Club. In the end, the hotel dropped the name which was designed to attract former Vancouverites living in Toronto.

Some of the best stories, however, have to do with club members themselves. Gordon Bell–Irving remembers being told this one:

> *Dr. Duncan Bell–Irving was appointed to propose the toast to the British Empire at the Club Dinner on Empire Day, sometime around 1908. When the time came he laboriously got to his feet (he was a large, very heavy man) raised his glass and pronounced: "Scotland for 'iver," and sat down firmly.*
>
> *Percey Shallcross, an Englishman sitting beside him, poked him in the ribs and said: "You can't do that, old man; really it's Empire Day you know." Dr.Duncan then got to his feet again, even more laboriously, raised his glass and said: "An' heer's to a' the 'ither odds and ends."*

Another incident connected with the dining room is related by John Rose:

> *My uncle, Harry Kirkland, was a hard drinking fellow.... He was at the club with a couple of friends for Christmas Dinner and he stole the boar's head. He took it up to his friend, Jim McGavin, and they had great fun, had a couple of more drinks and then he went home. He lived very close by. The committee eventually figured out who pinched it and Harry was hauled up before them. He was told his membership was suspended until the boar's head was returned. When it was returned he would be suspended for only two weeks but if it wasn't he was finished.*
>
> *So Harry got in touch with McGavin. This would be in the 1930's. When asked about its whereabouts McGavin said "Oh, Hell, I put it in the garbage." So they went out and here's this thing covered with ashes and junk. They got it out, turned the hose on it, and Harry Kirkland brought it back and was reinstated.*

A story that has been told frequently about a club member during the 1940's. "It is my understanding," an acquaintance of his wrote,

> *... that his wife, who did not drink, thought that he did not drink either, or at least she pretended to think so. It was certainly well known that you did not expect to get a drink in their home. He would therefore come to the Club after work where he would have a congenial drink at the round table. On leaving he would pick up, from the bar steward, a Coke bottle full of whisky which the steward knew to have ready for him. This I have observed myself.*
>
> *I have been told he then ... proceeded home and, before entering the house, attached the Coke bottle to a string which hung from the window of the downstairs washroom behind a flower bush. Prior to dinner he would go to the washroom from time to time and pull up the string to enjoy his before-dinner drink.*

Humour is always entertaining and club members have a quick

appreciation of wit. Space permits one more anecdote which involves a well-known billiard player, a past president of the club (who is presently chairman of the History Committee) and the club historian. Cornelius Burke, the billiard player, has had an interesting career. During the war he skidded around the English Channel and the Mediterranean in a motor gun-boat causing much distress and considerable damage to German and Italian naval and marine forces. Properly and deservedly honoured by a grateful government he and his friend, Thomas Ladner, another naval officer, returned to Vancouver to pursue quieter careers. Ladner went into law, Burke into the tugboat business and then into the travel business. Burke's World Wide Travel became the largest travel agency in British Columbia and was sold to P. Lawson Travel.

With more time on his hands, Burke pursued his wish to travel by bicycle in Europe and elsewhere, writing humorous accounts of his adventures. Several of these he loaned to this historian. The latter wrote him asking for permission to quote from them as an example of what some club members do "... when they retire." This resulted in a memo—Burke to Ladner: "I advised Dr. Roy that I wasn't retired and that if he dared indicate in the club history I was, then I would file a suit against him, the University of Victoria, the Vancouver Club and the chairman [Ladner] of the club history committee, jointly and severally."

An attached memo, Ladner to Roy, read: "Reg, I would be fearful of being a defendant in an action where the plaintiff was Bogus Enterprises Incorporated." What was this suspicious firm? The answer came in a letter from Burke to Roy. The letterhead read "Bogus Enterprises Inc., Dark and Difficult Deeds Done." Printed at the bottom of the page was a list of some of the deeds which included, in part: "Lips Sealed, Threads Lost, Bribes Taken, Laments Sung, Juries Rigged, Pigeons Holed, Tongues Tied, Saints Preserved, Bases Loaded, Scandals Mongered, Palms Crossed, Gooses Cooked, Webs Woven, Tracks Covered" and numerous other nefarious deeds. The letter, however, was explanatory and conciliatory, but advised: "The chairman of Bogus Enterprises is not ... retired from business. It is in fact his mission in life to attract as many clients to his firm as possible. To that end he spends much time walking up and down Hastings St., grasping likely candidates by the lapels and suggesting that they go away." With a club member admitting to being chairman of a syndicate or firm engaged in murky, devious and questionable enterprises, the historian decided to use the material in the letters rather than the bicycle travelogues. Burke we shall leave in the billiard room with some of his fellow veterans, cues in hand, as they knock their balls around the tables.

*   *   *   *

Since the members moved into their new clubhouse sixty-four years ago, it has not been possible to invite guests to join members in some of the more active games such as bowling, squash or tennis. But sports as an entertainment, although limited to the billiard room, has always attracted most of the members. When the city was young, many of the members were responsible for organizing sporting clubs which were to grow and flourish. Some of the leading organizers of the Vancouver Lawn Tennis and Badminton Club, for example, included members such as G. Gardiner Johnson, H. J. Crombie, R. G. Tatlow, Richard Marpole and others.

Polo was another popular game with some of the members. Eric Hamber, Clarence Wallace, Austin Taylor, "Chuck" Wills Sr., the Woodwards and A. E. Jukes were some of the early enthusiasts while after the Second World War, Martin Griffin, Jonathan Parker, David Graham and Patrick Oswald were instrumental in reviving interest in the Vancouver Polo Club and improving and enlarging its accommodation. Yachting has long been one of the favourite out door sports of club members and, once again, several founding members of the Royal Vancouver Yacht Club belonged to the Vancouver Club. A number of the Yacht Club's commodores ranging from Eric Hamber and B. T. Rogers to Ronald Cliff, Douglas Haitland, and Patrick Oswald indicates the range of interest and association between the two clubs' memberships over more than three quarters of a century.

What has been said of polo and yachting could be said of rowing, cricket, golf, rugby, fishing and other sports in which club members are involved. A recent book "The Vancouver Rowing Club, A History, 1888-1980," details the long association between club members and rowing which goes back a century. Original club members such as H. B. Abbott, H. J. Cambie, F. W. Boultbee and R. G. Tatlow helped to start the original Boating Club; R. Marpole, C. Sweeney and Col. Victor Spencer were Honorary Presidents of The Vancouver Rowing Club and several members, particularly Colonel Spencer, donated racing shells to the club. Two members, C. E. "Ned" Pratt and George Hungerford were to win Olympic medals for Canada in rowing competitions, Pratt a bronze medal in 1932 and Hungerford a gold in 1964.

Vancouver Club members have also contributed money to permit outstanding athletes attend Commonwealth and Olympic Games, and have provided equipment to local sports clubs to help them achieve the highest training standards. Although neither indoor nor outdoor sports (aside from billiards) can now be considered to be part of the entertainment offered by the club, it should not be thought that members are no longer interested in these activities. One example is R.

B. Spray, a member of the B.C. Sports Hall of Fame. He came to Canada from England in 1947 and was instrumental in re–establishing the Canadian Rugby Union in 1965. There are others such as Victor V. Spencer. A former member of the Hamilton Tigers Football Team, he was almost as interested in sports as he was in his own business affairs. He was one of the founding directors of the B.C. Lions along with such other club members as Eric Beardmore, John Davidson, Arthur Mercer and Allan Russell. One could go on, but sufficient it is to say that although many of the members are not as active in sports as they used to be, over the years they have given both their time and money to support sports clubs and activities and to help Canadian athletes compete in the international arena.

*   *   *   *

For club members the 1960's and 1970's were more than two decades when wining, dining and entertainment were uppermost in their minds. These were decades of considerable social and economic

Head Table at the Club Dinner in honour of Air Vice Marshall Leigh Stevenson, C.B., October 4, 1988. Left to Right: David Helliwell, guest of honour, Hu Chapman, Norman Hyland, Peter Richards.

change in Canada and in British Columbia. Within the club changes were underway also. If there were new drapes, rugs and furnishings, there was also the problem that the clubhouse itself was getting old and in need of considerable repair. Once again the question of selling and moving would be raised, and it is to those problems and their solutions we must now turn our attention.

Head Table at the Club Dinner for the Honourable John Fraser, Speaker of the House of Commons, October 23, 1987. Left to Right: Tom Ladner, George Hungerford, guest of honour, Hu Chapman, David Helliwell, Chief Justice Nathan Nemetz, Bill Armstrong.

CHAPTER VIII

A HERITAGE BUILDING AMONG HIGHRISES

The winds of change that were blowing in the decade and a half after the wartime years turned into a gale in the 1960's and 1970's. There was growth everywhere--in the city, in the province and in the nation. In 1941, for example, Vancouver had a population of 377,447. By 1961, this had more than doubled to 816,798. It passed the one million mark ten years later and by 1986 was up to 1,380,729.

Vancouver in this period was developing into one of the major seaports of Canada as trade with the Pacific Rim countries increased by leaps and bounds. In the 1960's alone, for example, Canadian exports across the Pacific jumped from about $371,000,000 to well over a billion dollars, and imports increased in the same proportion. This trend continued in the 1970's and 1980's, and shipping traffic in and out of Vancouver doubled and tripled. More people and more trade brought with it changes in the look of the city's core. Property values increased and the city's skyline grew higher, both of which were to affect the Vancouver Club.

With increased trade and employment, the annual inflation rate began to warm up as well. In 1962 the inflation rate was about one per cent. Ten years later it was close to five per cent and by 1974 it was over ten per cent. Between 1980 and 1982 inflation averaged between 10 and 12 per cent. To put it another way, in 1983 it took $2.77 to purchase what could be bought in 1971 for $1.00, and in 1971 it took $1.00 to buy what could be purchased in 1961 for 75 cents.

Here, again, there was a decided impact on both members and staff of the club. Naturally, staff wages went up, and also the cost of food, liquor, repairs, refurbishing, fuel, taxes and just about everything else. In 1974–75, to cover some of these increases, the cost of renting a liquor locker went from $24 to $36 per year. Owing to the rise in the cost of liquor the bar began to lose rather than make money, and it was difficult to break even on the dining room. Fees were increased in the billiard and card rooms, bedroom charges went up and so did the charges for private rooms for lunches and dinners. These were increased again in 1978, a year when a shoeshine went from 75 cents to a dollar. If this seemed a harsh increase, even harsher in the same year was the notice that the club's property tax would go from $46,000 to $63,000. By 1982 the taxes reached $77,733 and in the following year they were upped again to $84,125.

In November 1981, when the nation's annual inflation was at its height, the General Committee met to discuss the measures which had to be taken to meet the situation. The increases the committee approved would have seemed incredible a decade earlier. They agreed dues would go up by 20 per cent, meals by the same amount and bedroom charges by about 40 per cent. Card and billiard room charges increased by 25 per cent, and bar, locker and corkage charges by 15 per cent. As late as 1969 entrance fees had been $1500 for resident membership. At the November 1981 committee meeting, despite incremental increases during the past decade, it was agreed the new fee must be $4000. Annual dues, of course, were not overlooked in the process, nor could they be. Annual dues of resident members went from $695 to $835. Even those members in the "70 + 30" category (i.e. those members who were seventy years old with at least 30 years continual membership (a category established in 1980) were not spared since their dues, although only half that of a resident member, would have increased proportionately. In other words, between 1976 and 1981, annual dues doubled. These were difficult times for the club, and although inflation cooled off somewhat as the decade wore on, there is no doubt that one effect it had was to make potential applicants for membership think twice when they were approached to join the club. This was true not only of the Vancouver Club, but in gentlemen's clubs all over the world, perhaps particularly in the heart of "club land," London, where clubs were either closing or amalgamating at a considerable pace.

The steady acceleration of inflation was by no means the only disturbing element of the sixties and seventies. During these decades there were many challenges to what club members probably thought were the normal and traditional Canadian ways of doing things. In 1961, when a Soviet spaceman successfully orbited the earth in an hour and a half, whizzing about some 200 miles above the earth's surface, there must have been many who felt that the space age was truly launched. In the 1960's the Vietnam War was well underway and as American forces became more deeply embroiled with victory continuing to be elusive, there was growing resentment among American youth over conscription. This, coupled with a variety of other causes, led to a nation-wide confrontation on a massive scale between the radicals who demanded ideal solutions and the moderate element which sought compromise with practical methods. It was the decade when black Americans fought for equality, when race riots were endemic and when the assassination of the Reverend Martin L. King in 1968 led to further riots in 125 American cities.

The disturbance in the United States spilled over into Canada, but politically, took a different twist. The "Quiet Revolution" in Quebec did not go far enough for some of the more radical Quebec nationalists and, under the title of Front de Liberation du Quebec (FLQ), a small group in that province began to agitate for separatism. Acts of terrorism in the 1960's culminated in kidnapping and murder in 1970 and the imposition of the War Measures Act. Student turmoil in the United States brought a similar if more moderate activity on Canadian campuses. The new Simon Fraser University was establishing a reputation as having one of the most tumultuous student bodies in Western Canada while even the older and more sedate U.B.C. had its Faculty Club occupied briefly by radical students. This, in turn, led the Vancouver Club to make its own plan of action in case any attempt was made to force an entry into its premises.

In British Columbia the series of centenary celebrations, which started with the 100th anniversary of the 1858 Gold Rush, carried on with the anniversary of the Union of the Two Colonies (1866) and Federation with Canada (1871). By far the main celebration was the centenary of the birth of Canada in 1967. Ironically, while celebrating and extolling Canada's traditions, Ottawa took steps to eliminate many of them. The armed forces were integrated and unified and a dark green stain spread over the traditional distinctive dress of the three services. There was great debate about a new Canadian flag with hundreds of suggested designs sent in for consideration. Emotions were so high that one wit suggested the new flag should be a large white banner with the word ''flag'' on one side and ''drapeau'' on the other. Eventually the red maple leaf was found acceptable in 1965 and ten years later, almost as an afterthought, parliament declared the beaver

A Heritage Building among the high-rises. The Canada Pavilion at EXPO 86. The Vancouver Club at right centre.   *(Canada Harbour Place)*

to be Canada's national symbol. The beaver on the Vancouver Club's crest must have been pleased to attain Canadian "citizenship." It had been looking to the right and to the left for many years.

These were the decades when "bi–culturalism and bi–lingualism" were becoming "buzzwords" and when intellectuals and journalists were becoming quite vocal in their search for a "Canadian Identity," as if somehow it had been lost or misplaced. In 1968 Pierre Trudeau became the prime minister of Canada and for the next decade he was to bring both joy and exasperation to the nation and tremendous copy for the newspapers and caricaturists. Incidentally, he was to be a private guest at a luncheon at the Vancouver Club, and his host was impressed with an old club tradition—he was treated in the dining room as a private individual rather than prime minister, which is as it should be.

Closer to home, Vancouver was changing as well. In 1961 the city's first privately owned television station went on the air and four years later Simon Fraser University opened its doors. A sign of the times was the opening of the city's (and Canada's) first topless bar and restaurant. Protest rallies were becoming more common—against the Vietnam War, against American nuclear tests in the Aleutians and even against the Engineers' Club for not allowing female membership. In the early seventies young people had set up a campsite on the land where the Four Seasons Hotel was to be built and in Gastown there was a clash between police and "hippies". In the mid–seventies, the Knight Street and Arthur Laing bridges were opened to help ease increasing traffic problems and the first container terminal began operation to meet changing maritime commercial needs. In 1977 the Vancouver Centre opened with the tallest building in the city.

During the late 1970's and early 1980's, the face of downtown Vancouver was changing constantly, and as some of these changes were affecting the Vancouver Club, this might be the proper time to go inside and see what had been going on.

* * * *

The large number of new members who came into the club in the 1940's and 1950's, together with the increase in the permissable number of resident members, had an impact on the dining room, bar, and other areas of the club house. For various reasons, however, there was a decreasing use of the fourth and fifth floor bedrooms. There were a few which were occupied permanently, but the number of country members or guests from affiliated clubs using these rooms for several days or weeks declined steadily. As early as 1951 the General Committee had considered converting some of them for other purposes such as private dining rooms and cocktail lounges. There was even the suggestion that the billiard room be moved to the fourth floor. Owing to the need to improve the club's furnishings, replace carpets and drapes, renew the kitchen, redecorate most of the rooms, and so forth, it was not possible to obtain the consent of the membership to agree to the major expenditure required. In 1960 David R. Blair, speaking for the House Committee, again recommended that better use should be made of the upper floors, pointing out that a recent survey showed only an 11 per cent occupancy rate of the bedrooms. Two members who were architects, C. E. Pratt and P. Thornton, put in a great deal of time drawing up sketches showing how some of the rooms and space might be better utilized. A snack-bar on the third floor, for example, could easily take care of light lunches for those in the bar, the billiard room and the card room. Private dining rooms on the fourth floor could be serviced by a new elevator to enable members to hold mixed, private functions at noon or in the evening.

By the fall of 1960 the plans and sketches were ready and later that year the committee drew up a resolution to be presented at an extraordinary meeting of the club. It read in part:

> *1. That the committee be authorized to borrow on the club's credit a sum . . . of money not exceeding in the aggregate $250,000;*
> *2. That the proceeds . . . be expended by the committee on the following:*
> *a) the remodelling and renovation of the 4th floor . . . in such wise as to provide for the construction of three new private dining rooms and cardroom with proper related facilities;*
> *b) the installation and construction of a new elevator on the east side of the club premises;*
> *c) the construction of a snack bar in what is now the 3rd floor cardroom.*
> *3. The number of resident members of the club to be increased to 850 members. . . .*

Any General Committee wishing to get approval for a major change in the club which also involves a large expenditure of money must prepare its case carefully before presenting it to a meeting of club members. In the audience there will be bank managers, lawyers, auditors, architects, executive officers of large business firms, builders, and others who could unleash a barrage of penetrating questions should they spot weaknesses in the proposal or faults in the resolution. It is not unknown for presidents to have well prepared supporters scattered about the meeting--especially those who are well regarded and respected by fellow members--who will be quick to voice their assent to the motion with great vigor and some flourish. It is always wise, when possible, to avoid a long debate which can generate much heat but little light. A. D. Bell-Irving and David R.Blair, president and vice-president, prepared their case well, particularly as a similar proposal had been turned down earlier. The measure was accepted with little modification. Work on the alterations began in 1962, and after a year's trial Blair was able to report:

> *The changes made to the 4th floor in 1962 which resulted in the addition of four private dining rooms and a reception area, are proving to have been well justified. There was an increase of 16 per cent of the number of private dinners, luncheons and cocktail parties held in the private dining rooms in 1963 as against the previous year. There were some 500 of these private functions held in the new 4th floor facilities, the balance being held in the ladies lounge and the Blue Room. Since the use made of each of these sets of facilities was not at the expense of the other, it would seem obvious that there was a definite need for the new 4th floor rooms.*

The restructuring of the 4th floor was the first of a series of changes in the clubhouse which would continue over the next quarter century. In December 1963, the club president sent a circular letter to the members stating that the committee felt the lobby needed renovation and there was need for additional lounge area. It was felt that the most practical solution would be to develop, out of the small first floor bar and adjacent west coat room, "a facility, in keeping with the general decor of the club, which would function as a quiet lounge area in which drinks could be served to those desiring such service." This would involve converting the Ming Room into a coat room but, on the other hand, with four additional private dining rooms it would be easy for those who had used the Ming Room to move their locale upstairs. Work on this project began in 1964, and from it emerged the present Gun Room. While the workmen were on the site they undertook another job–reducing the little-used Silent Room with its soft chairs and book-lined shelves to a more practical size which, in turn, restored the Card Room "to its original proportions and handsome architectural design." The entire project was completed by the end of the year.

By the late 1960's, although much of the interior of the club had been redecorated, there were indications that the main structure of the building was going to need major repairs. In 1968, for example, it was evident that the central beams in the main lobby and the kitchen floor drainage system had to be attended to immediately. They were, but by the following year a committee member, A. D. "Peter" Stanley, questioned the wisdom of maintaining the existing premises in view of

The former ladies' entrance gives way to the installation of huge seismic steel beams during 1988 reconstruction.

Reinforcing the harbour side of the clubhouse with massive seismic beams.

its age. He suggested that some thought be given to the potential expenses which would be involved five, ten or fifteen years hence in maintaining both the building's interior and exterior.

During the next decade it seemed that just as one part of the club was fixed up, another part revealed faults that needed attention. In 1970 a considerable amount of work had to be done on the east, north and south exterior walls. The old fire escape needed repairing, and of course, these had to be attended to.

Early in 1973 the club's new secretary–manager, reported that the club was being continually beset by pigeons. "One had caused flooding in the bakery by getting stuck in a drain pipe," he said, and added "Their dung was rotting the woodwork on window sills, corroding the iron fire escapes and covering over escape lights." John Chutter, who had been hired as secretary in 1972 after a lengthy military background, had tried his hand at potting away at the pigeons with an air rifle but, despite his considerable score, they kept coming. One reason was that railway box–cars loaded with grain, after being dumped in the grain elevators further down the harbour, would be shunted about in the nearby railway yards which caused some spillage of wheat. This provided a feast for the pigeons and the Vancouver Club was evidently an attractive roosting area. The nuisance was taken care of eventually by using a bird repellant.

That was hardly done when the 600–gallon hot water tank in the club sprung a leak which could not be repaired. It was fifteen years old and a new one was required. Unfortunately the new one could not get through the doors in the club but the day was saved when Central Heat Distribution Ltd., which supplied the club with steam heating, came up with an "instant hot water system" which did not require a storage tank of any sort.

Another improvement was being made at the same time. The telephone system in the club was archaic. A check had been made in January 1973 and during the two five-day periods monitored, an average of about 1,500 calls had been made by members and staff, both internally and externally. A new, modern switchboard was needed and it was installed in March to connect the thirty telephones in the club.

There was another facility in the club which needed replacing at this time which was done over the vigorous protest of some of the older members. The men's urinals on the first floor were getting cracked and shabby. For almost sixty years they had provided comfort to the needy, a joy to those in distress and a place for brief conversations and greetings. The urinals were huge, wrap–around affairs, almost like a bathtub on end. They were shoulder high, and the brand name, "Adamant," made one member wonder whether the name was a warning or an exhortation. As Chutter said later: "We wrote all over the world to try and get duplicates . . . but the only place we could get them from was Scotland. They just could not ship them over and they told us over the phone the only way we would get them here [at a reasonable price] was to put them in the water and paddle them across. So eventually we had to get American ones."

It was in the mid–seventies, however, when the first of a series of major changes occurred which were to affect the club. In September, 1975 the club president, Brenton S. Brown, reported that

> . . . *a notice had been received from the City Clerk advising the Club that a public meeting would be held in the near future to discuss lists of buildings recommended for designation by the Vancouver Heritage Advisory Committee. Thirteen buildings had been recommended for category "A" designation (those which the committee feels should remain and be preserved or restored to their original condition). Twelve buildings had been recommended for Category "B" designation (those which the committee would entertain proposals for some alterations).*

The notice went on to say that the Vancouver Club was recommended for category "B" designation.

Members were proud of their clubhouse but being dubbed a "heritage building" was not the same as being selected as a prize-winning home for Christmas decorations. It implied outside interference with private property and just what the implications were the committee was determined to discover. Fortunately, Warnett Kennedy, a club member, was also a city alderman. He and Lawrence Killam met with the committee in November and explained that a major concern of both the Vancouver City Council and the Heritage Committee was the economic implicatons of designation. It would require weeks or months of further study. After hearing from them, the president felt it was time to write City Hall

> . . . *asking for a clarification on such things as: 1) restrictions on demolitions, alterations, changes of decor or furniture; 2) compensation for drop in sales value of designated buildings; 3) availability of maintenance allowance from City Hall; 4) whether such buildings would be automatically open to the public . . .; and 5) right of appeal and to whom.*

It took some time for the matter to go through the city's bureaucracy but in the late summer of 1976 Graham R. Dawson, a member of the club's House Committee reported that the clubhouse had recently been designated an "A" category heritage building. The club sent one of its newest members, David E. Gillanders, to represent it at a public meeting at City Hall on the matter in November. He reported that the question of compensation and economic assistance was still unresolved. He added, however, that "Mayor Phillips advised that the club site was one which the City of Vancouver would give favourable consideration to a transfer of development rights to adjacent properties."

Part of the reason for the city's slowness in responding to the question of economic compensation was owing to the lack of firm directives from the provincial government. In the Speech from the Throne in the Provincial Legislature, it was announced that compensation for heritage designation would be looked into. Mr. G. Buchan McIntosh, a lawyer acting for the club, meanwhile, pointed out that, in his opinion, one-half to two-thirds of the value of the club's land had been taken away by the heritage designation.

Like it or not, the club was stuck with its category "A" heritage designation, which meant that the exterior of the building could not be changed nor could its mass or style. In 1978, following an appeal to the city for a reduction in taxes owing to the club's designation and consequent loss of commercial value, the tax was reduced by $3,971. On the other hand legal fees were almost three-quarters of the amount saved. As the saying goes, "you can't beat city hall."

Despite the temporary loss of tax relief on the scale the club had hoped for, there was one development which helped compensate matters. When the club was built in 1913 it was one of the major buildings in downtown Vancouver. With each passing decade more and more highrise structures were built, and in the sixties and seventies many of these were demolished to make way for buildings of twenty, thirty and forty stories. This increased density of buildings, and therefore people, had a major impact on traffic and parking, to mention only two problems which concerned the city's engineers and planners. As a result the city imposed severe controls on new construction, especially on those wishing to erect tall buildings. Land values increased proportionately.

There were some buildings, only a few stories high which, under the city zoning guide, could be torn down and a new structure built in its place which would be twice the height of the old. In brief, it had what was termed "development rights" which were determined primarily by the zoning and allowable F.S.R. (Floor Space Ratio). If the owner of the building had no wish to increase the height of his property, he might be given permission to sell his "air space" or transferable rights to someone close by who wished to construct, shall we say, a twenty-storey-high building on land which city planners had designated for a building only fifteen stories high. The revenue from the additional five stories would be considerable over the life of the taller building, and thus development rights could be a very valuable asset. These rights were granted to the Vancouver Club after it was designated a heritage building. The question of their sale was to occupy the minds of the House Committee in particular and the General Committee as a whole for several years.

While these events were unfolding, at a meeting in February 1977, a member of the General Committee confirmed a rumour that the Daon Development Corporation intended to construct a nineteen storey office building immediately west of, and adjacent to, the Vancouver Club. The plans, he said, were being considered by the City Planning Department and he added that the club would be given the opportunity to see, discuss and comment on these plans before any construction was commenced. The member who spoke with such authority was Graham R. Dawson, and since the name of the development company was derived from his surname (Daon--Dawson with the two middle letters left out) he could make the announcement with some conviction.

Dawson had joined the club in 1955. He was in the navy during the war and on his return to Vancouver he studied engineering at U.B.C. After graduation he married the daughter of a former (1945) president of the Vancouver Club, Col. R. D. Williams, and began to work for his father's firm, Dawson, Wade and Co., later known as Dawson Construction. Following a stroke by his father, also a club member, young Dawson had to take over from him when he was only 31 years old, but he was to see his firm through a period of tremendous growth. As a heavy construction and civil engineering firm it was involved in building roads all over the province. In close association with other firms it constructed many of the office buildings in downtown Vancouver. It built hospitals, grain elevators, bridges, pools and schools. It was deeply involved in building both the Burrard and Granville Street bridges, and in later years the Dawson group was bound to have their equipment on site whether it was building a dam in the interior of the province or blasting a road through rocky terrain to create a modern highway. The club has always been fortunate to be able to draw upon men with such experience to serve on the committee, and indeed, Dawson was to serve as president in 1981. It is not every day, however, that a committee member announces he is going to build next door.

When the committee members saw the plans of the new building late in 1977 they were more than pleased. There had been some concern originally that, when constructed, it would cut off a good portion of the view over the harbour. However, the architects had designed the building so that, next to the club's property, it was stepped aside so as to affect the club's view very little. In 1978 work began on the demolition of the Seabord and Richardson buildings and in the latter part of the year heavy machinery moved in to start the work of excavation. A considerable amount of rock had to be blasted and this had an impact on the older club. In November, for example, John Chutter told the committee:

> *A serious water leakage caused by a broken pipe has flooded the ceiling and walls of the poker room on the third floor and the defective piping and ceiling had to be replaced. He was awaiting a report from K.D.Engineering as to how much blame, if any, could be attributed to the vibration caused by the underpinning carried out by Daon.*

By January the underpinning of the club had been completed. It resulted in the strengthening of the foundation of the clubhouse, but three months of blasting and excavation had caused a number of cracks to appear in some of the walls, ceilings and floors of the building. Another problem was caused by the vibration from drills which resulted in flakes of rust shaking loose inside the water pipes clogging the pipes at joints and elbows. Flooding had resulted on both the third and fourth floors with consequent damage to the ceiling and walls.

By the summer of 1979 the Daon Building was nearing completion. The club put in a claim for $6,500 to cover the cost of the repairs due to drilling, blasting and demolition. Daon offered to pay 85 per cent, and the club accepted. When the Daon Building was occupied it was decided to put a gold reflective plastic film on the west windows of the third floor bar "to prevent members from being scrutinized." The Daon Building, with its mass of triple glazed windows, had a somewhat similar reflective material incorporated in its windows.

During the time when the Daon Building was under construction and, indeed, going on well into the 1980's, the club was considering what might be the best use of its development rights. A special committee was established in 1976 to deal with the matter and the first thing it did was to meet with the City Planning Department. The latter would be a major factor in any proposed transfer of development rights, either in whole or in part. Moreover, with the tremendous amount of building and proposed construction going on in the city, there were considerations to be resolved respecting the best offer for the club's rights. In 1979, the club received a copy of the city manager's report on Marathon Realty's schematic plans which would bring tremendous changes and development on the Canadian Pacific Railway property. As reported in the committee minutes:

As Marathon's plan envisaged the erection of a twenty storey hotel immediately north of the Vancouver Club and the new Daon Building, and an even taller office building immediately behind the Terminal City Club, he [the president] considered this would completely cut off the view of the North Shore to all three. However, as the City Council seemed determined to press ahead with this plan, he could not see much hope of having the siting of the proposed new building altered.

To understand this problem, we must go back a few years to appreciate what was happening to the area in which the club was located. As early as the 1960's the club was aware of potential changes which might affect members' view of the harbour and the North Shore. Among the schemes proposed to improve the development and land use of Vancouver's waterfront was "Project 200." By the early 1970's, planning for the development of the waterfront between Granville and Burrard Streets had reached a stage where the club decided to strike a special committee consisting of G.Peter Kaye, J.Norman Hyland, R.S.Whyte and C.H.Wills "to meet with the developers and other interested owners of adjacent property in order to keep abreast of these proposals and to protect the interests of the club." The latter were defined at the Annual General Meeting in January 1974 as:

(1) to preserve the general atmosphere of the club premises; (2) to retain as much of our waterfront view to the north as possible; (3) to perpetuate this club's equity position in its investment in land and building and (4) to secure suitable parking facilities for the members.

The committee met with the planners of the Marathon Waterfront Project early in 1974 but it was not until March that they were able to see a model of the proposed plan. They were not pleased with the proposal. Among other things, after talking with the development manager, it was apparent that

(1) the club view of the North and West Vancouver would be cut by at least 50 percent by the proposed new hotel; (2) the proposal to make Hornby Street, north of Hastings Street, two-way traffic with traffic signs would mean that it would be impossible to stop one's car in front of the club, let alone park there and (3) the new hotel (17 stories) would be only 50 feet northwest of the Vancouver Club which is far too close.

This, to use a phrase made popular by protesters at the time, was not acceptable. It was time to rally and raise the fiery cross. If club members did not converge on City Hall carrying placards and chanting slogans, they did begin to organize an opposition based on the expertise within the club's membership as well as using such influence as it possessed.

In June 1974, a new plan and model was ready for examination which was more acceptable. Even if members would lose part of the view from the club it would not be as cribbed and confined as had been feared. There the matter rested until 1979 when, as we have seen, a new plan was developed which, among other things, proposed the erection of a 20-storey hotel directly across the railway tracks north of the club where the old C.P.R. docks used to be.

Since this time it appeared there would be little chance of persuading either the city or Marathon Realty to change their plans, and since the clubhouse was proving to be rather expensive owing to increasing maintenance costs, once again the committee was faced with the question of whether or not it should move to new premises. A sub-committee, chaired by Sydney W. Welsh, accepted the task of preparing a report on the options, keeping in mind the cost of renovations and maintenance of the building over the next five years and the cost of relocating the club in a space either leased or owned in a downtown building.

The selection of Sydney Welsh was a good one. He had been a member since 1957 and was to be president in 1983. Born in 1913 in South Vancouver, he can remember as a boy getting wooden slivers in his bare feet as he played with his friends on the planked sidewalks and roads in his neighbourhood. His father was a plumber, and young Welsh started as an apprentice plumber in 1933 at eight dollars for a 40-hour week. Ultimately, he and his father started Fred Welsh and Son, a plumbing firm which expanded to include air conditioning, electrical contracting and heating. Unable to join the services during the war owing to a back problem, Welsh was able to take part in the tremendous building boom which took place during the war. He was soon involved in defence contracts from Whitehorse in the Yukon to Vancouver. His firm worked on the Abbotsford, Long Beach and Jericho airports, the army camp in Nanaimo, the internment camp near Hope, and a variety of other places.

After the war his firm expanded from about 40 to 400 men. He was asked to undertake major industrial and commercial contracts and in the 1950's he became one of the pioneers in the cablevision business not only in Vancouver and Victoria, but in Ontario and Quebec as well. He expanded into a variety of other business enterprises, yet still found time to become involved in a variety of other interests. He was national president of the Kinsmen Clubs of Canada and president of the World Council of Young Men's Service Clubs. He put in two years' service on the Council of West Vancouver, six years as a director of the Lion's Gate Hospital and more time as a director of the Salvation Army's Grace Hospital. He was also president of the Vancouver Board of Trade.

There is an old saying that if you want to get a job done, choose a busy man. The club president, Larry Dampier, selected a very busy club member and Welsh, in turn, asked a number of other members--architects and engineers--to join his committee.

The report by Welsh's committee was presented on March 31st. Generally speaking, considering the age of the building, its mechanical and electrical systems were in fair condition. The old piping and the domestic water system were going to need repairs. These, together with other areas needing attention and refurbishing, would come to $85,000. With respect to a possible move to new premises, the committee spoke to a large number of the members. Only eleven showed a serious interest in the proposal and then only if they could be assured of no additional cost of operations or assessments. Twenty-seven did not want to change under any circumstances and 25 had a number of concerns about leaving the building.

The committee reported that the clubhouse had about 47,000 square feet of space, of which 40,000 square feet was being used on a full-time basis. Thus at least the new premises must have 40,000 square feet. The cost of dismantling the dining room and reinstalling it in the new premises, together with moving, was estimated at $1,300,000. The sale of the clubhouse, with its heritage designation, was estimated at $2,000,000. There would be a tax on the sale price and, taking everything into consideration, the club would be left with $450,000 which, if it had a 12 percent return, would yield $54,000 per annum. To lease 40,000 square feet of space suitable for the club over the next five years was estimated at approximately $467,500 per year, and that figure took into account the savings the club might anticipate from not paying taxes, insurance, maintenance and other annual building expenses. From a financial point of view, the committee concluded that "we are far better off ... in our own premises." It added:

> *In considering long-range renovation and maintenance recommendations for the Vancouver Club, the Premises Committee feels that it is on safe ground when it states that the most sincere desire of the members is the retention of the quality of accommodation and the quality of services which presently exist.*

The Premises Committee went on to say that although the clubhouse had stood up well against minor earthquakes, a nearby ship explosion and vibrations from blasting rock when excavating the Daon Building next door,

> *Nevertheless there has been some deterioration of the out-*
> *door and interior finishes and frequent repairs are necessary to*
> *the walls, rooves, openings and equipment. Maintenance, repairs*
> *and costs will increase annually and the committee suggests that a*
> *program designed for preventative maintenance is a mandatory*
> *responsibility for the club management.*

The report by Welsh and his committee was well received. It comforted those who did not want to move and confirmed the suspicion of many that if a move to new premises was necessary, it was going to be a costly affair. Fixing up the clubhouse was proving to be expensive but that was a burden to be borne.

Meanwhile, what about the view to the north and Marathon Realty's plans? In May 1980, two months after the Premises Committee had made its report, the General Committee was informed that the demolition of Pier B.C. was to begin in a month's time. A photographer from the City Planning Department had come to the club and taken panoramic pictures of the harbour and North Shore from the third floor to show the Director of Planning. Evidently there was some concern at City Hall respecting the loss of view when the new buildings were erected. In July the architects had drafted what was their final scheme for their development--at least in its first stage-- and there was to be a public information meeting about it early in August. The development of Pier B.C. would include a trade and convention centre, a cruise ship facility, a hotel, an office structure and a parking garage.

Once again the club sent representatives to the public meeting, had talks with the architects, consulted with their neighbours, examined models and so forth. Space does not permit the telling of the full story of this development project which, in time, passed out of the hands of Marathon Development into a project involving the provincial and federal governments as well as private financial interests. It merged, too, with a much grander scheme, "Expo '86." Nevertheless, the basic idea of a convention place, hotel and cruise ship facility, all grouped under the name "Canada Place," remained. By late 1982 Canada Place planning became the responsibility of a Board of Directors chaired by a club member, Robert G. Rogers, who had only recently stepped down as Chief Executive Officer of Crown Zellerbach. He had been on the club's General Committee. One or two years were to elapse before the building began to rise on the waterfront, and with each storey a portion of the view across the harbour with the snow clad mountains beyond would disappear. To the east and west, however, members could still enjoy scenery which few clubs in Canada could match.

There is one compensation which should not go unmentioned.

When Canada Place was completed, it was a beautifully-designed building. Also its length jutted out into the harbour, thus narrowing the degree of harbour scenery blocked off from the club. If members could no longer watch the "Princess" boats come in from Victoria, what better sight to watch than the large, gleaming cruise ships slipping into the docks on either side of Canada Place. It was enough to make members want to go on an ocean voyage, and many did.

There was one man on the General Committee between 1975 and 1981 who was keenly interested in the tremendous changes going on in downtown Vancouver. He was H.Clark Bentall. His father, an engineer, had come to Vancouver from England in 1908 and three years later started the Dominion Construction Company. His father's company had built a number of well-known buildings in Vancouver-- the B.T.Rogers mansion, the Capitol Theatre, the Yorkshire Trust Building and Point Grey Junior High School to mention only a few. In keeping with its name, the firm branched out to do major construction work all over the province and in Western Canada as well. After weathering the depression, the stimulus of wartime orders ranging from airports to cargo lighters led to further expansion until it became a truly national company engaged not only in construction but development and management enterprises as well.

Clark Bentall had taken over control of Dominion Construction from his father in 1955 and one of his proudest achievements was initiating the building of four large office towers which changed the look of downtown Vancouver probably more than any other structures built at the time. In the mid-seventies, at the time the Vancouver Club was given permission to sell its excess development rights, Bentall was no longer on the General Committee but his firm owned the land on the eastern side of the club. This, of course, was the original site of the Vancouver Club. At that time, and for a number of years previously, it was used as a parking lot. The taxes on the parking lot alone were high and getting higher, and it was obvious that the property, if built upon, would yield a very decent revenue.

In the late 1970's when some thought was being given to the possibility of moving the club, there had been some informal discussions about a joint endeavour to improve both properties. If the clubhouse were torn down, would it be a good idea to build a large modern tower encompassing the two lots and have the club established on two or three of the top stories? There members could continue to enjoy their magnificent view and, basically, remain on their old site. The idea of a club moving to an office tower has been put into practice elsewhere, but there were problems to consider as well. The heritage designation of the club had to be taken into account; the potential noon-time traffic of members using the tower's elevators might make other tenants of the building annoyed, and certainly by the time Sydney Welsh turned in his report, the membership was against the move. As a result, the informal talks of a joint venture never bore fruit.

On the other side of the parking lot, however, was the Terminal City Club. The two clubs have been friendly rivals for years and each has looked forward for decades to the annual billiards competition and bridge tournament. The Terminal City Club was in an old building which is not a heritage building. Dominion Construction executives began to consider the possibility of building a tower on their parking lot and the property to the east and, as such, they would still be interested in the Vancouver Club's excess development rights.

The questions of when, if and to whom the club would sell its development rights were discussed for a number of years, and there is no need to go into the complications of the negotiations, offers and counter-offers. There were discussions whether the rights could and should be sold outright, in whole or in part, for cash or for a share of equity securities. What was the value of a cubic foot of "air space"? Should the club hold on to some for possible expansion? How much space was there to sell? In 1983, when Bentall was giving some serious consideration to buying the development rights, the club hired some professional land surveyors and engineers to give it some accurate figures. The report to the General Committee stated in part:

> *The site area of the Vancouver Club is 16,537 square feet. The total net floor area of the club (basement plus five floors) is 51,913 square feet. The maximum floor space ratio permitted for Zone 'B' (the Vancouver Club zone) is seven. Thus if one took the site area times seven you got 115,759 square feet less the building floor area of 51,913 square feet which gave a surplus floor space of 63,846 square feet. The surplus floor space requested by the Bentall group is 60,000 square feet and thus the space remaining to the Vancouver Club would be 3,846 square feet.*

The initial proposal of Dominion Construction was to build a structure which could occupy 472,162 square feet, so aside from the development rights, the club was also most interested in the impact it would have on the club, just as it had when the Daon Building went up.

Discussions with Dominion Construction respecting what came to be called the Terminal City Tower building carried on into the late summer of 1984 when it was decided that no further action would be taken, for the present, to build the new tower. In April 1986, the club president, Hubert Chapman, inserted a small notice about the matter which summed up the situation at that time:

> *Bill Leithead, Roy Jessiman and myself met with Clark and*

Bob Bentall yesterday to determine the status of their proposed office tower development next door.... It was no surprise to learn that, while the project will undoubtedly proceed, the current oversupply of office space makes it unlikely that it will proceed in the near future.

* * * *

Although the club members were concerned with the new buildings being erected to the west and north, and a potential construction to the east, there was a fair amount of activity going on within the confines of the clubhouse itself during these years.

The fourth floor had undergone a major reconstruction which had been completed in 1963. The creation of several private dining rooms on that floor had served an obvious need. However, unlike the first three floors of the clubhouse, the fourth floor had low ceilings. The dining rooms were also rather long, there was no air conditioning in them, and the serving kitchen was not as efficient as it should be.

In 1977 there was some discussion in the General Committee about the need to redesign or redecorate the entire floor. The firm of Hopping, Kovac and Grinnell were hired to make recommendations of what could and should be done. The club had already spent a fair amount of money on redecorating and refurnishing almost every room, and it was only fifteen years previously that the fourth floor had been renovated. To do it again, and this time properly, called for a study of the problem in depth. The president in 1978, D.Michael M.Goldie, reported to the annual meeting the results of the investigation as follows:

The main effort of the House Committee over the past year has been the study, planning, designing and costing of a refurbishing project for the fourth floor of the club. The total cost of this project, if carried out during 1979, would be $200,000. It would include new carpeting throughout, new wall furnishings, drapes, lighting and air conditioning of the President's Room, Committee Room and reception area, and structural alterations to increase reception and dining room areas. However, at a meeting of a specially formed committee of all club committee chairmen and advisors, chaired by Geoffrey H. Tullidge, it was decided that it was not a propitious moment to undertake this expense.

The need for change was obvious, however, and the new president in 1979, Lawrence Dampier, continued to pursue the matter with some vigour. There were a number of factors to consider. At the time some six or seven banks and firms were using the private dining rooms on a monthly basis and it seemed unlikely this number would be increased unless the rooms were upgraded and better facilities for ladies provided. Only a few members used the rooms for private parties and if dues were increased to assist in covering the cost there was bound to be protest. If the rooms were improved and used more frequently, the 40–year–old elevator would require fixing up at a cost of about $10,000 and the consultant's fees would be a little more than that. Balancing this, however, was the fact that even a modified refurbishment, which the committee agreed to in February, was going to cost between $50,000 and $60,000. If the major reconstruction costs were put off, current inflation would make the eventual price–tag even steeper and there was the argument that better dining facilities would bring in increased revenue.

The committee decided to take the chance and present the proposal at an extraordinary general meeting in June 1979. To finance the scheme the club would borrow $120,000 and charge members extra dues over a twelve month periods only. At the meeting it was Dampier who persuaded the members to give their support. Turning over the chair to his vice–president, Tullidge, he gave a strong speech in favour of the proposal, answered the questions of opponents to the scheme with facts and figures projecting future costs, and persuaded the necessary 75 per cent of those present to agree to the scheme. The meeting approved and work began almost immediately.

When one begins to tamper with an old building there is a certain amount of intermingled excitement and apprehension about what lies behind walls and partitions. Building codes before the Great War were far different from what they are today, and though the clubhouse was built with the best material, even that will wear out. Moreover the architectural plans of the club had been lost and were not found until the late 1980's.

When the Dominion Construction Co. began work and started to demolish certain connecting walls, one of the things it found was a number of sewage and water pipes serving four rooms facing Hastings Street on the fifth floor. To fit into the new plans these would have to be removed or repositioned into the outside walls. To remove them would cost $1,500 and would eliminate toilets and sinks in some of the rooms. To relocate would cost $5,000 and spoil the ceiling decor in the President's and Vice–President's Room. This was only one of the problems that had to be resolved. It was done partially by switching the use of the rooms upstairs between staff quarters and members' bedrooms. Those members who rented Room 15 permanently retained their quarters, in part owing to the plumbing experience of Sydney Welsh who pointed out to the contractors a method of retaining the rooms' plumbing without changing the ceiling height of the floor below.

By the late Fall of 1979 the fourth floor was completed. It was a

dramatic improvement. The Lieutenant-Governor of British Columbia, the Honourable H. P. Bell-Irving, presided at the official opening. As a club member, and especially as he had served on the General
Committee himself before his appointment, he was well aware of the
tremendous amount of planning and work it took to create the lovely
dining suites which now became available.

The cost of renovation had been higher than expected. The
secretary manager, Chutter, reported that the total bill was $296,000,
or about $50,000 over the June 1979 estimate. Part of this was due to
unforeseen plumbing, carpentry and painting. This was taken care of
in part by the membership agreeing to extend the special year-long
dues increase for several months. One might conjecture that this
measure was passed owing to the members pleasure at what had been
accomplished and the difficulties that had to be overcome, especially
in the inflationary period. Originally, for example, the new furniture
was estimated at $10,000. The actual cost was $14,189. New drapes
were estimated at $5,000. The actual cost was $9,347. The air conditioning was marvellous but it required additional voltage and the
control panel had to be increased from 600 to 800 amperes. That cost
$4,000, and B.C. Hydro expected the club to pay a quarter of that
amount. And so it went.

Despite it all, it was worth the effort, even if it cost almost as
much as the original cost of the club, there were now three private
dining rooms and three private reception rooms available for private
receptions, luncheons or dinners. The President's Room (East) could
seat 32 persons, the Marine Room (North) could accommodate ten
persons. If necessary the two President's Rooms could be made into
one Dining Room seating up to 58 persons and so well designed was
the plan that 180 persons could congregate for cocktail parties and
receptions. The club's architectural advisor, William G. Leithead,
received a lot of praise for his help, and it was well deserved.

The interior work going on in the club was underway at the same
time the Daon Building was under construction. The clubhouse was
getting a good rattling inside and out, and when the Premises Review
Committee made its report in January 1980, it not only suggested that
the club should not move from its present premises but it drew up a
plan of what needed to be done. William Leithead told the General
Committee in April 1981 that

> *[it] gave first priority to replacing the old piping in the domestic
> system (at an estimated cost of $35,000) which is galvanized steel
> and badly corroded. When leaks have occurred, replacements
> have been made with copper piping. As a consequence, the mix-
> ture of steel, copper and iron fittings has hastened the disintegra-*

tion of steel pipe through galvanic action. Several pipes have burst over the past three or four months causing flooding. Last year $10,000 was spent on repairs and replacements. So far this year, replacement piping (copper) and fittings have cost $5,000 and the present KD Engineering project is scheduled to cost a further $10,000 this year.

These matters had to be attended to as well as some of the windows. Added to that it became obvious in time that both the roof and the exterior walls of the clubhouse needed looking after. Nothing was done to the latter until there was some decision whether the Terminal City Tower would be built but by the late Summer of 1985, with the good weather coming to an end and no further word about a tower being built in the near future, it was decided to re-stucco the walls. Early in 1986, Roy Jessiman, now the club's architectural consultant, advised the committee that repairs on the exterior walls of the building were almost completed. There had been an overrun of $24,000 on the original estimate of $80,000. The shoulders of the committeemen must have sagged. Once again repairs to the roof would have to be delayed.

This wasn't the only problem. The main sewage pipe from the clubhouse was getting plugged up and had to be fixed. The original estimate was that it would cost $35,500. As work progressed on its replacement, it was found that the large sanitary pipe in the rear of the property was buried 18 feet deep, was corroded and had to be replaced. This involved the use of heavy equipment and meant the small garden at the rear of the club would be no more. Jessiman also said that the city's building by-laws now made it necessary to separate the storm and sanitary sewers.

He had more bad news. After a careful examination it was discovered that the built-in down pipes, part of the roof drainage system, were badly corroded and as a result there was moisture damage to the interior walls. Their replacement would be costly, but Jessiman suggested that exterior PVC down pipes could be used at a fraction of the cost. It seemed that there was no end to the repair bills. Whether the water was coming into the club from the water mains, leaving the club by sewage drains or falling as rain from the heavens it was costing money.

The maintenance costs were bad enough. What was worrying were the expenses which did not come to light until after a job was started. In November 1987, for example, Roy Jessiman attended a meeting of the General Committee to report on work being carried out on the northern exterior walls. The minutes explain clearly the kind of unpleasant surprises the members dreaded to hear:

Jessiman stated that the repairs to the northern elevation are almost complete. After the erection of scaffolding, work commenced on 27 September 1987. First the contractor dismantled the stucco and masonry at the top north-east corner where stainless steel vertical bars had been installed to assist in stability. It was found that the anchorages of the bars were in the tile work which was barely three inches wide and severely cracked. Second, all the masonry adjacent to the northeast corner was dismantled and the six-by-six-inch rusted steel support beam was exposed. The beam is now encased in concrete on three sides. A concrete beam (above the steel beam) was found to be cracked and was rewelded by injecting epoxy resins. Third, both the northeast and northwest corners of the cantilevered section was rebuilt with reinforced concrete. On the removal of the stucco, it was found that the steel columns and beams were severely rusted, requiring them to be fully exposed, treated, further galvanized steel reinforcements attached, and concrete formed and repoured. Other damages were also found . . .

As a result the cost of the work on the north wall has been exceeded to the extent of some $23,500. Thus the original estimate of $79,150 was now up to $104,000.

Once again the repairs to the roof had to be delayed.

*   *   *   *

While priority had been given to repairing pipes and exterior walls, there was other work to be done inside the club. One area was the fifth floor. As early as 1974 the House Committee had discussed the need to upgrade certain rooms to be clean, quiet and adequate for themselves but, it was reported, "they did not consider them of a high enough standard to offer to their out-of-town guests."

At that time there was only one member living in the club, R.J. Elliott. A former pilot in the Royal Flying Corps, he had been living in the club for almost 25 years. He became increasingly disabled in the 1970's and relied more and more on the staff. Mrs. Ilmi Archambault, the club's housekeeper since 1968 did everything possible to help him until his death in 1975. He was appreciative of this help and in his will left a sum of money to each of the staff who had served in the club for ten or more years.

With Elliott's death the committee decided not to accept any more live-in members. Bedrooms would be rented henceforth by the day, week or month, but the old tradition of a member literally living in the club was ended.

But what of the bedrooms themselves? After Elliott's death a survey was taken and it was found that over the past three and a half years an average of four and a half bedrooms had been rented out daily, two of these (Nos. 13 and 15) had been rented to members of

"Room 15" on a monthly basis and one to Mr. Elliott. The demand for bedrooms was low, but was this because they were small and rather pokey or was it a trend? Of the thirteen clubs with which the Vancouver Club was affiliated at the time, only three had residential accommodation. It was decided to do some redecoration in a few of them, put a colour television set in them and increase the rent in 1977 from $18 to $20 per day for those bedrooms with a bath.

Thus matters stood until the mid–1980's when "Expo '86" began to take shape. It seemed that everyone in the city was making plans for this world exposition and since it was located almost within a stone's throw of the club, the committee decided it should re–examine the fifth floor as it was quite possible guests from affiliated clubs would want to use some of the bedrooms as well as the dining facilities. Roy Jessiman, who had been a professional architect all his life and who had been responsible for many of the buildings on the U.B.C. campus, had recently retired and, as the new architectural consultant for the club, set out to see exactly how the fifth room floors were being utilized. As he recalled later:

> *There were fourteen rooms on the fifth floor, and eight of them were occupied by staff. I reported this to the General Committee. They said: 'what do you mean eight of them are used by staff?' I said one is records storage, one is furniture storage, one is the secretary–ager's day room . . .; the chief steward has a room, the maitre d' has a room, the wine steward has a room, the housekeeper has a room, and so forth. That set the General Committee back on its heels.*

After hearing the report, and later examining plans showing how the bedrooms could be enlarged and all provided with baths for guests staying for a few days, the committee agreed to the conversion which took place early in 1986. Several rooms were retained for the staff but the bedrooms were enlarged by knocking down walls and making most of them into large comfortable rooms. Once again prices were increased to an average of about $60, but at that it was a bargain compared to the price of hotel rooms in downtown Vancouver. Several rooms were retained for the staff, but now they had to share.

When "Expo '86" did come the club was ready. When it was over Hubert Chapman, the club president, was able to report that the bedrooms had produced a gross profit of $23,909. He also reported that Expo '86 had a very positive effect on attendance at private functions in the club with an increase of about 2,100 persons using private rooms during the year.

*   *   *   *

During the years when the clubhouse was to be fixed, altered, repaired, reinforced and generally improved both inside and out, there was yet another drain on building and maintenance funds which might be described briefly at this point. Much of the repair work described above was owing to water. A great deal of money was also spent owing to fire, or to be more exact, fire prevention.

When the clubhouse was being built in 1913, fire prevention codes and regulations were not strict. Indeed, it was really in the post-1945 era that the city began to impose a series of regulations on buildings such as the Vancouver Club, and these regulations became increasingly strict in the sixties and seventies. As far as the city was concerned, the clubhouse was a building which had numerous bedrooms on its upper floors, and in a sense was a mini-hotel. Moreover it had the capacity to seat several hundred people for dinner and if, by chance, there whould be a fire when the club was crowded, provisions had to be made to get people out of the club rapidly.

The first major expense in this area came in 1966 when, in order to meet building codes, the General Committee decided to build a fire tower. The projected price was high but, as a House Committee member put it, "this project must receive priority . . . in order to protect life" and second, "it would be far less expensive and inconvenient to undertake construction work on the east side of the clubhouse now than after a building should be erected on the parking lot. . . ." The fire escape tower was completed early in 1967 at a cost of $53,564, somewhat higher--as usual--than the original estimate.

Several years later, in 1974, as a result of new fire laws brought in by the city, a number of changes had to be made in the club. For example, all doors and transoms in the corridor of the fifth floor were replaced. All doors to the enclosed stairs on the west side of the club were made into approved fire doors and made to open inward to the stair shaft. Provision was made to install illuminated exit lights and rated self-closing fire doors at the entrance of the snack room and billiard room on the third floor. This was estimated to cost $15,000, and an additional $2,500 was added to make a second egress for the staff in the basement.

In 1980 the Fire Commissioner's Office recommended further improvements--automatically closing fire doors, smoke detection installations, an alarm system and other measures. The estimated total bill was $52,000, but permission was granted to bring these measures into effect over several years rather than all at once. This was helpful and the burden made a little easier to carry with the knowledge that the members had decided not to move but remain in its own building. During the next three years all the suggestions made, and indeed more, were carried out. Magnetic door holders, thermal and smoke detectors, manual pull stations, the most up-to-date fire alarm system and so forth were all installed, and by the time all of this work was completed the total bill was well over $100,000. There is no doubt that the club has always taken fire precautions seriously and it can boast that its alarm and detection installations are the most efficient available.

By the latter part of the 1980's the members had spent a small fortune on restoring the club to a first class condition. Some of the renovations and improvements eventually generated additional revenue, but straightforward repairs and improvements such as the fire prevention installation yielded no income whatever, even though they improved safety and prevented further decay. The roof still needed attention and, with inflation, normal maintenance costs were causing some worry. Although designation as a heritage building eventually brought some tax relief, expenses were steadily rising. What was worrying, too, was the information coming in about other clubs being forced to close their doors, throw them open to female membership or amalgamate. These concerns, and the resolution of them, were to cause the Vancouver Club to make one of its most dramatic decisions in the 1980's. Fortunately, the decision taken was to be the correct one.

CHAPTER IX

TOGETHER WE STAND

In June 1986, the Reverend Edward Wallace left the University Club, walked past the Vancouver Club and made his way to Edward Chapman's, an old established men's wear firm. Wallace, born in Winnipeg, had been a school-teacher before he entered the Anglican ministry. He had served in a variety of parishes but he was happiest at St. Stephen's in West Vancouver where he had been for the past eighteen years. He knew Hubert Chapman quite well, partly because Chapman and he had been on the board of directors of the Canadian Club, partly because he became president of the University Club at the same time Chapman became president of the Vancouver Club, and also he sometimes went to Chapman's to buy clothes. Chapman invited him into his office and Wallace began to explain the reason for his visit. For both men, and ultimately for both clubs, it was an historic occasion. Wallace suggested that the two clubs should amalgamate.

According to Wallace he had to get "three of Chapman's more stalwart salesmen to come and help me lift Hu off the floor," [but] gradually the light began to dawn. 'You know,' said Hu, 'that may have some merit.' Then I said:

> *We are so much alike in the atmosphere and ambience in the two clubs. It makes good economic sense. The place to merge is in your building because ours is not a solid building. We've been having discussions for years on the future of our building . . . as to what might happen to it. It will cost a lot of money to upgrade it.*

Chapman could certainly appreciate the last remark since he had been on the General Committee for a number of years and was well aware of what the repairs had cost in his own club.

Chapman is a native Vancouverite. During the school holidays he used to work in his grandfather's store and when his grandfather died, he went to work there on a full-time basis. This was interrupted by the war, but when he returned from serving in the navy, he returned to the family business and was the guiding hand behind its expansion in the post-war decade. He was an early member of the University Club but eventually joined the Vancouver Club in 1967. For a while he was a member of both clubs, as were other Vancouver Club members, but in time he kept membership only in the Vancouver Club as it was closer to his place of business.

Since he had become a member, but more particularly as a committee member and then president, Chapman had witnessed a disturbing change in membership figures. When he joined in 1967 there was a total of 1,109 members of all categories. In that year there were 95 applicants waiting to enter the club and 41 applications had been received. A decade later the total membership was up slightly to 1,208 but the number of applications had gone down to 20 while 42 new applications had been received. By 1984 the number on the waiting list had dropped to nine and the applications during the year had dipped also, though not as dramatically.

Equally important was the increase in life membership. This category brings with it a well-deserved decrease in annual dues for older resident members who, for decades, have contributed to the club financially and in other ways. Many of the older members were on pension and, for some, being a life member meant the difference between enjoying the club or having to withdraw. In 1967 there were 44 life members. Within a decade this had increased to 102 and by 1986 the number had gone up to 156. If one considers the loss of revenue this represents in annual dues, and taking into account also the fact that, looking into the future, the number of life members would increase, there was cause to worry.

There was also the problem of resident membership. This category remained almost full during the seventies and eighties which meant that, unlike the late forties and fifties, there was no surge of new members who brought with them entrance fees which helped to pay for the renovations and refurbishments in the club. Between 1967 and 1975 there was an average of 52 new members per year coming into the club. This average dropped by about ten per cent in the next decade. With the waiting list going down, there was a trend which had to be watched.

The trend was not new. It was happening everywhere, particularly in England. At the turn of the century London was reported to have had 200 private clubs. Two world wars, a depression and a sickly post-war economy had reduced this number drastically. In 1979 the *Financial Post*, surveying the Canadian scene, came out with an article entitled "Clubs go a-courting while costs go awry," which pretty well summed up the reporter's investigation. He noted, among other things, that "since 1972, when the federal government excluded membership fees from its list of allowable corporate business expenses for tax purposes, private clubs, already hard hit by inflation, have watched membership dwindle." He went on to cite rising annual dues and entrance fees as a deterrent to new members and noted that to encourage members to use their club, new facilities were needed-- including parking space --to make the clubs more attractive. For the English clubs in Montreal, the reporter continued,

> *. . . the difficulties have been abetted by other factors: the exodus to the suburbs, meaning members do not want to drive all the way back into town at night; the continual growth in the number and the quality of restaurants, meaning that when they do drive in, they would rather sample something new instead of the old club restaurant; and changing tax laws, making write-offs more difficult.*

The Vancouver Club, of course, was familiar with many of these problems and had made vigorous efforts to attract its members to use the club through Consular Dinners, Father-and-Son Nights, Gourmet Dinners and so forth. All of these had helped. Some changes had taken place which could not be reversed. The third floor bar, which used to be full from late in the afternoon until the early evening changed so much that in the 1980's there might be less than a dozen members there. The card room used to be packed for several hours at lunch time and frequently busy in the evenings as well. This changed also. Both caused a reduction in revenue.

Of greater importance, however, was the tremendous increase in the cost of maintaining the building, both inside and outside. It did not require a brilliant mind to project membership and maintenance graphs and to come to the conclusion that an amalgamation would be a good idea. Aside from the financial benefits, the two clubs had many things in common. Both were men's clubs. Both were in the same general location, the one only about five hundred yards from the other. Over the years a great many members of one club held membership in the other. Their joint aim was social rather than commercial and, basically, their entertainment program, form of government, elections and rules and regulations were not that different so as to make an amalgamation an insurmountable task.

By 1986, too, one obstacle to amalgamation had long been eliminated. The University Club, shortly after it was formed, had agreed on a policy that no potential member would face discrimination because of race or religion. The Vancouver Club's constitution, with all its amendments through the years, said nothing about the subject one way or another, except for the provision made after the Great War which excluded Germans for about a decade. Nevertheless, although members' application forms did not ask for an applicant's racial origin or religious persuasion, the club's membership in the inter-war period shows no members of Oriental origin, whether they had been born in the Far East or were second or third generation Canadians. It is apparent, too, that the potential member was assumed to be a Christian. It was obvious that the membership did not want to bring into its midst people who, it was felt, would not fit in comfortably with other members.

This attitude began to change after the Second World War. As more young members joined who no longer held the prejudices of the older members, and as the acceptance of Canada's cultural mosaic became widespread, a growing number of members wanted to eliminate any remnants of racial or religious prejudices presumed to exist within the club. This was accomplished in 1976 when the General Committee took steps to amend the constitution to increase the number of negative votes (black-balls) necessary to deny an applicant's entry into the club. The amendment was accepted and within a year the old pattern was broken as the Vancouver Club's membership policy became similar to that of the University Club.

During the 1970s and 1980s, the University Club began to suffer from falling membership. In 1971 it had a total of 812 of which 637 were resident members. By 1978 there were only 565 resident members. There was an improvement in the early eighties but, in the middle of the decade, despite a membership drive, the projected membership numbers pointed downward just as surely as projected costs pointed upward. It was little wonder, therefore, that when Wallace and Chapman met to discuss amalgamation, both agreed to present the idea to their respective governing bodies and propose that steps should be taken to test the opinion of their members.

There was another event which took place in 1986 which was to play a role in the amalgamation process. Early in 1986 the Vancouver Club's Secretary–Manager, John Chutter, left the club. He had held his position for about fifteen years, so long that it almost felt as if he were a resident member. Before he left, a search was made for a replacement and after some time and a considerable amount of interviewing, four prospective replacements remained. One of these was George W. Smith. He had considerable experience in Great Britain and Canada in hotels and clubs and for the past eight and a half years he had been Secretary–Manager of the University Club. As he put it later: "I was advised that I was on the 'short list'. Considering my height of five feet seven inches (fully stretched) I thought the wording was somewhat appropriate." After considering applications from all over the continent, the Vancouver Club decided to select Smith, who worked only a few hundred yards away. It was a good choice, but it would be some months before Smith could leave his club. He was replaced in the University Club by Tom Marshall, a former club president who was retiring from the legal profession and agreed to assume the task.

Hu Chapman had to find a replacement for Chutter until Smith could take over. He decided to try Darrell Braidwood, a retired lawyer and old friend. As he related later:

> *I phoned Darrell and told him Chutter was leaving the next morning and asked if he could fill his place temporarily. 'I'm too old, I'm too lazy and I'm too dumb.' I said, 'I agree with the first two but I don't agree with the third one. But do you have any ideas?' 'Well,' he said, 'Let's have lunch tomorrow.'*
>
> *At lunch he said, 'What do you think of Bob Orr?' 'I don't know him.' 'He's a practicing but semi–retired lawyer.' 'How can we get him?' 'He's down having lunch on the second floor.' I got Michael Sikorra to bring him up to have coffee with us. The three of us sat down and I told him what the problem was. Orr said, 'When do I start?' 'Tomorrow morning at nine o'clock.' He said, 'I'll be there.'*

> *I'll never, ever be able to thank Bob enough for doing that [job]*
> *until George Smith came over on September 15th.*

As a result, Smith was at one club when the early initiative was taken there towards amalgamation, and he was at the other club when the talks became more serious and detailed. His knowledge of both clubs and their respective staffs was to be especially valuable in the months to come.

When Chapman met with the General Committee in June 1986 and told them about the conversation he had with Edward Wallace, there was a great deal of interest in the idea and a consensus that the prospect of amalgamation should be pursued. There was an equally warm response when Wallace did the same thing at his Board of Directors at the University Club. It was generally agreed at the outset that the University Club would sell its building, estimated at about $4,000,000, and the money and the members would move to the larger Vancouver Club. There would have to be major changes in the latter club to accommodate the extra numbers. It was soon to become apparent, too, that the "new" members felt strongly about a separate entrance for the ladies, and there were one or two other accommodations the Vancouver Club would be expected to make. Moreover, there were a great many other things to consider. The by-laws of the two clubs would have to be rewritten. Membership categories would have to be examined and the merging of the two staffs would have to be sorted out. Club affiliations needed looking at and, of course, there were many legal aspects of the merger which would have to be considered.

With the General Committee backing him, Chapman struck a committee on amalgamation consisting of himself, Philip Owen (his vice-president) and George Hungerford, the past president. As Chapman said later:

> *The three of us had meetings with our opposite numbers at the*
> *University Club in early July [1986]. By the end of September we*
> *had had numerous meetings and were getting to the point where*
> *we felt we had to get the decision from the membership as a whole*
> *as to whether we should proceed on the possibility of amalgama-*
> *tion or not.*
> *On October 7th we had our first information meeting and we*
> *asked for a show of hands as to whether we should proceed with*
> *that possibility. We had 125 members turn out to our meeting and*
> *I think we had four dissenting votes. We just asked for an*
> *expression of opinion. It was a good meeting and the same was*
> *true when [University Club members] had their meeting on the*
> *following night at their club. . . . Obviously the majority of both*
> *clubs would like to entertain the possibility.*

We then started working on the by-laws. Bill Armstrong, a lawyer, was on our committee and was extremely good at that type of thing. In their club they had Sholto Hebenton and Tom Marshall. They, together with Armstrong and David Helliwell from our club, were the by-law committee members. From November 1st right through until our special general meeting in 1987 their committee was very active. It met every Tuesday morning at eight o'clock for three hours in Bill Armstrong's office to develop the new by-laws. Other committees worked on house rules and the constitution, and there was one on the amalgamation agreement which was the resolution we had to pass at the two special general meetings.
There's been a tremendous number of hours of work put in by the by laws and amalgamation committees of both clubs.

The Special General Meeting on June 10th, 1987 at the Vancouver Club brought out 381 members, probably the largest the club had experienced since its inception. The Dining Room was packed and many had to stand. This was not an "opinion" meeting or a meeting of information. This was the time when the members would cast their votes for or against amalgamation, a time when they could speak out for or against the proposal. Members, both old and young, expressed their thoughts on the matter with considerable verve, some quite emotionally, both for and against. Then the ballots were cast and the scrutineers made the count. There were 325 in favour, 52 against, and two spoiled. The Vancouver Club had voted almost 86 per cent in favour.

Over in the University Club, Wallace and some of his executive members were waiting for news of the outcome of the voting and then went over to the Vancouver Club to join in the rejoicing of the members there. The next evening University Club members held a similar meeting. "We had three people who spoke out very strongly and very heatedly against the proposal," he said. He didn't argue with those opposing amalgamation and he could appreciate the reasoning of their arguments. As he put it later:

We have an incomparable view but . . . Marathon Realty owns the property right along the waterfront and the day will come when the view will be gone. We were faced with harsh reality. As I put it . . . the moment of truth lay about five years down the road for us.... And I said, 'I'd be quite happy if things could stay the way they are, but I don't see that happening.'
I felt, and others agreed with me, that we had much more in common with the Vancouver Club than we would have with the Terminal City Club [or the Engineers Club], both of whom had approached me regarding amalgamation.

Despite the last verbal arguments against the measure, when the vote was taken over 80 per cent of the ballots favoured the measure.

With both clubs in agreement, the University Club could now proceed with the sale of its property and development rights to Bell Canada Enterprise Development (BCED). This was done on September 25th, and the terms were such that the members were allowed ample time to remain in their premises and make all the innumerable arrangements necessary before moving from the building.

One of the major concerns in both clubs was the ultimate disposition or placement of the two staffs. Again, Edward Wallace describes what happened:

> *[The merger of the two staffs] has been very well handled. We were well served by the fact that George Smith has been secretary-manager of both clubs. He knew intimately almost all of our staff people. We insisted from our side that our members not be sort of fitted in … where there were holes or vacancies but rather that the staffs from the two clubs be pooled, and each position in the new club be considered and the best available be put in that place. The two staffs were treated equally and that has worked very well.*
>
> *We have been well served by our staff. We kept trying to keep them informed and finally, just before Christmas [1987] we were able to tell them pretty much who would be coming over and who would not.… Both clubs have had a very generous settlement arrangement for those who couldn't come.*

There were numerous other settlements and agreements which were negotiated. With amalgamation all members and their guests, male or female, would now enter by the main door. The "ladies' entrance" or "evening entrance" was to be a thing of the past. Women as well as men would serve in the hall porter's office. Special arrangements were made so that ladies could be invited to lunch as guests of members. Those who had been corporate members in the University Club could switch to resident members of the new club, but could not retain corporate status. The governance was to change somewhat, but democracy would be the essence of the voting procedure even if some of the titles changed. The screening of membership applications was to remain, and although sons of members--after screening--need only to pay half the entrance fee, this benefit was to be widened to include potential applicants under 30 years of age. Affiliations made by both clubs had to be reviewed and renegotiated. There were a great many things to be done, but with patience and goodwill, all the problems were resolved as both clubs reached the point when the two officially merged as one. The two resolutions which legally made the two clubs one were accepted unanimously at

Special General Meetings of both clubs on the 20th and 21st of October 1987. The effective date for amalgamation was December 29th of the same year. To celebrate the union, the Vancouver Club invited University Club members to a reception and buffet on December 8th. Some 400 members from both clubs attended and all judged it to be a very happy affair.

*   *   *   *

There had been a lot of work going on both inside and outside the Vancouver Club building prior to amalgamation. The fourth floor had been completely renovated and on the fifth floor the bedrooms had been greatly improved in anticipation of many out-of-town guests during the Exposition year. During these years, Roy Jessiman acted as liaison between the General Committee (renamed the Board of Directors in 1988) and the architectural firm engaged to oversee the work. As a retired architect he had served for several years on the House Committee, but in 1988 became one of the busiest men in the club. To accommodate an additional 400 or more members in a clubhouse built originally to handle about 600 members meant there was a lot of work to be done, and Jessiman was to do a first rate job under a great deal of pressure overseeing the major renovations.

There was much to do but almost from the outset the planners and the Finance Committee bumped into a problem which was not unlike one of the popular jokes which include the words "I've got good news and I've got bad news." The good news was that the City Planning Department approved the proposed renovations. The bad news was that since the value of the renovations had reached a certain percentage of the assessed value of the building, the club was automatically required to bring the building up to current seismic standards by installing earthquake bracing.

The potential of earthquakes along the Pacific Coast varies from area to area, and earthquake zoning categories can change. Vancouver recently had paid more attention to this potential danger and revised its building codes which affected both old and new structures. To do what the city demanded would cost an estimated $700,000. It had become almost a club tradition that the estimate would not meet the actual cost. Tradition was to triumph again.

The earthquake bracing took the form of installing an "A" frame of eight-inch boxed steel girders stretching from the basement to the roof in four walls of the clubhouse, and an exterior "H" frame on the north wall. It meant drilling and jack-hammering through five floors, ripping out sections of walls and ceilings and, where necessary, altering plumbing and wiring as it was encountered. It was to affect almost every part of the club. At one time, George Smith reported, there were six jack-hammers at work on the same day so that even in the most remote room from the workmen the noise was never absent.

The contractors' schedule was from January 6th to May 13th, although the club was warned there "might" be an overrun of "maybe" two weeks. According to George Smith,

> The contractors had told us that we should be able to continue to use the club during the renovations period--on a limited basis. They would stop working with the noisy equipment over the luncheon period. Of course, this did not work out. It was impossible to remain open. Fortunately we were able to provide limited service to all members within the former University Club building. The Vancouver Club was completely closed down for a two-month period.

In the final plans for renovation and construction there was far more done than making the clubhouse safer against an earthquake. In fact it would be true to say there was more work done on the building in 1988 than there ever had since the building had been erected, and the amount spent would have bought half a dozen clubhouses back in 1913 when it was being built.

To begin, a completely new roof was laid. Additional fire exits and walkways were constructed and there were extensions to some of the private room facilities. Two new service kitchens were built. The old kitchen area was completely redone, and 15 tons of new stainless steel kitchen equipment was installed. Altogether, including the girders in the walls, it was estimated that 70 tons of steel were put into the building. For some members, two new features were most welcome-- the installation of two wheelchair access to washrooms and an electric wheelchair lift at the club entrance. In the basement one improvement made Hans Kummer happy. The wine cellar was expanded to hold hundreds of extra bottles which, in turn, permitted a somewhat wider variety of wines to be stored as well as a greater quantity of stock. The staff quarters in the basement were improved as well.

Probably the greatest interior changes made were on the first and third floor. On the latter, two rooms remained basically unchanged-- the billiard room and the third floor bar. Another large room on that floor, the card room, which had a small room off to one side--a combined Library and Silent Room--underwent major reconstruction. In former years the Card Room, measuring about 25×75 feet, was one of the busiest rooms in the club. This large and gracious room which overlooked Hastings Street, held at least sixteen bridge and cardtables. In the inter-war period and for some time after, the room would be packed with players, many having a light lunch while they played. There were plenty of players in the evening, and not infre-

quently on the weekends. Poker players played games which sometimes would go around the clock, and the amounts of money won and
lost during the time when the Card Room was being put to maximum
use must have run into the hundreds of thousands. In recent decades,
however, fewer and fewer players were using the room and it was
decided to make major changes to it. Most of the space was used to
create a new dining room, now called the UBC Room, presided over
by Assistant Head Waiter Josef Hlavacek. Although it does not
provide the full menu available in the main dining room, it provides a
gracious setting for luncheons and, of course, it can be used in the
evening for full dinner service if necessary.

What about the card players? During the summer of 1987 they
were asked to use the Gun Room. Perhaps an English guest peeking
into this room and seeing men playing cards surrounded by display
cases of old Colt revolvers might have thought that he was getting a
glimpse of the "Old West"! Later the card tables were taken back to
the third floor and placed in the new Card Room. It used to be part of
the original Card Room but some years previously it had been converted into a Grill Room. The latter had been popular for several years
but its popularity waned and it had closed down.

There were other changes to the Card Room as well. Although
most of it was renovated to create the UBC Room, about one-third of
it was made into another private dining room, and what had been the
Silent Room and Library was converted into a reception room.
Shelves of books were taken down to the Gun Room and the latter
became a sort of all purpose lounge and reading room.

The main Dining Room was not touched during this period of
major reconstruction. There would have been a major revolt if anyone
had suggested it. The Blue Room, however, did undergo some slight
conversion. Half of it reverted to its original use, a dining room, but
this time it was to be used for luncheons where members could invite
ladies.

With the Blue Room no longer available as a mixed reception
area for evening dining, where were they to meet? Roy Jessiman, who
had made a thorough study of the club, described the solution to the
problem just before the work started on it.

*This room [the Reading Room on the first floor] is one of the
more handsome rooms in the club. There has been quite a bit of
controversy about this room. My utilization studies and recommendation was that this has been the potential of a very handsome lounge. This has all sorts of connotations. What do you
mean by lounge? You mean ladies would be allowed in here? That
caused a few feathers to fly! I knew it was being under-utilized.*

We had to look at it in terms of the additional numbers we were going to get. . . . I used to do a periodic check [and] at any one time you might get six, or at the most eight, people in this room, either reading or snoozing behind their papers. . . . The directors felt that a compromise had to be reached. It will stay as a reading room during the day but in the evening it will become a mixed lounge.

There were other alterations on the first floor as well. A new bar was added between the Gun Room and the Reading Room, one which could serve patrons of both. In a modified way, this almost marked a return to the original plan of the clubhouse when the first floor bar used to be one of the most frequently used bars prior to 1928. The lobby itself was enlarged to provide a new ladies washroom and cloakroom, and even before the major renovations, the Secretary-Manager's office--the old "Strangers' Room"--was divided to provide space so that his secretary could be next to him.

During the peak of the conversion period some 75 tradesmen were working on the site. The total labour used during the period from January 6th to June 6th, 1988 was estimated at about 26,000 man hours. The total bill for the complete renovation work during the year came to a bit more than two and a half million dollars.

Perhaps one of the most pleasant results of this major reconstruction was that, when the members returned that summer to re-occupy the club, they found that the ambience of the club had changed very little. Great care had been taken to restore what had to be ripped apart. Where there was something new, the panelled walls and subdued lighting, the carpets and drapes, the furniture and decor, were all selected and installed to blend into what had existed before. Roy Jessiman and the House Committee had done a superb job and the newly appointed president and vice-president, Hu Chapman and Ed Wallace, were more than pleased to see the members of the amalgamated club settle in comfortably once the tradesmen moved out.

There was one benefit the year brought to club members which was not part of the building plans or even the building. When the original clubhouse was built it contained a bowling alley and, outside, there was a squash and tennis court. The new club had no such amenities. As early as 1960 various suggestions were made respecting the building of some sort of "health" or "exercise" room in the club, but other more pressing demands, together with the greater availability of these fitness facilities in downtown Vancouver, precluded the construction of one in the club. However, while the members were waiting to re-enter the club in the summer of 1988, arrangements were made for members to use the Impco Health and Fitness Centre on the lower floor of the BCED (formerly Daon) Building next door. The

Centre contained everything most members wanted.

There was an extension of the number of clubs with which the Vancouver Club was affiliated. By July, 1988 arrangements had been made for affiliation with 52 other clubs around the world. Eighteen of these are in Canada, eleven in Great Britain, five in South Africa, four in Australia, New Zealand and in the United States, and one in Hong Kong, Ireland, Malaysia, Singapore, Sweden and Japan. Here, again, is a reflection of the tremendous amount of travelling by club members, both for business and pleasure.

An inevitable change has been the turnover in membership, but a particular loss in 1988 was the death of Air Vice Marshal K. G. Nairn. He was one of the few members who was acquainted with many of the club's original founders. He had joined in 1922 and his fondness of the club and the friends he made in it are well and clearly expressed in a taped interview in the club's archives. There is only one member who can claim a longer relationship--though not membership. Major-General H. F. G. Letson, a member since 1929 (the same year Prentice Bloedel joined) can remember going to the old club house as a young boy, invited there to attend a Children's Party which the General Committee used to host in the Christmas Season. These are the only two members still on the club's "List of Members, 1988" who joined in the 1920's. There are a few more who can claim membership in the 1930's: the Honourable A. Bruce Robertson (1933), George Milburn and A. D. Lauder (1934), David R. Blair (1935), H. R. Malkin and F. C. Sweet (1936), and the Honourable J.V. Clyne and Ron Wilson (1939). All the rest are newcomers.

*   *   *   *

In the Spring of 1889 a number of gentlemen in Vancouver decided to form a club. Even before they built a clubhouse or even united formally and legally to establish a club, they decided to come together and have a sumptuous dinner, to enjoy the good fellowship of friends and probably to engage in more serious talk over dinner about the best way to go about forming the sort of club they would like to see in the still young and raw city of Vancouver. The result of their vision has been the topic of this book. Their persistence in the face of adversity during the early years led to a firm foundation being laid in 1893, the club's official hundredth birthday. During the century which followed the club has been like a second home to its members, and that is what it was intended to be in the first place. That continues to be its purpose today and, one hopes, for the next century to come.

CHAPTER X

THE STAFF

In many ways a good club may be compared to a good marriage; that is, there should be a warm relationship between the two groups who are involved in the smooth running and functioning of the institution--the members and the staff. From time to time there may be certain strains and complaints but, in general if there is goodwill and understanding on both sides, together with a willingness to compromise and understand the other's point of view, the relationship should be long-lasting and based on mutual respect.

The present-day members appreciate the staff at the Vancouver Club and the professional way they perform their duties. One member, who for several months in 1987 was the unpaid acting secretary manager, was in a special position to observe the staff. One day, when talking to the club president, he said:

> *Hu . . . what the hell have we got in the club? . . . Really all we've got is a good dining room and a magnificent staff who, for some unknown reason, enjoy making our lunch and our dinner pleasant. They do not feel diminished to be "servants" at all. They are proud of it. They do it well and they just love to see that you enjoy yourself. They make an effort and it rubs your ego the right way. When you walk in, any of the old ones can call 95% of the members by name. So you walk in and they say, "Good morning, Mr. Orr." And if your wife is there--"My, it's nice to see you, Mrs. Orr."*
> *I think it's the staff that makes the club, I really do.*

Another member, who has been with the club over forty years, had this comment on the staff:

> *They're absolutely magnificent. They are so well trained. New staff members know new members' names in no time flat, it seems to me. Not only do they know your name, they know what you like and what you don't like, and they make a point of knowing it. This makes the club a very attractive place.*

An honorary member since 1945 reflected on his relationship with the staff in these terms:

> *At Christmas time one gets a little card with all the employee information on it--those who have retired, their years of service and those who are presently serving, . . . goodness gracious, some have been there practically all their lives. They're loyal, dedicated people. They have maintained very high standards in the club in their years of service. We are all used to those standards and accept them as part of the course which makes the club such an outstanding, distinctive place and such a pleasure to be in.*

Opinions such as these are common, and they refer primarily to those employees with whom they are most frequently in contact--those in the dining room, the bar and the hall porter's office. There are almost as many again who work behind the scenes to ensure the comfort of the members. All contribute in their own way, and the club has been fortunate in having enjoyed the service of so many first rate men and women for almost a century.

Not too much is known about the number and classes of employees who served in the old club house. Occasionally references are made

—" I'm SORRY MADAM,— he's just LEFT the CLUB"!

—WITH BEST WISHES AND DEEPEST
GRATITUDE TO THE VANCOUVER CLUB
From J.E.Broome
CAPT.R.N., HMS "BEGUM" DEC/44.

*A wartime R. N. officer, guest of
the Club, expressed his appreciation
and in doing so fixed permanently
in many members' memories this
familiar picture of R. F. Pyne, who
for thirty years until he retired
at 79, was helpful to members.*

in the minutes to them, and they reflect something of the flavour and attitudes of the time. Many of them lived in the club house itself--a situation which continued into the 1920s. It was common for the club secretary to live in as well.

Some of the Committee Minutes speak for themselves. In 1902, for example, the club secretary was given permission to employ Japanese servants, "if necessary." In the same year a Hall Porter was hired, possibly the first, since the secretary was ordered ". . . to have the needful alterations made for his accommodation. . . ." After being there for five years this gentleman asked for a raise of $5.00 per month--which he did not receive. The club's employees were not unionized.

From an early date the club was faced with the problem of retaining good and ambitious employees, especially in an era of economic growth and expansion. One example of this occurred at the turn of the century. A number of club members were senior executives with the Canadian Pacific Railway. One, G. McL. Brown, evidently appreciated the capability of the club steward and in 1902 offered him the position of managing the C.P.R. hotel in Field, B.C. The steward accepted, and when word of this got around, the committee sent a letter to Brown requesting ". . . some explanation of your conduct in the manner in which you induced the Steward . . . to leave without previously ascertaining whether such action would not prove detrimental to the interests of the Club." Mr. Brown replied rather tartly, writing in part: ". . . business must at all times take precedence when the duties to the employers and the Club conflict." Despite the power wielded in Vancouver by the C.P.R. at this time, the reaction of the committee was swift and blunt. In replying to this unsatisfactory explanation the committee stated:

> *This view of a member's relationship to his Club is entirely erroneous. A member is elected as a private individual and not as an employee or representative of any one or any company. A Club cannot be looked upon as an 'open market', a labour bureau or ordinary place of business, but on the contrary is a private house.*

The letter went on to say that if Brown had approached the committee beforehand they might have agreed to the steward leaving, but it was for the committee to decide. Further, they requested Brown to write a letter of regret and assurance that his action would not be repeated.

Although Brown's reply is not on record, the committee decided to make sure there would not be a repetition of the incident. On 11 March 1903, at the Annual General Meeting, the following new rule was added to the constitution: "No member shall engage or take into his employ any servant of the Club without the consent of the Committee until such servant shall have left the Club employ at least three months." It is reasonable to suppose that the steward left the club not only for a higher position but for better pay as well.

Finding extra rooms for the servants as club membership expanded, as well as coping with slowly increasing salaries, was a constant problem. Early in 1908 consideration was given to raising the housekeeper's wages to $40. per month. Four years later her salary had risen to $55. In 1909 the secretary was empowered to increase the salaries of the bar tenders to $75. and of the waiters to $50. By 1910 the dining room steward had his wages upped to $125. per month. Two

Hans Kummer, Assistant Manager,
at the Christmas Buffet, December
1988.

Michael Sikorra, Maitre d'Hotel,
(with son Robin).

years earlier the club decided to engage a chef and the secretary was told to write the Superintendent of the P. and O. Co. for assistance in selecting one. This important gentleman was to be offered a salary of $140. per month, but his "travelling expenses [to the Club] were to be deducted by degree from his salary until paid for." This chef, incidentally, came from London. Thirteen years later a new chef, E. C. R. Cocks, was hired at the same salary.

Although these salaries may seem low, one must take into consideration the cost of living in Vancouver at the turn of the century. A glance through the "Daily News Advertiser" early in 1901 reveals that the Palace Clothing House on Cordova Street had a sale. Men's socks, regularly fifteen cents, were selling for five cents; a ten-cent hand-kerchief was on sale for two cents and a man's cotton night shirt was marked down from one dollar to fifty cents. A fancy tweed suit, regularly $8.50, was going for $4.90. One could get a dozen white and gold cups and saucers made of the "best English China" for $1.50, attend a Victoria Opera House performance for as little as twenty-five cents, or buy a pair of white wool blankets for $1.50. Mr. R. Byron Johnson (incidentally a club member), who was in real estate, was advertising a house for sale on Cardero Street for $1,785, while one of his competitors had a seven-roomed house on Richards Street for only $950. Even four years later one could buy a nine-roomed house on a lot and a half on Burrard Street near Davie for $3,400. And as a final example of prices and wages, the "Daily News Advertiser" itself would be delivered daily for only fifty cents a month.

Despite these comparatively low costs, wages at the club were not particularly high, and wages paid to Japanese and Chinese staff were generally lower than that paid to what was termed white labour. During the Great War when a labour shortage began to develop and the cost of living went up it became necessary to increase the wages of the Chinese help. "Also," the Secretary noted in the Minutes of the General Committee, "in view of the fact that there was a tendency among some of the Club's permanent employees to seek more remunerative employment, it would be necessary to consider a revision of the scale of wages as occasion may arise in order that the present standard of efficiency may be maintained." Among those listed receiving increases in pay a few months later were the "Japanese Boys," as well as I. M. McAucliffe (Steward), R. W. Catton (Head Waiter), P. Worrall (Billiard Marker), P. Howard (Bartender) and H. Holton (Receiver).

The Japanese boys ran the elevators and acted as bellboys. They occupied one or two rooms in the basement when the new club was built and, as with most teenagers, now and then got a little out of hand. This prompted the committee to pass a motion in 1920 that "in order to have the boys' rooms under proper surveillance, it was considered necessary that the Secretary shall have access to all parts of the Club at any time for inspection."

Aside from wages, the club also had to pay for liveries. In 1919, the full uniform for the Hall Porter was estimated at $65, the same as that for the Billiard Marker. The uniform for the Bellboys and Ele-vator Boys cost about $50. No estimate is available for the waiters' uniforms but apparently the club paid only for the trousers and instructions stated that they must wear white coats at all times. One can assume that one of the more expensive uniforms the club had to purchase was for the doorman, hired in 1925, who had to work both inside and outside the club.

During the course of the Great War, resident membership slipped from a total of 401 to 310, with a peak of 90 members at one point being on active service. In the decade after the war, membership bounced back to the pre-war level and by the end of the 1920's it had topped the 500 mark. This, of course, had its impact on the staff. In 1919, following a reduction of staff in wartime, half a dozen additional employees were hired which added about $4,000 to the club's payroll. In the early 1920's, wages increased slowly also. By 1922, for example, the Steward was earning $175 monthly, the Head Waiter $120 and the Assistant Head Waiter $85. A decade later wages had increased further, and a random sample of the monthly wages of some of the forty-eight employees of the club is revealing.

Secretary	$275.00	Waiter	$50.00
Steward	$250.00	Bar Steward	$75.00
Chef	$200.00	Cleaner	$50.00
Head Waiter	$140.00	Storekeeper	$90.00
Stenographer	$110.00	Housemaid	$50.00
Head Bar Steward	$100.00	Bellboy	$50.00
Hall Porter	$ 90.00	Kitchen Man	$50.00

By 1932, however, the country was in the grip of a paralyzing depression. Club resident membership was falling and the club had just faced two yearly deficits of about $10,000 and $11,000 which had to be addressed. As a result the House and Finance Committee suggested a cut in wages of up to 20 per cent for those earning over $100 but much less for those earning less than that amount. These cuts were to be temporary and it was resolved "that wages be restored to the former scale as soon as conditions warrant the change." The club was able to start restoring some of the cuts by 1934, but it was not until early in 1937 that all wages were restored to their previous level.

From the beginning there was no pension plan for the club's employees, a situation which was quite common with most of the Canadian workforce at the time. It was not that club members were indifferent to the idea. Indeed, even during the Depression, to quote part of the minutes of the General Committee,

> . . . various schemes were proposed periodically with respect to providing a pension for the employees. However, the financial difficulties of the times precluded it. Even as late as October22nd, 1940 there was a general discussion in the General Committee regarding the proposed scheme for the Club employees and it was then resolved 'that having regard to the present condition and the

general uncertainty prevading on account of the war, the question
of adopting a pension scheme be left in abeyance for considera-
tion at a later date.'

Although a Group Insurance Plan covering death and disability
had been instituted in 1931, and a Staff Health Insurance Fund
established in 1930, it was pretty well left up to the individual
employee to make provision for his or her retirement years. Some
employees, of course, worked only part-time at the club and might
earn extra money at other jobs even though the job situation was very
tight. Overtime work might provide a few extra dollars, and it was not
uncommon for club members to hire bartenders and waiters to serve at
private parties at their homes. If a member was planning a major
dinner at his home, he could usually find an off-duty cook from the
club to prepare the meal. Aside from these extra jobs, employees
looked forward to the Christmas bonus to which all members contributed in December. This was divided among the staff according to rank
and, in a way, it helped to make up for the no tipping policy which had
been instituted in the club from the beginning and which is still in
force.

Tivadar (Ted) Simon, Head Bar Steward, and John Bratus, bar steward, at the third
floor bar, (known as Bar 3).

We can get a glimpse of a few of the club's employees in the early period. Mr. R. Catton, for example, came to the club in 1913. Born in England, his father had died at the age of thirty–five, leaving his wife and four small boys to fend for themselves. Young Catton started work when he was nine, was self–educated, and in time began to work in the catering business. At one point he helped cater to the group that organized the first London to Brighton automobile race. After working at one or two of the older London clubs he was persuaded to come to the Vancouver Club, following a stint in the Garrison Club in Quebec. He was to serve the club for over thirty years, primarily as Head Waiter.

Although earning a modest salary, Catton was determined to own property of his own. As a result, according to his son (now a member of the club):

> . . . in 1917 he moved to Burnaby which, at that time, was like a garden municipality, very undeveloped, a lot of it under quite heavy trees. He bought ten acres of land which, in due course, were cleared and he set up a little mixed farm which was his hobby all though his life. We maintained 400 chickens, had half an acre in raspberries, grew all the winter food for the chickens, had 20 fruit trees. We were self-sufficient on that property. We sold eggs to the Vancouver Club and to the members . . . that was the nature of the hobby which was very successful, really; out of that he built five houses . . . on the property and had quite a success.

There is a fair probability that, during the Depression, Catton was more financially secure, in a small way, than some of the members. Catton's son remembers coming to the club to wait for his father on a Saturday. He loved to visit the boiler room where the engineers kept the coal–fired furnace highly polished. He was allowed into the kitchen where, as he recalls,

> I knew all the kitchen crew. They were mostly Chinese at that time. [My father] was responsible for hiring a lot of the people in the dining room and the bars. They were very largely an English crew because he leaned towards Englishmen at the time, and there were some people like Fitchett, Teddy Bush and Arthur Hull [whom I knew].

Arthur Hull and George Cave were two employees who were to have 43 and 42 years of service with the club when they retired in 1968. Cave, a Yorkshireman, came to Canada in 1923. After trying a variety of jobs he eventually was hired by the club as a busboy in the dining room and eventually became head waiter. Arthur Hull, born in London, left England for Saskatchewan to homestead with his brothers.

In the mid–1920s, like Cave, he, too, tried a succession of jobs and when advised of a job opening at the club he applied and became a barman and valet. At that time the fourth and fifth floors contained two dozen bedrooms, most of which were constantly occupied either by members or occasional visitors. "I would see if their clothes needed seeing to," Hull recalls, "and then I would go down and work in the bar for the rest of the day."

Listening to these two men reminisce brings back something of the flavour of the club in the interwar years. When hired, both men were given rooms in the basement which helped with the wages. Each had a small cubicle with rather Spartan furnishing, a change of bed linen and towels, and of course ate in the staff quarters. Living in the basement lasted only a few years until the General Committee decided to do away with the system.

When they were there, up until the Second World War, it was quite common for club members to pay for their meals or drinks either by signing chits or cards, as is done now, or by using "club money." The latter consisted of a small booklet of printed tickets, each worth five, ten or twenty-five cents, and each about the size of a postage stamp. The club's crest was printed in the centre of each ticket as was the denomination . Packets of tickets could be purchased at the club, and arrangements were made with several other Vancouver clubs for an "exchange of tickets." This was particularly useful when a member belonged to several clubs and could use the same tickets to pay at any one of them.

When Hull first arrived, the present Gun Room was the main bar. There were only a few tables and lockers lined the walls. Eventually drinking spread into connecting rooms until in the late 1920's the third floor bar was expanded. One member Hull remembers was F. W. Peters, a senior executive in the Canadian Pacific Railway and one-time president of the club. He used to take a number of members to the Cariboo country in his private railway coach, and they would return with numerous boxes of duck, geese, etc. and bring these to the club to be defeathered, frozen and later eaten. "He would come into the bar and order a Collins," Hull relates. "In those days you made each one with fresh lemon, gin and soda. He would get a spoon and stir it up and up and every time it would spill over the floor. He liked it but his whiskers would get in it. He was a nice old boy."

Another member Hull remembers well was Sir George Bury, who is mentioned elsewhere in this book. Hull recalls that Bury, "dressed up like a little soldier" used to sit at the round table in the third floor bar with some of his friends. Sometimes he would show Hull the diamond–studded cigar case he received from Czar Nicholas II of Russia. Cave remembered Bury also. "He told me the story," he said, "of when he went to London where he always had his shirts made. He went to a store and they fetched out bolts and bolts of material. He didn't want any of them. 'That's what I want, up there on the shelf.' 'But, Sir George, that's pyjama material.' 'I don't give a damn if it is,' he said, 'that's what I want.''' Sir George had a mind of his own.

When Cave started working in the dining room he began to notice some characteristics of certain members. At that time, incidentally, the hardwood floor of the dining room was bare except for three strips of carpets running up the centre and either side. One member Cave remembers was B. T. Rogers, the sugar man.

He had "his" own table, "his" own seat, and if any stranger or new member came and sat in that seat he would walk around the table and stand and look at them all the time. They would get so embarrassed that they would move to another table and then Mr. Rogers would go and sit down.

Then there was Mr. Elliott. He used to come in the dining room, sit down and jump up and say, 'Give me another chair. This is a hot seat. Someone has sat in it. Get me a cold chair.'

I had a couple of tables with members who routinely sat there and I got to know their habits. I used to look at what was on the menu and guess if Mr. So-and-So came in I would give them this or that. Sometimes they would come in and wouldn't order--they were talking and once I just put in front of them what I thought they would like and they would look and start eating. I had one member come in, Mr. Molson, talking to another man. I gave him what I knew he would like. Later he called me over and said: 'I've been sitting here for half an hour and nobody's taken my order and I'm not going to stay any longer.' And I said: 'Mr. Molson, you have had your lunch.' 'Oh, what did I have?'

And then there was another member who, when he was dining, would jump up and raise the roof if anyone touched his chair when he was passing his table.

I remember, too, a stout elderly waiter named George Moore who used to gamble on the horses and also took bets from some of the members. On one occasion he was arrested for gambling and on being fined by the judge, a club member, said 'Take it out of what you owe me.'

Cave and Hull continued to serve at the club during the "Roaring Twenties," through the "Dirty Thirties" and into the wartime years. Both got better paying jobs for a few years as the war brought slightly higher wages and better opportunities outside the club, but they returned to serve for another two decades after the war.

The war brought with it a number of problems both for the staff and the club. One curious incident occurred in 1939. In August of that year a member wrote to the General Committee regarding the employment of Japanese servants. His letter is not in the club archives. In any event, on 26 September the General Committee passed a resolution: "That all Japanese employees be immediately notified in writing that their services be dispensed with as of October 31 next, and that those Japanese employees who have sleeping accommodation in the club be notified that they must vacate at the same time on September 30 next." Although there is no reason given for this motion, there was a considerable reaction to it in the club. Seventy members protested and as a result a ballot on the question was sent to all resident members. Of 394 members voting, 228 disapproved the committee's action--a rare occurence in the club's history--and as a result the Japanese-Canadian employees remained.

Following the Japanese attack on Pearl Harbour on 7 December 1941, it was decided "in view of the changed war conditions" that all the club's Japanese employees should be dismissed and one month's wages given in lieu of notice. At the same time the club secretary was authorized "to convey the committee's regret at the need for this action, and also appreciation of their services during the time of their employment." This action by the club was similar to what was taking place in many other parts of the city and the province. Japanese-Canadians were caught in a situation over which they had no control and so high was the feeling against them at the time that they were even refused permission to join the armed forces to show their patriotism to Canada. Early in 1942 most were forced to leave the coastal cities and move inland.

The wartime years brought with them some disruption among the staff. The combination of more, better-paying jobs in war industries together with the government's clamp-down on increases in wages led to the first work-stoppage ever experienced among the luncheon waiters early in September 1941. The wage scale of these men was not high, and eventually a raise of $1.75 for service during the meal was accepted. In 1942 an unusual and disagreeable event occurred when the Chief Steward was dismissed. From the beginning, one of the rules of the club was that no gratuities be paid to any members of the staff. Early in 1942 a member complained of the special attention being paid to a particular group in the dining room and claimed, also, that he had seen money passed to the Chief Steward. This was a serious charge and led to a full scale investigation which resulted in his dismissal. He had held his position for 21 years and he had been appointed to replace a Chief Steward who had been dismissed for drinking on the job.

Although staff wages crept up slowly during the wartime years, a major advance was made when the General Committee decided to establish an "Employees Retiring Allowance Fund" in 1943. All resident, country and imperial members were to be assessed five dollars each year to create the fund which was to be looked after by a committee of three members. The fund was to be used solely for staff pensions and could be contributed to through the club sweepstakes, Christmas donations and other sources. Retiring allowances were to be made "at the discretion of the Committee."

From the staff's point of view, this was an initial good start, but to look ahead, it was only a first step. It was intended for long service employees, and since the pensions were low, the club tended to retain the services of older employees well beyond the normal retirement age. In 1960, for example, a survey of the 62 employees was made and and it was found that twenty were 60 years or older, and ten of that number were seventy years or older. The oldest employee that year was Wong Chew who was 81 years.

The Pension Fund, although carefully invested, grew slowly. By 1956 it had reached $45,000. About $5,500 was being contributed to it each year from members' assessments and certain amounts from the club sweepstakes. Periodically the committee would authorize special payments into it. But annual pensions were costing $6,600 each year and, moreover, the number of permanent and casual employees was increasing steadily until 1963 when it reached a peak of 89. In 1964 the General Committee decided that the retirement age for all employees should be 65 and this, if anything, put additional pressure on the club to bring the pension plan up-to-date. In October 1968 an Extraordinary General Meeting was held to resolve the matter. As the notice of the meeting stated:

> *Some twenty-five years ago the members decided to assess themselves $5.00 annually to take care of staff benefits, especially retirement. Since 1943 and earlier a percentage of club pools has gone to the staff fund; interest on a modest accumulation of capital has also augmented the fund available; but, generally speaking, we have not kept abreast of the times, as anyone conversant with employee compensation and inflation will quickly discern. The loyalty of our employees demands that we bring ourselves up-to-date.*

The pension plan accepted was basically one controlled by the General Committee with the benefit of professional advice. Employees made no contributions. It did have the benefit of flexibility which permitted members to ease themselves into any other plan according to the time and circumstances. However, the plan was not good enough. It was underfunded, no provisions were made for payment to wives after an employee's death, and increases to pensions to cover

Ed Wallace, last president of The University Club of Vancouver: Hu Chapman, first president of the unified Vancouver Club.

inflation placed increasing pressure on the funds and the number of pensioned employees kept increasing. By 1978 members' annual contribution to the fund had increased to $40. However, it was not until five years later that the club's staff retirement fund was superseded by a Registered Retirement Pension Plan which satisfied everyone. As the club's annual report summarized it: "This formalizes our arrangements with the staff, allows the pensioner to claim up to $1000 per annum pension deduction from their income for tax purposes and allows us to provide, on an actuarially sound and consistent basis, the appropriate funding for present and future pensions."

In the post-war decades there were quite a number of old time members of the staff who retired after long service with the club. P. F. Pyne, the hall porter, retired in 1949, aged 77, after 30 years of service. William M. Bugeden, aged 66, retired the same year with 33 years of service. Mrs. C. McCollam, the housekeeper, retired in 1955 having started in the club as a maid in 1920, and five years later, after 33 years of service as a receiver and storekeeper, Jack Saunders retired also. A lady who had worked "behind the scenes" as an accountant, Mrs. Edna Smith, retired in 1960 after 32 years of service. She was particularly missed as she was probably the only person in the office who could decipher members' signatures on their order cards. In order to identify the cards from the dining room and bar, members were later requested to print their names on their cards. Philip Vignal, who took over as Chief Steward in 1942, retired in 1961, and the billiard marker, Sid Boys, who had been with the club for 26 years, retired in 1965 at the age of 78.

It was in 1965 the General Committee decided that something should be done to recognize those staff members with 25 years or more service to their credit and those pensioners who had served the same length of time. Suitably engraved gold watches or sterling silver trays were suggested and in 1966 arrangments were made that

> *after the club's business had been [completed] at the Annual General Meeting held on March 9, 1966, the president and chairman, T. E. Ladner, would present to six active and four retired employees, with a total of 352 years of service behind them, inscribed watches as a token of the club's deeply felt appreciation for service well rendered.*
>
> *The six active employees were: George T. Cave (41), head waiter; Arthur Hull (41), head barman; Scotty Young (41), master carver; Ted Bush (39), head hall porter; Bert Ainge (38), bar steward; Charlie Hardcastle (29), head waiter; and the four retired were Arnie Gremmell (38) dining room steward; Christine McCollam (36), house- keeper; Jack Saunders (33), storekeeper and Sid Boys (26), billiard marker.*

This event has now become a tradition in the club.

Not all gifts to the staff were made publicly. In 1975, for example, it was reported at a meeting of the General Committee

> *That an unnamed club member had approached past-president P. R. Brissenden with a request that he be allowed to make a bequest in his will to all club staff members and pensioners. He did not particularly want it to go into the staff pension fund. The sum would be in excess of $5,000. Mr. Brissenden wanted to know*

George Smith, first Secretary-Manager of the unified Vancouver Club.

*if the Committee would agree to this bequest provided that the
Committee was empowered to organize the distribution as they
saw fit. [The] proposal was unanimously accepted.*

The General Committee itself, incidentally, sometimes saw fit to
be generous to a staff member. For example in April 1980, the club's
Garde Manger, Hiro Yoshinaga, was given $2,000 to attend the
Frankfort Culinary Olympics in October as part of a ten–man team
being sent by the B.C. Culinary Olympic Committee. While there he
won a gold medal, to the delight of all the members, and the team
manager wrote that Yoshinaga "is one of the best cold kitchen chefs in
the province."

So far little has been said about the senior employee of the club, the gentleman who is responsible--under the direction of the General Committee--for all members of the staff, either directly or indirectly. Working in close cooperation with the chef, the chief steward (or catering manager), the housekeeper and one or two other senior staff members, the secretary (or secretary-manager as he is now called) occupies a key position in the smooth functioning of the club. He holds a particular position of trust. He attends all the meetings of the General Committee and is responsible for recording committee minutes. He is the official correspondent of the club, oversees all club business, carries out the wishes of the General Committee and has a very special relationship with members.

In the early decades of the club life it was not uncommon for the secretary to be a club member. An example was a gentleman, very definitely of Scots ancestry, named McIver McIver-Campbell. He was hired in 1904 at a salary of $100 per month. By the time he resigned in 1907 the club had increased his salary to $150. His place was taken by B. M. Humble who had previously worked at the St. James's Club in Montreal. He was offered $150 per month plus room and board at the club. He must have found the volume of work heavy and one of the things he arranged six months after his arrival was to get an office assistant. His office hours were from 9:00 a.m. to 6:30 p.m. every day except Sunday and he could anticipate an annual two-week vacation. In 1908 he asked for a raise but he was told the club could not afford to pay him more than $1800 per year, especially as he was also getting room and board as well as an assistant.

Mr. Humble handed in his resignation and he was replaced by H. B. Helbert. He was to get $100, stay at the club, and he too was allowed to have a clerical assistant (L. K. Williams) at $65. per month. Mr. Helbert lasted less than a year. He had been requested to post bond and ultimately was unable to do so. An examination of the books resulted in the club prosecuting him for misappropriation of funds.

Helbert was replaced by Major A. B. Baker, DSO in April 1909. One of the first things he did was to fire the bookkeeper whom he replaced by hiring a gentleman who was to serve the club for many years, H. A. Acton. Little is known about Major Baker. He was given permission to play billiards and squash in June, and five months later he was asked to resign forthwith. Evidently there was a deficiency in the secretary's accounts. Fortunately it was only $293 and, since he had been bonded, the club was reimbursed.

But what about Helbert? It took a while, but in time it was found he had swindled the club of $2594.03. This may not seem like a very large sum, but one must multiply that amount by twenty to appreciate

Roland (Roly) Sauviat, Head Hall Porter, at his desk at the entrance of the club.

its present day value. When the extent of the swindle was appreciated the club president who had hired Helbert, J. G. Woods and his vice-president, G. L. Smellie, made out a cheque for the amount and sent it to the club with the request that it be used to cover the amount misappropriated. This gesture speaks volumes and needs no elaboration. The General Committee, however, did not feel that these two gentlemen should bear any burden of guilt for hiring Helbert and returned the cheque to them.

The club was fortunate to have Mr. P. McNaughton as its secretary for the next several years. When he left in 1913, he was thanked for his "integrity, efficiency and unfailing courtesy" and was granted two months leave with pay. As usual, Acton filled in the post while the General Committee looked for a replacement. After interviewing one applicant, who demanded a long term contract the committee was unwilling to grant, the committee evidently approached B. M. Humble again. He was agreeable to take the position on the following terms: his title was to be secretary-manager and his salary would be $400 a month if he lived outside the club. He was to have some entertainment expenses, complete and absolute control over the staff and the backing of the club president and General Committee in carrying out his duties. By this time the new clubhouse was nearing completion and the sooner a secretary manager was appointed the better. Despite his demand for twice the amount he had been getting a few years earlier, Humble was found quite acceptable. He decided to live in (using a sitting room, bedroom and bathroom) and accepted $300 per month salary with meals at the club on a two year contract. He was also permitted to purchase club supplies at near cost.

Mr. Humble was on the job for only a week or two when he was given authority to visit Winnipeg, New York, Philadelphia, Minneapolis "and any other points . . . to look into the economic arrangements, systems of payment and service of the principal clubs of those cities." The move into the new club was only months away, and the members wanted their club to be as efficient and as good as any in the country.

When war was declared in 1914 Humble, like many of the members, went overseas and once again Acton became acting secretary–manager, a position he held until 1920 when he was appointed in his own right. Humble returned early in 1919 with the rank of colonel. His position was kept for him but, as the committee minutes record, "he fully realizes, however, the financial condition of the Club and, coupled with the fact that his health is not very good, would prefer to remain free for a time." He stayed at the club for about a month and during that time found other employment. He was married later that year and the last mention of him is a note saying the club sent him a handsome wedding gift.

Space does not permit even a brief sketch of the various secretary- managers who served the club after the Great War. Periodically, as they retired owing to age, illness, or other reasons, Acton would step forward from his main job as chief accountant to fill the post until another man was hired. Acton himself was finally retired in 1945. It was always a difficult task to find a person who had both the ability and tact to fill the position especially, perhaps, when the salary could not compete with those offered in large hotels where similar skills were in demand. As late as 1939 a newly appointed secretary–manager was offered $300 per month with room and board, and when he was replaced a year later the new man was offered $50 per month less. Not until 1954, when Arthur Brown had been secretary for six years, did the salary range reach $7200 per annum. With increasing membership and a larger staff the secretary–manager's task became more demanding. After the Second World War his office was moved from the basement to the main floor, occupying the space formerly known as the Strangers Room. The office staff has increased, word processors have replaced the old typewriters and photo- copying machines now save hours of work which used to be done manually. Despite the modern equipment in the office, the task of the secretary–manager continues to be the same as it was over ninety years ago.

The Second Half Century

By the end of the Second World War the club had been in existence about 52 years. It was middle–aged, or perhaps "mature" would be a better term. After some fifteen years of economic depression and war the club was still carrying on much as before, but the post–war decades were going to witness considerable changes––most of them for the better. Some of pre–war staff were retired and not replaced. Automatic elevators meant an elevator boy was no longer necessary, nor were the half–dozen Japanese messenger boys to be seen in the club. The engineers were let go as heat for the club changed from a coal to an oil–fired furnace and then to steam heat supplied from a source outside the club. To pare expenses the doorman, looking elegant in his many–buttoned maroon coat, was not replaced when he resigned. Valet service was no longer provided as bedrooms became increasingly fewer as they were converted for other purposes. Many of the "old timers" on the staff left the club, but not before they had the opportunity to train and advise the new staff members who replaced them, and they, in turn, made their way up the ladder to head the various divisions today. This might be a good point to look at the staff and their work through their own eyes.

One of the main reasons for the existence of the club is the dining room, and quite naturally the members anticipate good food to be served every day and exceptional meals to be served on special occasions. This places a great deal of responsibility on the chef. During the past few decades, the club has been fortunate to have Ivan Wheatley as its chef and since his service with the club spans some 42 years, one can see some of the changes which have taken place as well as old traditions carried on.

Wheatley had been working on board one of the Union Steamship vessels and was unhappy with the long periods he was away from home. A friend of his family happened to be A. E. Veronneau, the club's chef who had been appointed in September 1946. Wheatley was offered the job of peeling vegetables in the club kitchen, a task he took on in October of the same year. He was to learn to cook by observation and experience, and was to become a master of his craft.

When Wheatley started the kitchen staff consisted of a chef de cuisine, a sous–chef, a butcher, baker, two salad girls, the fry cook and himself. Each had his or her own particular job. For Wheatley it was, as he stated, a case of "on the job training." As he recalled later:

> *It was a case of when there was other work to do, if I was well enough ahead in my own work and there was something else to be done, the Chef would say 'Come and give us a hand here.' So you would go from maybe the vegetables to the butcher shop, bone*

*Urs Gerber, Executive Chef, and Serge L'Ecuyer, Sous-chef, and their fine kitchen
staff in their modern milieu.*

*out some chickens or trim up some meat. . . . I would watch other
people to see how they did things and they would ask for a hand
and I gradually worked into a position where I could handle these
things.*

When he reached the position of sous–chef, Wheatley came more
directly under the supervision of Veronneau. "He did a lot of the
things I should have been doing, but until I gained that knowledge . . .
he would work in along with me." Wheatley continues:

*It didn't seem to take very long. At first I was working on the
breakfast shifts, coming in early in the morning (7:00 a.m.) to
prepare the soups, put the roasts in the oven, and any of the dishes
that were prepared ahead of time I would start them. Then when
the other cooks came in they would take over their priority job
and finish it. I also made sauces and stews and that sort of thing.
At that time . . . not many members came for breakfast––maybe a
dozen or so. Then there was the staff to feed for breakfast––we
had living in engineers, the hall porter, the housekeeper, some
kitchen staff and breakfast waiters.*

Until the practice was stopped over a decade ago, members could bring in duck, partridge, quail and other game to be prepared by one of the kitchen staff. "At one time," Wheatley recalls,

> *. . . it was done during our working hours and then it became too much. We had a butcher who agreed to do these on his afternoon break. . . . He would sit downstairs and pluck these [birds]-- feathers flying around everywhere. He was paid extra for this. At times members would arrange a luncheon or dinner party and send in their birds. We would pluck them and cook them and serve them. Sometimes members would send salmon in to be poached and be prepared for a cold buffet. There wasn't too much in the way of larger game like deer. They would send in a roast or different cuts and have a dinner party with that.*

Sometimes as a special favour the club chef or sous-chef might go to a member's house to help prepare for a special dinner, and now and then he might be asked to prepare the food for a party going fishing. In the immediate post-war era, a member could also ask the kitchen for help in providing for a family picnic. As Wheatley stated:

> *At one time we would set up the cold meats, hams, turkeys and we would have it all pre-sliced and make up salads and all the garnishings that went with it. But now . . . this has been cut back to cooking a ham with slight decoration. We will cook prime ribs or roast sirloin and just send it out in pieces. Occasionally members will ask for it sliced which is no problem to us.*

Among the many things which he did well was a favourite among club members--veal and ham pie. Chef Wheatley believes it was Cornelius Burke who arranged to have it listed on the menu as Ivan's Veal and Ham Pie as a mark of honour, and even today it is not uncommon for a member to telephone and ask if he can have one of Ivan's pies to take away for the weekend. Wheatley was awarded the citation of "Man of the Year" by the British Columbia Chef Association in 1973. One suspects club members would have endorsed that choice every year he was chef de cuisine.

Although some staff work very much "behind the scenes" there are others who come in daily contact with club members and their guests. Those who serve behind the hall porter's desk are typical of the latter. The present hall porter, Roley Sauviat, is a comparative new-comer. Born in Quebec in 1916, he worked as a blacksmith's helper at the Burrard Shipyards during the early part of the war and, to earn a bit more money, he would work in the bar at the Dufferin Hotel on weekends. During the war he went overseas and on his return, as the shipbuilding industry declined, he went full- time into the hotel business, advancing from waiter to assistant manager. When the hotel chain changed hands Roley was looking for a job when the club needed a new hall porter. Roley got the position and was hired by the then secretary-manager, John Chutter, in February 1975. Almost from the first day he enjoyed it. "I think this is one of the best jobs there is," he said. He continued:

> When I first came here somebody remarked: 'Have a nice weekend,' and I nearly fell through the floor. In the hotel business you work ten to thirteen hours a day. They couldn't care less whether you're there next day or not. . . . Over here they care. It's a nice place.

The hall porter is rarely idle and because of the traffic in and out of the main entrance he usually has an assistant during the busy parts of the day. The main telephone exchange is there, and the office acts as a mail and message exchange. The visitors' book and the suggestion book are in the hall porter's care, and so, too, is a modest supply of cigars, cigarettes, liquor, wine and playing cards. In the old days members bought packages of "club money" from him, and since club rules forbid the carrying of briefcases into the building, these are left at the hall porter's office and reclaimed later. He checks on all the magazines and newspapers subscribed to by the club and a number of the latter are returned to his office from the reading room for re-sale to club members who want to keep them permanently.

One of the things the hall porter must do is to keep abreast of what is going on at the club. If the messages or telephone calls are to reach club members promptly the hall porter must know where they can be reached. Some club members, however, prefer **not** to be reached, even by their wives, and leave word to that effect with the hall porter with the result that many a white lie has been told over the telephone. Sometimes a little wifely ingenuity could overcome that obstacle. There is a story told that there were two brothers, both members of the club, one who was always available to answer his wife's call, the other never. If the wife of the latter really wanted to reach him, she would get her sister-in-law to call her husband and have him tell his brother to phone his wife--or else.

While greeting members entering the club, the hall porter also had the responsibility of keeping non-members out, a task recently made easier with the installation of security alarm and television systems. One never knew who would wander in however--salesmen, drunks, tourists, curiosity seekers, cranks, and so forth. One time when Sauviat was away from the desk for only half a minute he returned to find a lady in the vestibule. "What do you think she was doing? She was feeding her baby, and not from a bottle! I said, 'I'm sorry, this is not the place—this isn't a dining room.' She said her baby had been crying, apologized and left.''

Another person, now retired, who used to work at the hall porter's desk was George Symington. He, too, was a watchful guardian of the main entrance, especially on days when the weather was warm and the main door was open. One couldn't leave the front desk for a moment. ''One morning I had to nip up to the kitchen for a second,'' he said, ''and when I came down I found three teenagers walking nearly into the reading room, so I had to turf them out.'' At times certain religious evangelical couples would try to enter the club and convert the inhabitants, and on another occasion Symington recalls ''two beefy young men coming and saying 'could we see the facilities?'—evidently thinking it was a sports club as they had their equipment with them.''

When Symington first started to work at the club he was surprised at the reaction of some of his acquaintances.

> *People asked me if I could get liquor at wholesale prices because I was working there. And someone asked me if I could get them Irish Sweepstake tickets. And people said, 'Please tell me, if you can, everything about silver prices' or 'If you hear any good tips about stockmarket shares will you tell me.' And someone had the nerve to ask me if I could get them a list of names and addresses and phone numbers of the club members.*

Occasionally someone would get into the club on false pretenses. On one Friday evening, for example,

> *A very smartly dressed man arrived in a taxi wearing a tuxedo. He said he had an appointment with a member in Bar Three so naturally Charles sent him up to wait for him. He asked the barman for a drink and was given one. He gave him another drink and, claiming his friend was late, got another. One of the members got a bit suspicious so he rang up the member's home. He was away on business. The 'guest' was shown the door—but that man knew all the moves. He was an artist at it.*

Sometimes there were situations which had to be dealt with which were very unpleasant. Symington recalls two of them.

> *The man working at the hall porter's desk that evening was Bill Bryan. A man came in wearing a sort of zip-up jacket and jeans with a sawn-off shot-gun, and shouts at Bill to give him money. Bill did a very good act. He looked a bit vague and said: 'There's*

> *no money here. All the money has gone up to the office.' The man was nervous. At that time Bar One on the ground floor was being used as a cocktail bar for the ladies because the Blue Room was being re- decorated. Just at that moment, when the young man thought he was going to get tough, Mr. and Mrs. Lundell, the nicest, quietest people you could you could wish to meet, and their guests, came out of the bar and the young man ran for it. The Committee gave Bill a cheque for $100 for his quick thinking.*

Although one of the main duties of the hall porter was to act as a guardian of the main entrance and make sure no one but members and their male guests use that door, there was one occasion when the strict enforcement of the rules was somewhat overdone. Late in 1962 an elderly member in the third floor bar appeared to be in need of a doctor. It was late at night, someone rang the doctor's office and was informed help would be coming. The task was given to a young female doctor. She and her husband had only recently arrived in Vancouver. Her husband described the events which followed.

> *She had a vague idea where West Hastings was. We looked at a city map and I thought 'Oh boy, that's probably a bad part of town. I'd better drive you down.' So we drove down trying to find the address and there was this sort of a big house . . . and we didn't know what it was. She rang the bell at the main door and this fellow in a uniform opened the door and asked her what she wanted. She said: 'I'm Dr. Lau; I've been summoned here to attend an emergency.' The fellow looked at her and said, 'Women are not allowed here.' She said, 'What do you mean? I was called. I'm a doctor. Do you need a doctor or not?' He went back inside to talk to someone else and returned. 'Well, we'll let you in but you have to go through the side door.' So we went to the side door.*
> *By that time I got a little suspicious and she was quite nervous because we didn't know what it was like. I thought it was some kind of a house of ill repute or some gambling casino.*
> *We got to the side door and the man said, 'Come in' so I followed my wife. He said to me, 'You can't come in.' I said, 'I'm her husband and insist I go in as well.' He said, 'No, you can't.' 'Why not?' 'You're not wearing a jacket and tie.' Anyway we went into the lobby. My wife said, 'Where's the patient?' He was upstairs. So she said, 'Let's go,' so she proceeded to walk upstairs and the man cried out, 'You can't go up there. No women are allowed beyond this threshold. You're not allowed up the stairs.'*
> *My wife is Hungarian and quite outspoken. I think she called him something in Hungarian--I don't know exactly what it was. She said 'If you have a patient, let me see him. If I can't go up, bring him down.' So these two men went up, brought the old gentleman*

down and put him on the sofa. She examined him and the out-
come of the examination was that he was suffering from a severe
hangover. Other than that there was nothing wrong with him so
she told these two fellows to take him back upstairs, put him to
bed and let him sleep it off.

Club rules are club rules, even if at times they might seem mysterious to non-members.

In the post-war era, there was probably no one person who brought more improvement to the dining room than John L. New-cliffe. Actually his proper surname was Neuenschwander, but he felt Newcliffe was easier to pronounce. He came to the club as chief steward in 1961, a title which was changed in 1972 to catering manager; and held that position for 22 years.

Newcliffe was born in Switzerland where he was trained in the hotel business. He was a professional and a perfectionist, and his sole purpose was to make the Vancouver Club the best club in Canada. "People took a long time to appreciate John Newcliffe because in his stiff, well-trained and precise way he was difficult to get to know but once you did . . . you appreciated his value. . . ." This opinion, by one member of the club, is reflected by others. A staff member stated that "it was difficult to work under him." "As soon as Mr. Newcliffe came along," a former waiter recalls, "everyone was on guard and nervous. He ran around like a whirlwind and when he disappeared everybody relaxed." He continued:

He had real ability. He used to come into the Dining Room and
say 'Are you all set up?' 'Yes, we are all ready.' 'That table over in
the corner, there is no salt or pepper on it.' He would immediately
pick those things up. 'That tablecloth over there, it is not
straight.' He had an eye for it, and could tell at some distance if a
tablecloth was upside down.

One of the things Newcliffe did was to streamline the organiza-tion and make things more efficient. One man who served under and later replaced him recalls that when he came to the club in 1962, the dining room staff were not professionally trained. Many were old and some were ailing. Moreover there were a number of new restaurants being opened and skilled young waiters were in demand, usually at salaries which the club could not match. Evidently Newcliffe approached the club president, R.M. Hungerford, about the pos-sibility of hiring waitresses. Hungerford was well aware of the prob-lem: "We were hiring men who might make good plumbers but were awful waiters," he remarked later. On the other hand, what would the members say to having waitresses in the dining room?

Actually the idea of hiring waitresses was not a new one. In April

1920 at the Annual General Meeing, a member suggested the club should get female help in the dining room. The secretary was instructed to write some of the clubs in Eastern Canada to find out what experience they had had on the subject and, possibly as a result of their replies, the General Committee decided on the following month that it was inadvisable "to make any changes at present."

Forty-four years later, again at the Annual General Meeting, there was a motion

> . . . *to consider the introduction of a few carefully selected and well-trained middle-aged women as waitresses in the dining room for both luncheon and dinner in the event that currently proposed wage increases do not produce a better type of waiter or bus-boy.*

Even two months later the Committee seemed to be approaching the inevitable with considerable reluctance. It resolved that "at the appropriate time" the secretary and chief steward be authorized to engage two waitresses, a number later increased to four. The first waitresses started to work at the club in November 1964, all of suitable age and experience, and all rather drabbly dressed so as not to excite the members. There were, of course, some complaints--one member telling the Committee that they wouldn't have dared to introduce females if Sir George Bury were still alive. Bury, of course, was a very clubbable member, but with his imagination one wonders just what he might have said. R. M. Hungerford, then club president, said later: "We got a very good type of waitress in there . . . and there were no problems . . ., but God, there were strong objections to it at first."

Newcliffe, having got his waitresses, began to shape them into the mold he wanted. He was not an easy man to please, and there were some tears, but eventually things settled down and the waitresses soon were serving in other parts of the club.

Aside from improving both the service and variety in menus, et cetera in the club, Newcliffe worked to improve wages for his staff and, in particular, he was responsible for bringing in the incentive system. As we have seen, no form of tipping or gratuity is permitted in the club. However, in almost all the city cafes and restaurants waiters depend on tips as part of their income. A known "good tipper" will get preferred service, and naturally the more tables he serves, the more tips the waiter can expect.

To bring something of this incentive system into the club, New-cliffe decided to try something he had known was in operation in Switzerland. Waiters, working on a straight four or eight hour shift with no tipping, were paid their normal salaries plus an additional small amount for each person served, the amount--the equivalent of a tip--being more for dinner than for lunch. In brief, it made the waiters happier, more attentive to latecomers, and led to less complaints when some waiters felt they were being asked to serve more guests than others despite the same wages.

Newcliffe was only 51 years old when he retired in 1983. Aside from his pension he was given a handsome sum in appreciation for his work which was summed up in the club newsletter as follows:

> *He was instrumental in introducing and perfecting a system of food presentation and service in the club of the highest order, [and] was a major factor in the raising of the standard of our club's cuisine and service to one of the highest in Canada.*

Newcliffe was succeeded by Hans Kummer. Also born in Switzerland, Kummer began his apprenticeship in the hotel business when he was not quite sixteen. He was 23 years old when he came to the Vancouver Club to be its banqueting manager in 1962. As the fourth floor of the club was being refurbished and private dining rooms replacing the old bedrooms, he worked for a month or so as a waiter. Comparing the dining room twenty-five years ago, Kummer said:

> *There were double the number of staff in the dining room then. Many of them were elderly waiters, who were ex-stewards from ships. . . .*
> *We had a couple of male nurses from St. Paul's Hospital working here as waiters. One had a permanent leg problem. . . . I've never seen a crew working in a dining room like I've seen here when I started. It was a bit of a shock. They were not professionals, but they were very obedient when it came to looking after the members. But everyone had his own style. There were two head waiters at that time in the dining room, a wine steward and twelve stations. We now have six stations, but we have less business-- about 140 luncheons compared to 180-200 twenty years ago.*

When he was banquet supervisor, Kummer's position was fairly straightforward. The new private dining rooms were proving to be popular and club members found it convenient to have luncheon or dinner parties for guests, business associates, professional groups and others. The food was excellent, the service first class, the ambience very agreeable and the location very convenient. It was Kummer's task to ensure that everything went well from the moment the banquet was ordered until the last guest left the premises.

Sometimes, if things were a bit slow, the headwaiter in the dining room would ask Hans to help him. At that time there was a "no reservations" policy at the club which, for the staff, could create a severe problem. If there was a cocktail party at the club or at a nearby hotel, there might be a sudden large influx of members walking in quite unexpectedly. Thus when the club's headwaiter left and Kummer was asked to take the position, he refused. "It's a disorganized mess," he told Newcliffe, "and I don't want any part of it." On the other hand, Kummer's salary fluctuated with the seasons. In the summer the banquet rooms were only rarely used, and he needed a more stable income. When approached again he agreed to take it on condition that some sort of reservations system be implemented. As he recalled later:

> It took a long time . . . but slowly it got better. I was also given authority to close the door of the dining room to members without reservations if a certain breakpoint capacity we had planned for had been reached. The idea was that we would rather look after 50 people and keep everybody happy than look after 65 and get complaints. It was always difficult to convince the member who came to the door without a reservation that the dining room was closed because, with all those tables, how could you tell him it was closed when the dining room is half filled. That created some ugly confrontations at times.

Kummer succeeded Newcliffe in October 1983, when the latter moved to Morocco to enjoy his retirement. At one time both men, together with a third partner, had pooled their resources to start the William Tell Restaurant. It turned out to be a successful venture with the third partner buying out the other two some years later.

As catering manager, Kummer continues to uphold the standards set by Newcliffe. Although the chef orders the food, Kummer is ultimately responsible for its quality. He has the responsibility for hiring many of the staff, which he usually does in consultation with the chef and head waiter. The chef and catering manager go through gourmet magazines and come up periodically with new dishes which, incidentally, are tested by the Dining Room Committee at their luncheon meetings. He organizes private and club functions requested by members or the General Committee, oversees the menus with the chef, supervises the wine cellar, keeps an eye on the staff, and attends to other managerial matters relating to the efficiency and well being of the club.

When Kummer was promoted, his former position as head waiter was filled by Michael Sikorra. Born in West Berlin in 1949, Sikorra came to Vancouver when he was nineteen to join his brother. He has worked in various jobs, and by following his career over the past twenty years, one can get yet another glimpse of the club as seen through the eyes of an employee.

Sikorra, after a brief time with a construction firm, was looking for work when his brother noted a newspaper advertisement by the Vancouver Club seeking help. Michael's English at the time was poor so his brother telephoned Newcliffe, explaining that his young brother had just arrived, was willing to work but had a problem with the language. Newcliffe accepted him and, since both he and Kummer spoke German, he felt Michael would be suitable. Moreover, New-cliffe preferred to train his staff from the beginning.

For the first few months Sikorra worked as a busboy. As with the waiters they worked five days a week from 11:00 a.m. to 3:00 p.m., then from 6:00 p.m. to 10:00 p.m. Since at that time the club gave full service on Saturdays, there was one day off during the week plus Sundays. In the mid-afternoon break, during the summer, he would hop on his motorcycle and head for the beach. At the time, he recalled later, "I felt it was just great. For me the shift work was just super." Working in the dining room with only a limited amount of English and new to Canadian custom resulted in one humorous incident. "When I was a busboy," Sikorra said,

> *My English was terrible. I was learning as I went along and I just hoped the diners wouldn't talk to me because I only understood half of it. I was running around with my plates and one person called me over and said, 'I would like some hot mustard.' 'Oh,' I said, 'right away.' So I took off, grabbed the mustard, went into the kitchen and said to Sous Chef John Thompson, 'Can you heat the mustard up?' He looked at me and said, 'What?' I said, 'Yes, heat it up.' 'Why?' 'A fellow out there wants some hot mustard.'*
> *In Germany we don't call it hot mustard, we call it* **spicy** *mustard.*
> It caused a great laugh in the kitchen.

By coincidence a German friend whom he had met on the boat coming to Canada had also been hired by the club. He worked as a barman in the lounge in the Blue Room. Sikorra would chat with him and his friend taught him how to mix drinks, take orders and serve them. His friend quit suddenly so, having been a waiter for six months following a three month stint as busboy, Sikorra was promoted to barman working a straight 4:30 p.m. to 11:30 p.m. shift, six days a week.

Serving in the Blue Room acquainted Michael with some of the problems he would encounter later. People who use the club regularly tend to select certain chairs or tables where they like to sit. In time they tend to think of them as "their" tables and resent it if they come and find someone else occupying them. Club rules forbid reserving a specific table, and club members phoning in a reservation frequently expected to get "his" table and expected it to be held for him. Getting to know the members and their tastes and habits takes time and tact. Among other things there are members who know wines and others do not. Sometimes they ask for a nice white or red wine and leave it to the waiter to select it. 'We've got some people,'' Sikorra said, "who don't mind spending $50 or $60 on a bottle of wine and others who would have a heart attack if they were charged that much. It takes a little bit of skill to suggest a wine.''

For a while, following the Saturday closing of the Lounge and Dining Room, Michael worked for a few hours at noon in Bar One on the main floor. It was a busy place and Johnny Derbyshire needed help when an older barman, named Rudi, retired. A regular customer always called out "Hi, Rudi" when he came in and "Bye, Rudi" when he went out even though Sikorra had taken his place. This went on for a long time before he realized that there was a new face behind the bar. Then one day he gave his usual greeting and suddenly realized there was a new face. "Where's Rudi?" he said. Sikorra said, "He's dead." "Oh, my God, I was talking to him just last week"--and it wasn't until that moment he was aware that Rudi had retired two years earlier.

When Sikorra arrived in 1968 to work at the club, the new incentive wage scale was being considered and came into effect on January 1st, 1969. It was brought in, according to the General Committee, "in view of the current wage situation, the cost of living increase since November 1st, 1967 and the continuing difficulty in retaining and recruiting suitable staff for the preparation and service of food.'' Wage increases became an annual affair in the years that followed. In 1973 the club had to take into account the new law which stated the minimum wage must be $2.75 an hour, and the Finance Committee was forced to consider giving merit raises and adjustments due to outside competitive wages. As inflation roared ahead in the mid-1970's, across-the-board wage increases went up to 15% in 1974 and 18% in 1975, but cooled down to between 8% and 11% during the remainder of the decade. Between 1980 and 1985, aside from a sudden lurch of 12% in 1981, it levelled off at 5%-6%.

During this period the overall age of the staff went down as did the number of employees in the club. Automation of some services, as has been seen, accounted for part of the loss of personnel and a more efficient employment of others brought reductions elsewhere. A doorman, R. H. Dowler, hired for a three-hour shift in 1961 was not replaced following his death in 1965. Even though club revenues were going up owing primarily to entrance fees and increased charges, the Finance Committee was not having an easy time making ends meet. All during this period the Committee had been keenly aware that earlier pensions were not sufficient to cover the needs of the older employees and had done their best to increase them yearly as circum-stances would permit. Old Age Benefits from the federal government helped, but club members felt their responsibilities as well.

For almost one hundred years the relationship between members and staff in the Vancouver Club has been exceptionally good. It is probably a truism to say that the better the members get to know the staff as individuals, the happier the relationship will be. Pride in service must be matched by appreciation of the recipients, and if this is continued with the courtesy and respect one expects at the club, the next hundred years should be as pleasant as the last century.

CHAPTER XI

HISTORICAL MISCELLANY

THE CLUB CREST

The origins of the club crest are somewhat of a mystery. Quite possibly it was designed at the time when the club was formed in 1893, but who was responsible for its design we do not know. The first mention of it appears in the club minute book where, on 10 May 1905, there is an entry stating: "The Secretary presented various samples of crockery with prices and was instructed to get a cut of the Club crest from Messrs. Apsley, Pellatt Co. [a London firm] and await the samples now en route before doing anything further."

The club crest was placed on everything where one might expect to see it--club stationery, official notices and bills, bulletin board announcements, invitations, business cards for senior staff members, menus, dining room dishes of all descriptions, club ties, and so forth. In 1927 it was resolved by the General Committee that "in future all

Club linen be crested …," and two years later the Secretary reported to the General Committee that "the Imperial Tobacco Company has consented to put up Millbank cigarettes in a plain package embossed with [the] Club crest." It should be noted, incidentally, that it was one thing for the club to ask a tobacco company to do this sort of thing but it was quite another to have a company attempt to take advantage of its name. Around the turn of the century a member reported seeing in the Hudson Bay Co. a box of cigars called The Vancouver Club. Whether the title was accompanied by the crest is not known, but evidently immediate action was taken and the Vancouver Club cigars quickly disappeared from the store's shelves--at least in Vancouver.

The centre piece of the club's crest, of course, is a beaver, sitting beside a lake--or a river or a stream--with a branch in its mouth. Fortunately there are in the present club some samples of the original crest which go back to the earliest days. Early in 1971 Mr. Morris L. Green, president of Capital Iron and Metals Ltd. of Victoria, and a member of the Union Club, sent as a gift two reconditioned brass door plaques from the original club house. These historical pieces were accepted by the Committee with great pleasure. Then in 1974 a used-furniture dealer in Spokane, Mr. Byron Culkin, sent to the club a metal plaque with the club crest on it similar to the ones on either side of the main entrance to the club. He had found it in an old trunk amongst furniture he was disposing at an auction a year previously. Apparently the trunk's owner was a woman who had divorced her husband sixty years ago. Evidently he was a heavy drinker, had been invited to the club in 1913 and had removed the plaque as a souvenir of what must have been a particularly good party. The General Committee consulted Norman Whittall, Claude Thicke, and several other senior members but none could remember the circumstances of the incident. Mr. Culkin was thanked for his courtesy and the committee minutes report that it was decided "that the plaque be kept for some future use to be decided in due course."

Over the years the design of the crest changed in detail. In 1972 the committee, wishing to bring the crest back as close as possible to the original drawing, hired a commercial artist to do the task and his version was accepted by the Picture Acceptance Committee. The choice was approved unanimously by the General Committee in

August 1972. However when the newly-elected committee assumed office early in 1973 the members began to ponder the wisdom of their predecessors. The minutes sum up their decision very nicely: "A second look should be taken at the revised Club Crest approved . . . in August 1972. The latter half of his tail had been removed, and the part showing was braided! It was recommended that the beaver's appearance be restored to credibility. After discussion, it was agreed that the design be referred 'back to the drawing board'."

While the beaver was being re-drawn and getting his proper hair and tail, evidently the artist--or someone on the committee--corrected a major error which had gone unnoticed for forty-five years. There was not even a mention of it in the suggestion book where members are quick to voice their complaints about any changes in the club. From 1893 to the latter part of 1928, the beaver in the crest was always facing to the right. After that time, on the club stationery and later elsewhere, he began to face left. When this was brought to the attention of a club member recently, his comment was "there's nothing the matter with him looking both ways. If he was smart he **would** look both ways to see what was going on!" This businessman's observation may have been widely shared by others and the whole matter quietly accepted.

It was not until 1986 that the beaver affair was brought up once more--this time in a letter from a club member to Robert Orr, then the Acting Secretary of the Club. The letter bears reproduction in full.

September 9, 1986.

Dear Mr. Orr:

I write to advise you of my recent humiliation in the presence of a distinguished guest whom I had invited to dinner, in the company of my wife and daughter, in the club's dining room, with pre- and post- prandial refreshments in the blue room.

During the course of the evening, my guest felt it incumbent upon himself, (and I do not blame him in the least), to point out to me that our club beaver, Castor Canadensis, is no better than an equivocating, two-faced quadruped, unworthy to represent our club, its aims and ideals.

My guest alerted me to the fact that on the club's crest, which adorns each side of the main entrance, our beaver, like all right-thinking persons of conservative leanings, faces to the right. The beaver continues to maintain that posture and stance on the club's matchbooks, after-dinner chocolates, demi-tasse coffee cups and note-paper. However, as my guest also demonstrated to me, this inconstant rodent has turned sinister, in more ways than one, on our saucers, (which are used with the above-mentioned coffee cups), and on our paper napkins. On those two articles at least, he faces to the left. I recoil from imagining the other club articles of household use and adornment upon which our beaver may be depicted as facing to the left.

I can only conclude that, owing to the subtle and insidious influence of some of the newer and younger members whose political leanings were not carefully enough screened by the membership committee at the times of their applications for membership, the person on the club staff whose duty it was to order the saucers and napkins in question, abandoned that duty to the extent that he ordered those goods to contain left-leaning beavers that should prove totally unacceptable to all right-leaning members of the club.

While I refrained from pointing this out to my guest, I have noticed that, while on the club's notepaper, our beaver is suitably shaded by a branch of the Canadian maple tree, on the club's paper napkins he is o'er shadowed by some piece of vegetation unknown to the writer, (deadly nightshade, perhaps?)

Mr. Orr, I urge you, in order to save other members the embarrassment that our schizoid mammal has visited upon the undersigned, to draw the above situation promptly to the attention of the committee, which august body will, it is to be hoped, take immediate action to rectify this unfortunate situation.

I remain, sir,

Yours etc.,
John W. Walsh

Mr. Orr's reply to this question was initially brusque. "May the club beaver relieve himself on your sinister side." However, he did promise, "out of consideration for your friend who is so knowledgeable of heraldry," to bring the letter to the attention of the club president. Since then, minutes of the General Committee reveal no further action.

It should be noted, for the sake of historical accuracy, that the club crest is really a logo. It has never been registered legally, so really the club doesn't "own" it. Perhaps it is time the members should legitimize the animal and make him an honest beaver. Maybe he has been looking left and right searching for his parents!

SUGGESTIONS AND COMPLAINTS

Several years after the club was founded a Suggestion Book was bought and left with the Hall Porter. If a member had a suggestion or a complaint he wished to bring to the attention of the General Committee, he wrote it in the book and signed his name. In later years there was a margin on the side of the page in which the secretary-manager would indicate what action, if any, was being taken to satisfy the complainant or comply with the suggestion. Fortunately the first

Suggestion Book is still in existence though in a somewhat tattered state, possibly because many club members, when faced with the task of giving an speech at a club dinner, have used the book to inject some humour into their remarks. This old book, which covers the period from 1898 to 1963, casts some light on what the early members found irritating. Reading some of their comments today one cannot help but be amused--or at least entertained.

Something of the pioneer state of the city can be gleaned from this suggestion on August 4th, 1898: "The Committee [should] either interview or write the City Council complaining of the disgraceful state of the Burrard Street sewer and the unbearable stench which at low tide permeates the precincts of the Club."

There was another disagreeable smell about which a member complained. Apparently a horse-drawn wagon would come early in the morning to take away the kitchen refuse from the previous day. The covers were taken off the large swill pails in the wagon while the refuse was dumped in. Members coming for an early breakfast did not take kindly to the odours emanating from the wagon and complaints were registered, evidently with some effect.

Several other complaints were recorded respecting odours. One was brief and to the point: "The urinals stink," wrote B. T. Rogers. Seven members signed this remark: "Suggest that to avoid the disagreeable smell of sulphur and also to add to the cheerfulness of the hall, the dogs and logs be replaced in the hall." It should be noted that one of the features of the entrance hall in the old clubhouse was a large fireplace with, evidently, a stack of firewood nearby. One other feature of both the old and the new clubhouse was that they were close to the C.P.R. rail terminal. For decades the engines burned coal as a fuel and if the wind was in the wrong directon, windows had to be closed at the rear of the building to prevent smoke and soot coming in. Oddly enough, there were no complaints in the book about that, probably because nothing could be done about it.

Some complaints speak for themselves. "The appearance of some of the [messenger] boys is anything but what it should be. Can we not put them in uniform." The club could and did. "No attention having, apparently, been paid to suggestions or complaints in this book, it would appear a useless institution." This, written in 1898, was to be echoed time and again. In April 1899, Leonard Keyser suggested that "the writing tables be better looked after." He continued: "It should be the duty of some servant to place clean blotting paper on each table daily, to see that there is a good supply of writing paper and envelopes, and that there should be at each table at least three different kinds of pens and these should be renewed often; it would be convenient if a small candle, sealing wax and a [seal] be provided, and also a reliable machine for weighing letters. The state of the writing tables compares very unfavourably with those of other clubs.'' This comparison with other clubs came up two months later when a billiard player suggested that **ivory** balls, ''being generally part of the equipment of the billiard room of a **first class club** (such as the Vancouver Club is supposed to be), should be supplied as well as the imitations now in use.'' Another billiard player put it later: ''A game played with . . . composition balls is interesting, but it is not billiards.''

Then, as now, most club members frequented the bar, and one of the first complaints about this popular area was from William Salsbury, one of the founding members of the club. In September 1899, he wrote:

> *Myself and a number of other members of the Club desire to draw the attention of the Committee to the small portion served for drinks. This evening we insisted on measuring them for ourselves and each drink served in a long glass measured less than a liquor glassful. If the Club profits are to be secured by thus reducing the quantity below the standard charge, then the effect can only be to drive the custom of the Club elsewhere. Small drinks may be good morality--if* **not** *too frequently repeated.* But in the same spirit, make the charge commensurate.

If the drinks were small, the prices were low. At this time a drink in the club cost five cents. It was not until 1907 that the charge was doubled to ten cents. The club at this time was also charging $1. per night for a room and a member suggested this was too high and ''should be reduced.''

At the turn of the century it was not uncommon for members to bring their children and their dogs to the club. The first complaint against the former came in 1900 when a member drew the attention of the Committee to a club rule regarding ''strangers,'' later referred to as ''visitors''. This rule permitted a member to bring in friends, non-residents of Vancouver, for meals and others (presumably residents) only if they wished to view the club. Using this rather vague rule, a member remarked, ''If there is no rule regarding the age of members or members' friends, still members' children are residents of Vancouver and by the rules are not allowed in the club. . . .''

Dogs were more a problem than children. One must keep in mind that many members lived within walking distance of the club and even if one took a horse and carriage, a dog might easily trot alongside. In any event, dogs frequently accompanied their master to the club, which brought this complaint in July, 1904:

> *I beg to draw the attention of the committee to the fact that one of*

the members persistently feeds his dog on the front steps of the club which, to say the least, is anything but cleanly. Besides it has a tendency of making the dog in question snap at members coming in or going out of the club. If every member of the club exercises the same right, the front of the club would soon have the appearance of kennels. The **back yard** *is a proper place for a dog to be fed.*

The committee agreed with the complainant about the feeding but said nothing about dogs on the front steps. Two months later a member complained that a "Red Setter attacked me when coming into the club. I think in the interest of members that dogs not be allowed on the steps." Evidently this was asking too much and, as a consequence, in 1906, another suggestion was made that dogs "be not allowed at the entrance to the club" and, indeed, that "no dogs should be allowed on club premises." The Committee agreed to pass a rule regarding dogs on the front steps but it was difficult to enforce. A climax to the problem came in 1907 when Mr. Wolfjohn's dog bit not one but two members! This was too much. Wolfjohn was warned that "he must keep the dog off the club's premises entire[ly] and if this was not done the authorities would have to be called in and the dog destroyed." In 1908 the Committee finally ruled that no dogs would be allowed on club premises.

Other matters were raised, both large and small, as time went on. A member suggested that "a small bell be placed on each table in the dining room," and this was done. In 1906 a member asked the Committee "to take steps to prevent periodicals and papers being taken from the Reading Room." Eleven years later the same complaint was registered. "There has grown up a practise of removing the morning papers from the Reading Room--evidently with the purpose of reading [them] in the Breakfast Room or lavatory. . . ."

Periodically, over the years, complaints were written about the cost of food at the Vancouver Club compared with that served in the Union Club in Victoria. As early as 1907 one member wrote: "I understand oysters are sold in the Union Club for twenty–five cents a half dozen. Why should we pay thirty–five cents?" Twenty–five years later, in the depth of the depression, another member once more compared meal prices of the two clubs as follows:

Having just spent a week living in the Union Club [I] was impressed by the apparent suitability of the excellent seventy–five cent dinner provided each evening there and, as far as I could guess, general use of the service. The average meal so supplied could not be purchased on the Vancouver Club tariff for less than $1.00 and would probably cost more. To even a layman it would *seem that, in these weird times, popularity of such a dinner service as the Union Club enjoys would result in considerable economy and simplicity in kitchen operation. I have had in the Union Club for seventy-five cents: fruit cocktail, choice of two soups, choice of three joints (including roast chicken which costs fifty cents on one menu), two kinds of very tastefully prepared vegetables, choice of four or five courses of sweets and puddings or two savories. I would suggest that specimen menus be secured from the secretary of the Union Club and serious consideration be given to this suggestion of initiating its service in respect of its sensible dinner.*

The dining room service was most frequently mentioned in the Suggestion Book as the following extracts show.

(March 7th, 1907) "At 1:30 p.m.--impossible to get seat for three in dining room and eight members waiting for single seats."

(June 1st, 1911) "2:25 p.m.--the waiters resumed the detestable custom of sweeping the dining room while members are at lunch. Is this a quiet hint that the lunch hour is over? Is there no better way of signifying this than by sweeping dust into the plates of members?"

(July 5th 1923) "Would suggest that if it is considered necessary to secure the fingerprints of the kitchen staff, some more desirable substance than butter be used for the purpose."

(February 20th, 1927) "I would suggest that only a very necessary minimum of canned or preserved commodities be used in the service of food in the dining room. Oxtail soup served today so faintly answered the description that on enquiry I learned that it was a canned product. Consomme last week so reminded me of pioneering experiences that similar enquiry elicited the information that 'Oxo' entered very materially into its preparation. . . ."

*(June 19th, 1930) "For some time the so-called 'pies' have consisted of stewed fruit with a small piece of pastry cast upon them. Apparently the Chinese element is again getting control of the kitchen. It is respectfully suggested that when pie is on the menu, that **real** pie be served. . . ."*

(September 8th, 1941) Wartime labour shortages must have led to some consideration of hiring waitresses in the dining room. The concept was premature but it resulted in three members suggesting that consideration be given to placing girls in one-half of the dining room and boys on the other side, ". . . leaving members to choose who they desire to wait on them."

(April 4th, 1949) "[My] first complaint in fifty years of membership. Twenty cents for ice cream is O.K. by me for a reasonable

helping, but the portion served by the club is scandalously small."
(Colonel Kirkpatrick was assured a larger scoop would be used in future.)

*(April 17th, 1950) "May I suggest, with proper respect and humility, that you appoint Mr. Roaf, as an expert of long standing, and Mr. Church as a more recent authority, a committee of two to acquaint the steward and the chef with the fact that Steelhead (not Steel Head) is a **trout**. In 'compleat' defiance of Hardcastle's advice they persist in showing it on the menu as a salmon."*

(February 16th, 1977) "I wonder whether the commercial 'logos' are appropriate in the dining room--might the butter pats be turned upside-down so as to disguise the logo? Or better still, bring back hand rolled butter."

(February 11, 1986) "The crab cocktails served at dinner are becoming short on crab and long on lettuce filler. Fresh crab is a delicacy this club has been noted for and we ought not to short change ourselves."

From the above it might be thought that the Vancouver Club had the worst dining room in the city, that the kitchen was filled with incompetents and that the dining room staff had the manners and charm of a cannon ball. This, of course, would be completely false. Dining in the club was a pleasant experience, and members wanted to keep it that way. They sought perfection, but among hundreds of members there were naturally varying tastes and demands.

The suggestion book did (and still does) provide the reader with a glimpse of changing times. In the summer of 1907 a member suggested that "two suitable metal posts for tying horses to be placed on the curb in front of the club." The death of King Edward VII led a member to suggest that the club erect a flagpole either on the grounds of the club or on the building itself. "The King is dead," he wrote, "And there is no way of showing the club's grief or respect." Two years later a member had a complaint that was to be repeated half a century later. "Is it usual in any club except this," he complained, "that the servants should practice the bagpipes on the club premises. There seems to be a total lack of discipline."

The move to the new club house caused only a momentary slowdown in the usual volume of suggestions. There were always members who wanted the club to subscribe to their favourite journal or newspaper which, of course, they expected to see in the stands when they went into the Reading Room. One member noted a gap in the library holdings which was quickly tended to. "The attention of the committee," he noted "is respectfully called to the fact that there is not a copy of the bible in the club. The Word of God appears to be a very scarce commodity. I trust this oversight will be remedied at once.'' Five clocks on the ground floor, each showing a different time, brought a sharp rebuke from R. S. Akhurst. With so many members who were former or serving railroad executives, it is surprising someone hadn't picked on the clocks earlier.

Sometimes a sub-committee would come up with an idea which resulted in an immediate spate of complaints. During the 1920s, as noted elsewhere in this book, the club accepted numerous heads of wild animals shot by members in various parts of the globe. An unusual trophy given to the club was a 20-foot-long anaconda skin. This immense snake was captured in South America. Where it hung in the club prior to 1927 is not recorded but in October of that year the trophy was placed in the main bar on the first floor. This room had been called, for many years, the "snake pit," the term derived from decorative snake-shaped mouldings on pillars in the main lobby. Adding the snakeskin as part of the decor was a bit too much for some members. "Suggest that the suggestive snake over the bar should be removed for the sake of the nerves of some of the members," wrote one. Another added: "As a very ordinary and humble member of the club I suggest that the python skin in the bar should be donated to the Provincial Museum." A third saw no merit in displaying the trophy and he stated bluntly: "The presence of the snakeskin over the bar is a disgrace and degrading suggestion to the members of this club." Club records do not reveal the fate of the anaconda skin; probably it went into storage and ultimate destruction.

An innovation in the dining room in 1977 roused the ire of a number of members who rushed to the Suggestion Book to voice their complaints. As early as 1964 someone had suggested there should be a public address system in the dining room. (Immediately below this entry was the comment: "Suggest the suggestor write legibly"). No reason was given for the suggestion, and possibly it may have been for the use of occasional guest speakers. In any event in 1977 the General Committee approved the expenditure of several thousand dollars to install a first-rate P.A. system which would be used to "pipe" suitable music to members and their guests at dinner. It started on a trial basis in February and the reaction was not long in coming. "I usually dine here on Mondays and Wednesdays," one member fumed. "Last week and last night some dreadful kind of insipid music(?) was piped into the dining room. . I consider it inappropriate and banal. . . . I hope this desecration of a room dear to [my] heart will cease." Another added: "I am not in favour of canned music in the club." "Anti-canned music," wrote a member; "Ditto above," wrote a fourth. "Such music might be appropriate at MacDonald's or the White Spot," added a fifth and a sixth member seemed to sum up the matter when he wrote: "Want to record that I prefer dinner music on a 'live' piano to silence, and silence to taped music, in our excellent Dining Room." Taped music was ruled out.

The Suggestion Book continues to be a treasury of the club members' likes and dislikes. The entries, as one past president put it, "receive the attention they deserve." The comments in the book, however, are not ignored. Those that have merit are acted upon and others which cannot be carried out are at least explained to the complainant.

THE LADIES

From the outset the Vancouver Club was organized as a club strictly for male members. The only women working in the club were the housekeeper, one or two maids and later some female help in the kitchen. When club members arranged a ball or a special social evening involving dances or, presumably, the annual children's party, ladies were invited. Indeed, such invitations were highly prized, particularly as there were only a few establishments in Vancouver at the turn of the century that could have a ball which could rival a similar function at Government House in Victoria.

Although club members enjoyed these occasions as much as their guests, it was a club rule that ladies could not be brought to lunch or dinner. It was not until 1915, twenty-two years after the club was founded, that a resolution was passed stating that any member wishing to entertain guests at dinner in the private dining room "shall be permitted to have ladies among the guests. . . ." What events inspired this resolution are not recorded, but one can imagine a certain amount of wifely pressure being exerted behind the scenes.

During the wartime years there was a surprising resolution passed at an Extraordinary General Meeting on 17 April, 1918. It stated:

> *That the [General] Committee be empowered to arrange for the use of the Ladies Dining and Reception Rooms by the wives, unmarried sisters of members of this Club for luncheon, afternoon tea and dinner during regulation hours. Any or all of these privileges [are] to be extended at the discretion of the Committee; and an annual fee [is] to be charged as the Committee may see fit to impose, such fee to be not less than $10 per annum each, and shall be payable by the male relative. Ladies availing themselves of these facilities [are] to have the right to include amongst their guests ladies non-resident in Vancouver. Any lady under the age of 18 years [is] not to be admitted or entertained.*

It was estimated that at least 50 applications were necessary if the scheme was to work. It would not be sound financially to have even a small staff and kitchen help hired to cater to female guests if the demand was not there. As it turned out, only about 26 applications were received by June and as a consequence the resolution was left in abeyance. Once again the club's minutes give no reason why the resolution was proposed. The club's membership was down owing to the number who had joined the armed forces. It may have been a gesture to wives of members serving overseas who would not be able to enjoy dining in the club while their husbands were overseas, or it might have been a means of increasing the revenue of the dining room. Whatever the reason, the offer was not made again. In the following year the club's constitution was amended to allow lady visitors to enjoy unlimited attendance in the Ladies Dining Room, thus lifting a restriction for ladies which still applied to gentlemen guests in the main dining room.

The areas where ladies might go in the club had always been restricted. When members moved into their new building in 1914 arrangements had been made for a ladies entrance. This door led to a small lobby with a cloak room and, much later, an elevator. From the lobby ladies were to be escorted up the stairs to what is now referred to as the Blue Room, but which was termed originally as the Ladies Lounge and Ladies Dining Room. Beyond these confines ladies were not supposed to go. Even as recently as December 1944 the General Committee approved the ruling "that Lady Guests receiving telephone calls at the club may not be called to the telephone; the Caller being required to leave the number which will be given to the Guest." When a telephone was placed in the lobby of the Ladies Entrance this ruling fell by the wayside. The alternative would have meant ladies using one of several telephone booths in the main lobby and that area was strictly out of bounds.

Nevertheless club members, doubtless after considerable debate, made another major decision respecting ladies during the Second World War. Early in 1944 it was decided to convert the ladies private dining room into a lounge and admit lady guests to the main dining room for dinner. A referendum on the question was passed by a large majority of the members and in December 1944 the first ladies entered this former male preserve. "Since that time," the club's annual report noted, "there has been a steady up-trend in the number of dinners served. In practice, it would seem that the move is a popular one and that members are making more use of their club as a consequence."

It would appear, at first glance, that it took two world wars to have club members change their attitude towards having ladies dine in the club. In many ways the results of both wars were going to have even more profound effects in the longer run since the traditional role of women was undergoing considerable change. The shortage of labour in both wars brought more and more women into the work force and even into the armed forces. After the First World War women were granted the right to vote and women were elected to public office. Following the Second World War women made tremendous advances in every field of endeavour. They could be found in all the professions, they were appointed to the bench and to the Senate; they were making great strides in the business community, in politics and in all levels of management.

It is not surprising, therefore, that there was some impact on the club. Traditionally the club had accepted diplomatic members, provided they were properly proposed and seconded. Should this be changed, now that women were being appointed consuls and consuls-general in Vancouver? It had long been a custom to grant honorary membership to the lieutenant-governor of the province. Some recent appointments to this office--though not in British Columbia--were women, and indeed a woman now filled the office of governor-general. The club's private dining rooms were frequently used for business executive luncheon meetings, and female executives were becoming more common. In a word, pressure was beginning to build up to have the club modify its rules which, to an outsider, were beginning to appear archaic in a society which was undergoing rapid change.

Some external cries for change, which were particularly noticeable in the 1970s, were strident. Judge Nancy Morrison made the front page of the Vancouver "Province" on 24 May 1975, when she lashed out at the Terminal, University and Vancouver Clubs when giving a speech on leadership to the University Women's Club. She condemned the downtown clubs for not allowing female memberships, for allowing women on their premises only as guests and suggested that women who enter clubs on these conditions "enter as second class citizens and thereby encourage discrimination." If members' wives refused to go to the clubs with their husbands it would be a serious financial blow to the clubs and would probably be their deathknell. She went on to say that both political and business meetings went on at the clubs and she felt it was "very serious when we are excluded from premises where decision-making goes on."

The theme of Judge Morrison's speech may have been the result of an incident at the University Club. Dr. Pauline Jewett, who recently had been appointed president of Simon Fraser University, was nominated for membership in the University Club. This required a change in the club's by-laws which, when it came to the vote, was turned down two to one. Indignant at being excluded because of her sex,

Jewett issued a memorandum asking faculty and staff at Simon Fraser University to boycott the University Club. She was supported by Kathleen Ruff, an official in the Human Rights Branch of the provincial government.

One of the modest desires of the Vancouver Club is to keep its name out of the newspaper. During the 1970s, however, it was not an easy thing to do, especially when some female reporters felt the urge to bring to public notice the club's rules about women in the club. In July 1978, a woman reporter of the Vancouver "Sun" attempted to attend a lecture in the Terminal City Club, was turned away, and after trying to get information on the status of women in all clubs, wrote an article on what she uncovered. The president of the Vancouver Club at the time, Michael Goldie, was unavailable to answer her queries but Cornelius Burke, a long-time member, was quoted as saying in defence of the men-only rule that "men's precious bastions are falling away from them on all sides and we clutch on to one of the few things that's left to us."

Nevertheless, the club's strict rules were beginning to weaken. By 1978 the club was permitting women who were directors of businesses to attend lunches in private rooms of the club. In September 1978 a past-president, P.R. Brissenden, suggested to the General Committee that women be allowed to attend luncheons in private rooms without any qualification. From the staff point of view, there was no problem of ladies being included in luncheon parties on the fourth floor where they could be taken by elevator from the lobby of the ladies entrance. It was possible for them to use the ladies lounge at lunch time but the Blue Room posed a problem of having no ladies' powder room. The matter was handed to the Dining Room Committee to resolve and in November it agreed ladies could be allowed to lunch in the club in the private dining rooms between 12 noon and 2:30 p.m. The only provisions laid down were that the luncheon was not to be "of a purely social nature and approved or ratified as such by the Committee." Under these circumstances, for example, it was now possible for a businessman to hold a business lunch and invite ladies who were not necessarily involved in management. Three years later, in February 1981, this new rule was amended again to allow members to invite guests of either sex for luncheon in the private dining rooms for social functions. It was a sign of the times when this recommendation was approved unanimously.

There was one notable occasion, which must be mentioned, when women were permitted into Bar Three. With the exception of special dinners and club balls when ladies had general use of the club, this area had been a strictly male preserve for years. One of its main features, of course, was that it had a magnificent view of the Vancouver harbour and waterfront. Directly below it it was Pier B.C. and on 9 March 1983 **H.M.Y. Britannia** was moored there as Her Majesty the Queen and Prince Philip were visiting the city. When it was learned that the band of the Royal Marines would be beating retreat on the pier at 10:30 p.m., past president Geoffrey Tullidge asked the General Committee whether, as a special dispensation, members could take female guests into the oak-panelled bar to watch the ceremony. One can only assume most of the committee members were married men. The request was not only approved, but the secretary said he could arrange to have coffee and drinks served to this unique gathering. What Sir George Bury would have thought is hard to imagine.

A tradition in the club of many years was that only members could come in by the main entrance. When the new club was built with a special ladies entrance, that had to be used when members were bringing in even male guests. Although this regulation did not last very long, the rule remained that ladies were not allowed into the main lobby by way of the central doorway. In 1945, a female news photographer from the "Sun" got through the main entrance on assignment to photograph a visiting guest. As the "Sun" reported, "Despite her shrill cries of 'But I am the press' she was turned away," and the paper reported that she announced "that all Vancouver Club members were barred from her darkroom."

There seems little doubt, however, that by the mid-1980s there was a growing irritation among members' wives about segregated entrances. In order to modify this feeling, it was decided that after 6:00 p.m. the main entrance would be closed, the Ladies Entrance renamed the Evening Entrance, and all members and their guests would use the latter means of coming into the club. This new rule upset a number of older members who were quick to let the president know about their disapproval and dissatisfaction with the new arrangement. George Hungerford replied to one irritated member in part as follows:

> *Whilst appreciating your feeling on the subject of closing the main entrance at 6:00 p.m. each evening, the committee has asked me to point out that this action was taken as a result of the replies received to the large questionnaire sent out to all members a year ago. A substantial number of members stated that their wives refused to come to the Club if they had to go in by a separate ladies entrance. It was finally decided that, to avoid discrimination, the ladies entrance would be renamed . . . and all members, with or without guests, would use it. This compromise seems to have worked well so far. It is appreciated that a certain number of senior members are not happy about this change but the committee hopes that such members will accept it as being in the present best interests of the club.*

In the same year this change took place, the question was raised respecting women being allowed to lunch in the main dining room. After the proposal was discussed in the General Committee, it was decided that the members should be polled. Allowing ladies to dine in the evening had presented no problems to the staff nor did it impose any strain on the kitchen. Indeed, the number of members using the dining room in the evening had been steadily declining in the post-war period. Once ladies were permitted to join their friends or husbands, there was a noticeable increase in the number of dinners being served. However, the dining room was usually very full during lunch-time. More members made use of the club at this time than any other period during the day, and although there was a good percentage of members who were not against the idea, in practice--perhaps especially with the increased use of the Club during Expo year--no firm decision was made.

One decision was made in 1985, however, which passed easily at the Annual General Meeting. For some time other men's clubs had made provision for the widows of members to maintain certain privileges at their husband's club. The Vancouver Club decided it would make an amendment to its rules to conform to this trend as well. It was agreed, therefore, that widows of members who died, provided the member had ten years with the club, could be proposed for evening signing privileges. She would have to be proposed by another member, approved by the General Committee, and once that was done she could dine, with guests, at the club as often as she wished. This privilege would be cancelled should she re-marry, but the idea of allowing ladies to continue their long association with the club was a good one and mutually beneficial in many ways.

FINE ART IN THE VANCOUVER CLUB

A guest being shown around the Vancouver Club today would be impressed by the number of oil paintings, drawings, sketches and prints which decorate the walls of many of the club's larger rooms and reception areas. Some individual pieces are quite valuable. Some of the paintings have been bought, others have been donated by members, the wives of members or visiting guests. In all, the club has an eclectic collection and, although in so large a group one is bound to have differences of opinion about the aesthetic value or particular merit of certain paintings as well as their location, an effort has been made to cater to the taste of the majority of members. There are always some, of course, who when viewing a new picture acquisition, feel that the members of the Fine Arts Committee must have lost their heads. Others will complain that certain paintings are unsuitable, being in the wrong room or shouldn't be hung at all. Although there are few examples of what is termed "modern art", there are probably some members who feel that prints of English hunting scenes or of battles fought long ago, are really the only appropriate pictures to hang on the walls of a gentleman's club. Whatever their opinion might be, there is little doubt that the club today contains a far better collection of art and artifacts than it did several decades ago.

What pictures hung in the first clubhouse is not known. There are records in the old club minute books about some of the early donations of artifacts. The first one mentioned was a "handsome cigarette box" presented in 1906 by the wife of an early member, S. K. Twigge. It was to be called the S. K. Twigge Trophy, played for yearly as a prize for pyramids or such other game on the billiard tables, "as may from time to time be determined by the Committee." The trophy was to remain the property of the club but the winner was to be in possession of it for a year. The secretary, MacIver MacIver–Campbell, wrote Mrs. Twigge to say that the cigarette box would remain the club's most treasured possession and "would ever serve to remind the members of her husband's most kindly feeling towards them." The trophy has disappeared.

In the following year a club member, T. F. E. Kinnell, presented the club with a telescope which was used for the next two decades in both club-houses. The view over Vancouver harbour was unexcelled from both locations. The telescope also disappeared and was replaced by a pair of binoculars presented by Messrs. J. F. Belyea, R. D. Williams and H. A. Stevenson.

In 1910, some of the donations began to pose problems. In that year the Committee gave permission to several club members "to hang some skins and heads (Trophies of the Chase) in the club, and that the said skins and heads be kept . . . insured at the expense of the club." A year later another member donated a wapiti head. In 1927 Captain Henry Munn was thanked for his donation of three muskox heads and later that year Frederick Buscombe gave five more mounted animal heads to the club. In 1928 Colonel J. E. Leckie gave the club a 23 foot long Anaconda snake skin which, at one point, was moved to hang in the club bar until some members objected to its presence. Early the following year the President, at a committee meeting, ". . . reported that A. L. Hager intended to present the club with three of his hunting trophies (one moose and two caribou) and had invited the Past Presidents and the present Committee to be his guests at Dinner. . . ."

One might be a little suspicious of the intent behind the dinner invitation. Was Mrs. Hager, for example, complaining that there was no more room in their own residence to hang them on the wall? Or was her husband merely keen on displaying his trophies to his friends at the club? In any event the Committee accepted the donations and more followed as club members continued to shoot game in various parts of the British Empire. In 1932 W. P. Alderson presented the club with the head of a Cape buffalo he had shot in South Africa. Evidently Colonel Leckie went there a few years later and, as a consequence, the club became the possessor of two "very fine" kudu early in 1936.

Leckie's kudu heads were the last reported gifts of animal heads to the club. A minute in the General Committee's notes of November 1943 states that "the question of replacement and rearrangement of trophies be left to House sub-committee." Shortly after the Second World War a Mr. T. A. Hamilton requested the loan of any surplus animal heads--for what purpose is not stated. The last reference to the game heads in the minutes was in 1953 when it was noted that Mr. Hager's moose and cariboo heads were "in such poor condition that they could not be used again and should now be disposed of."

A number of heads hung in the main lobby of the club, but when it was being redecorated around 1949-50, these and others were quietly removed to the basement. At one time it appears that there was also at least one if not two stuffed bears in the club. Where they came from and what their fate is not recorded.

Not all of the gifts were animal heads. Following the Great War, Colonel R. G. E. Leckie wrote the Committee "offering to loan the club two machine-guns which had been captured from the Bolsheviki," an offer which the Committee was pleased to accept. Presumably these were displayed in the lobby while they were on loan. A photograph entitled "The Surrender of the Fleet" was accepted from F. C. Wade in 1920 but it was not until the late '20s that the first painting was donated. This was done by a Japanese artist and was presented by the Japanese consul, Tatsuo Kawai, who had become what was termed an "Imperial Member" in September 1927 and presented the painting two months later.

Photographs, or copies of paintings, appeared to be the favourite gifts for some time, however. A picture of the Coronation, 1902; the S. S. Beaver (the earliest steamship on British Columbia's coast); a picture of railroad builders Lord Strathcona and Sir Thomas Shaughnessy; "Rod and Creel;" "The Interior of Fort Garry;" "Romantic Copper," "Barren Ground of Northern Canada" and "The Vimy Front" were hung where room permitted. One of the club's most welcome gifts--and one which is still looked upon with great nostalgia by older members, was a whimsical cartoon sketched by a visiting British naval officer, Captain Broome, in 1943. It depicts the Night Hall Porter, R.F. Pyne, who had entered the club's employment in 1919 and was to serve it for thirty years. Pyne is shown seated at the old telephone switchboard answering a call, presumably from a member's wife, enquiring about the whereabouts of her husband.

"I'm sorry, Madam--he's just left the Club" is Pyne's traditional answer.

It was not until the end of the Second World War that the General Committee decided to pay more attention to its collection. In 1945 the club received a painting from F.W.Tiffin and a group of six steel engravings from A.F.Nation. In the annual report for 1945, the president expressed the opinion "that a permanent Art Committee should be appointed from amongst those members who are interested in these matters." Such a committee "should concern itself with the acquisition of suitable paintings and pictures for the decoration of the clubhouse...." In the spring of 1946 the Art Committee was formed and Colonel R.D.Williams, who had just retired as club president, was appointed its chairman.

During the next 15 years a great deal of renovation and improvement took place in the club and considerable sums were spent on new carpets, furniture, drapes and so forth. By 1960, however, the club president mentioned to the General Committee that there had been some discussion regarding members donating paintings to the club. A committee member, D.McK. Brown, felt that "the committee should consider having an art authority advise them on paintings for the Blue Room and lounge." His colleagues agreed and Brown was authorized to make arrangements to have such paintings (that are recommended by the authority) hung in the Blue Room and Ladies Lounge." It was not until 1965, however, that a Picture Acceptance Committee became an authorized club committee rather than an advisory subcommittee. This new committee consisted of R.W.Underhill, P.R. Brissenden, G.P.Kaye and Fred Auger. The latter, who was the publisher of the Vancouver "Province," said:

> *Although we had a beautiful club building, the halls and rooms were noticably lacking in pictures by British Columbia and Canadian Artists or of subjects representing our province and our country. One of our most respected and best loved members, George Cunningham, had passed away recently and I suggested to then President, Tom Ladner, that some of us who were friends of George would subscribe to a fund that would provide a fine picture as a tribute to his memory, to which Tom agreed. The response to the prosposal was astonishing. The contributions provided not one but two lovely pictures, "Eagle Pass at Revelstoke" by E. J. Hughes and "Howe Sound at Horseshoe Bay" by W. P. Weston. These acquisitions were the first of what might be called pictures of "gallery quality" in the club's possession and prompted others to donate first class paintings which have formed the nucleus of a fine art collection that had surpassed anything the club had acquired up to that time.*

Space does not permit a detailed description of the art which was added in subsequent years but one might be mentioned to illustrate how donations were encouraged: Fred Auger relates how he was invited for cocktails at the home of H. R. MacMillan:

> *Mr. MacMillan had some nice pictures he had collected over the years. He said he would like to give a picture to The Vancouver Club and asked for my suggestion. I chose a picture by Diego Rivera and he said, 'Fine. That will be it.' But a few days later he called and said, 'Some of the family are disappointed that I gave you this picture but I have something at my office I think you would like better, a painting by Emily Carr.' I said I was sure that would be just great, and he said, 'You go over to my office in the morning and get it.'*

This painting, titled "The Crooked Staircase" is now probably the most valuable among the club's collection. Quite appropriately, it is by Emily Carr, one of Canada's finest artists, a native of B.C., and depicts a British Columbia scene. As Auger stated,

> *When the picture came to us the canvas was stretched on a frame of four boards that obviously had been taken from a pile of firewood, one still had some bark on it. We arranged to have the picture sent to the National Gallery in Ottawa where it was restretched on a proper frame, varnished and otherwise treated to preserve the painting because the paint was beginning to dry. They did a fine job of restoration.*

During the 1970s the club received a number of paintings relating to British Columbia. "Snow Geese on the Fraser Delta," "Douglas Lake Ranch Country" and "Gill Netters, Fraser River" are examples. There were other donations of works by European painters as well as prints and lithographs. One gift accepted by the club was not a painting but a large grandfather clock, formerly in the possession of B.W.Fleck, a club member since 1908. It was presented in his name by T.E.Ladner, his son-in-law, in 1969 and stands in the foyer to the main diningroom. Another grandfather clock, also a gift, stands in the entrance lobby. The latter has had the dignity of showing the "official time" of the club according to a minute passed by the General Committee years ago.

Situated where it is, overlooking one of the busiest harbours in Canada, there is a close connection with marine and shipping activities among any of the club's members. Quite naturally there are paintings depicting aspects of life on the high seas, whether it be fishing or early sea exploration. To emphasize this connection, a member of the Picture Acceptance Committee made a proposal to his colleagues in

1970. On a visit to the New York Yacht Club he had admired a room filled with excellent ship models. He felt, considering the number of members who were in the marine industry, that there might be some who would donate or lend to the club some of the excellent models of tugboats he had seen in their offices. Permission to go ahead with the idea was given and soon, in the third floor bar, a collection of excellent models was installed. They ranged in size from one to two feet and were complete in every detail. Since this bar and lounge commanded the finest view of the harbour, it began to have a distinctly "marine" flavour.

Any changes in the decor of the club's rooms, whether real or proposed, was bound to bring forth some objections by members who wished to keep things as they were. Such was the case with the model tugboats. Early in 1971 a member wrote in the suggestion book that the models be removed as these introduce an uncalled for commercial flavour to the club. "Imagine if all the members with firms did likewise." The club secretary was instructed to reply that the tugboats had been donated on the invitation of the committee and, further, that "This innovation was, for the time being, only experimental." It was true that the models did carry the house colours of the tugboat companies and, in that sense, may have had a slight commercial tinge to them. Any sort of commercial advertising in the club has been frowned upon by the membership. In one case, for example, the General Committee received a complaint that the pats of butter in the dining-room were impressed with the logo of a palm tree, a symbol used by a well known dairy firm. Instructions were issued that, henceforth, when serving the butter pats the palm trees must be face down. Although some ten or twelve tugboat models decorated the third floor bar for several years, it was decided in 1973 that they should be removed. Most of them were sent to the Maritime Museum in Vancouver while others, which were on loan, were returned to their original owners.

Another collection met with a kinder fate. In 1973 a club member, Arnold B. Cliff, offered to lend the club for five years a number of antique Colt pistols which he had collected over the years. They were in excellent condition and many were collectors items. Mr. Cliff died before any decision was made but in 1975 his wife and his brother, Ronald, again made the offer either to present them permanently or for an initial period of five years. They were displayed in four large and two small cases. The Picture Acceptance Committee recommended "that this generous offer be accepted and displayed in lighted cases around the wall of Bar I on the main floor of the club." Arrangements were made to have the twenty-seven guns appraised and insured. By July, 1976 the cased pistols were hung and eleven members of the Cliff family were on hand when the redecorated room, now called the Gun Room, was re-opened. The collection of Colt revolvers and derringers is among one of the best in the city, and the Gun Room is shown to visitors with considerable pride.

The Gun Room, incidentally, contains no other guns nor was it the club's intention that it should. In 1979, for example, the club's then oldest member, C.S.Thicke, offered the club a Luger pistol from the First World War and a Walther pistol from the Second World War. The offer of this 96-year-old veteran was politely declined.

One set of pictures commissioned by the Picture Acceptance Committee caused a certain amount of worry for several years. They were the paintings of Her Majesty The Queen and H.R.H.Prince Philip which hung in the Blue Room. The first mention of a picture of Her Majesty in the Blue Room was in 1953 when the club was donated a colour photograph, "taken and presented by the Hon.M.W.Elphinstone of London, England in appreciation of privileges extended during visits to Vancouver...." It was placed over the fireplace.

Some twenty years later the club commissioned A.Bruce Stapleton to paint portraits of the Queen and Prince Philip which were due to be completed by the spring of 1973. These were not completed until 1975, and when the portraits were hung there was considerable discussion regarding their merit. Even two years later the General Committee, which had been receiving comments about them from members, noted that "the oil paintings of Her Majesty the Queen and Prince Philip... should be referred for consideration of either replacement or alteration." The portraits still hang there, which leads one to reflect that old saying, "Beauty is in the eye of the beholder." And sometimes in the eyes of General Committee.

Actually, according to one former club president, when the Blue Room was being redecorated in the early 1970s,

> *...the House Committee and the General Committee at the time accepted the recommendation [of the interior decorator]... that there would never be any pictures hung there. The design was such that to [display]... even pictures of the Queen at one end and the Duke of Edinburgh at the other, or Emily Carr or whatever, would spoil the whole concept of the decoration of these two rooms. One of the hardest jobs we had was to prevent the incoming House Committee from deciding that we should have some pictures in there. And when I was... on the General Committee, I discovered that the pressure wasn't coming from certain members from time to time, it was from their wives.*

Wifely influence on club members and their decisions respecting interior decoration of the club is never mentioned in committee minutes, but there is no doubt it exists and probably--and quite rightly--will continue to do so. It is likely, too, that "wifely influence" may have had something to do with the decision to remove from the Blue Room a large canvas, donated by F.W. Tiffen, depicting a group of comely nude maidens bathing by a sylvan pool. It didn't leave the club, but rather is hanging in a somewhat less frequented room.

The Picture Acceptance Committee, renamed the Fine Arts Committee in 1980, continued to do excellent work during the next decades. It made a permanent list of all the club's pictures which were donated, bought or on loan and began to display pictures the committee proposed to buy in order to get members' reactions. In 1972, it decided to dispose of some fifty or more old photographs and pictures that had been stored away for years. A notice in the main lobby invited members to claim any of those listed, but no one came forward. Prints, lithographs and photographs no longer thought suitable for display in the club house when rooms were redecorated were donated to various institutions.

In 1970 it was decided that the club's pictures should be appraised and insured, and further, that the appraisal should be carried out every three years. The first valuation was approximately $52,500 for fifty-three items. By 1977, owing partly to the increased number of items and the rise in value of one or two particular pieces, the appraisal increased to $121,000 and then to $152,000 by 1980. The annual grant given to the Fine Arts Committee increased steadily as well. The original grant of $1,000 had quadrupled in 1980 in order to keep slightly ahead of inflation. Nevertheless, although it was buying or commissioning more oil paintings, water colours, and so forth, the generosity of members or their wives donating art continues.

During the 1980's two chairmen of the Fine Arts Committee, George M. Hungerford and Robert G. Brodie, sought to bring somewhat more definite terms of reference for the committee. In April, 1981 Hungerford received approval for the following terms of reference for his committee:

1. *To ensure that the club maintains an inventory of items of fine art either owned by the club or on loan.*

2. *To ensure there is a regular appraisal for insurance purposes to determine the value of all items of fine art and collections....*

3. *To maintain the club's fine art collection and to advise the General Committee on repairs and/or restoration as required.*

4. *To negotiate exchanges on loans of works of fine art and where and when appropriate for the benefit of the club.*

5. *To recommend the purchase of fine art with the approval of the General Committee.*

6. *To periodically examine the location of the fine arts collection in the club....*

7. *In co-operation with the House Committee, to recommend... approval of the design of all items of decor and furnishings, carpeting, draperies,... which are important to the visual quality of the club's premises.*

8. *To recommend to the General Committee the employment of consultants with respect to all of the above items as is necessary.*

Most of these recommendations had been made from time to time over past years and as such this was primarily an attempt to coordinate responsibilities into an accepted and recognized guide for the committee. Item No. 6, however, gave the committee the power to change the location of pictures. Item No. 7 was completely new but at the same time logical, since the visual quality of the club is a mixture of both pieces of art and the rooms and hallways in which they are displayed.

One of the decisions of Hungerford's new committee was to reverse an earlier proposal that one of the fourth floor committee rooms should have an Indian motif. With that in mind, the club had purchased in 1979 a Hok Hok Indian mask for $1250. It was sold, at a slight profit, to the Museum of Anthropology at the University of British Columbia in 1981. One or two paintings of Indians were sold at the same time and so, too, were some other pieces of fine art which no longer seemed suitable.

For some time club members had donated prints, sketches, oil, pastel and watercolour paintings, engravings and photographs. Periodically, too, the club was pleased to accept such art on loan for a specific period. In 1980, William G. Leithead, then chairman of the Fine Arts Committee, visited the Vancouver Art Gallery and made arrangements to exchange the club's Emily Carr painting for another by the same artist entitled "Totem Poles--Kitseukla." Both were returned to their original owners in 1983, but the idea of borrowing pictures from the Art Gallery was continued. Partly as a result, when he was chairman of the committee in 1984 Robert G. Brodie added a few more general terms of reference. He felt that the club's principal traffic areas should be hung with paintings "of museum quality" and, further, that "these paintings should be carefully selected to be historical or traditional in nature and should be appropriate to the interior design, style and quality of the leading club in Vancouver." He suggested that this could be done at no cost to the club, and further that the club should no longer purchase any works of art.

Within a short time the club was able to borrow twelve paintings from the Vancouver Art Gallery, and there is no doubt that the addition of this collection has enhanced the collection already on display. The addition of further items from the University Club added more to the fine art collection when consideration was given to redecorating the newly renovated club building.

There are one or two areas in the club where pictures are hung which have a close association with the members. In one corridor, for example, photographs of former presidents of the club line the wall. In the Reading Room on the first floor there are autographed pictures of Governors-General and some of their wives who have been guests of the club. By tradition, Canada's Governors-General and members of their staff have always been offered Honorary membership in the club. Those who have visited the club and accepted membership have had their portraits hung in the Reading Room along with their wives, provided the latter have been guests of the club. In 1973 one member suggested that the portraits of the wives should be removed as the Reading Room was "a room for men only and . . . women should have no place in it." His suggestion was not followed but one result, apparently, was that the Committee's attention was brought to the portraits and instructions were given that they should be uniformly reframed.

Tucked away in the Reading Room also is a small replica statue of Sir John A. Macdonald, Canada's first prime minister. This was donated by the Sir John A. Macdonald Society. At first some members of the General Committee felt that such a statue might strike some as having political overtones but discreet enquiries by Robert G. Rogers, then chairman of the Fine Arts Committee, revealed that no one seemed to think the offer was made on political grounds. Nevertheless, it does lead one to reflect what the reaction in the club might be if a MacKenzie King Society had offered a statue of any more recent prime ministers.

The three frames of historical menus which hang at the entrance to the Reading Room were found by T. E. Ladner who had them framed during the 1960s. They represent a selection of dinner menus prepared over the years for special dinners given at the club. Their designs are imaginative and the menus are a tribute to a succession of excellent chefs over the decades.

Fine Art in the club has undergone dramatic changes in the last 90 years, changes for the better. Many hours of work by committee members have made this possible, and both those who have served and are still serving on his committee have every right to feel pleased with the results of their work.

Past Presidents
Vancouver Club & University Club
1988 Amalgamation Celebration Dinner

Bill Laurie, Hu Chapman, AVM Leigh Stevenson, Ed Wallace,
Chief Justice N. Nemetz.
Fred W. Charlton, Mike Hobbs, Larry Dampier, Dave Leaney, Sholto Hebenton,
Don Wheatley, Cliff Wyatt.
David Freeman, Bill Clark, David Sinclair, Michael Goldie, Dudley Darling,
Bill Leithead, Ron Webster.
David Brousson, Stin Clark, Doug Maitland.
Peter Sharp, Rod Hungerford, Geoff H. Tullidge.
Bill Jackson, W. Thomas Brown.
Tom Marshall, Judge J.D. Taggart.
Peter Stanley, Syd Welsh.

APPENDIX "A"

PAST PRESIDENTS of the VANCOUVER CLUB

HONORARY LIFE PRESIDENTS

1902–1915 H.B. Abbott   1923–1938 Campbell Sweeney

1907 F. M. Chaldecott

	President	Secretary–Manager
1893	J.M. Browning	
1894	J.M. Browning	A. Holmes
1895	I. Oppenheimer	A. Holmes
1896	I. Oppenheimer	A. Holmes
1897	J.C. Keith	A. Holmes
1898	H.B. Abbott	J.C. Kinchant
1899	H.B. Abbott	(R. Kerr Houlgate
		D.S. Wallbridge)
1900	H.B. Abbott	R.R. Slade
1901	H.B. Abbott	M.MacIver Campbell
1902	D. Bell–Irving, M.D.	M.MacIver Campbell
1903	D. Bell–Irving, M.D.	M.MacIver Campbell
1904	D. Bell–Irving, M.D.	M.MacIver Campbell
1905	H. Lockwood	M.MacIver Campbell
1906	E. Mahon	M.MacIver Campbell
1907	F.M. Chaldecott	B.M. Humble
1908	J.G. Woods	H.B. Helbert
1909	Sir C. Hibbert Tupper	
	K.C.M.G., K.C.	A.B. Baker
1910	Sir C. Hibbert Tupper	
	K.C.M.G., K.C.	Peter McNaughton
1911	W.F. Salsbury	Peter McNaughton
1912	W.F. Salsbury	Peter McNaughton
1913	E.P. Davis, K.C.	B.M. Humble
1914	E.P. Davis, K.C.	B.M. Humble
1915	F.W. Peters	B.M. Humble
1916	F.W. Peters	B.M. Humble
1917	G.S. Harrison	B.M. Humble
1918	G.S. Harrison	B.M. Humble
1919	A.H. MacNeill, K.C.	H.R. Acton
1920	J.A. Macdonald, M.D.	H.R. Acton
1921	F.W. Rousefell	A. Malins
1922	W.J. Blake Wilson	A. Malins
1923	J.H. Senkler	A. Malins
1924	F.W. Tiffin	A. Malins
1925	H.St.J. Montizambert	A. Malins

	President	Secretary–Manager
	President	**Secretary–Manager**
1926	George Kidd	D.B. Robinson
1927	J. Fyfe Smith	D.B. Robinson
1928	R. Kerr Houlgate	D.B. Robinson
1929	R. Kerr Houlgate	D.B. Robinson
1930	J.E. McMullen, K.C.	D.B. Robinson
1931	J.E. McMullen, K.C.	D.B. Robinson
1932	K.J. Burns	D.B. Robinson
1933	K.J. Burns	D.B. Robinson
1934	W.G. Murrin	D.B. Robinson
1935	W.G. Murrin	D.B. Robinson
1936	J.K. Macrae, K.C.	D.B. Robinson
1937	Hon. W.C. Woodward	D.B. Robinson
1938	Hon. W.A. Macdonald	D.B. Robinson
1939	Hon. W.A. Macdonald	D.B. Robinson
1940	E.H. Adams	R.O. Kennedy
1941	E.A. Cleveland	B.C. Binks
1942	F.J. Burd	B.C. Binks
1943	C.A. Cotterell	B.C. Binks
1944	J.F. Belyea	B.C. Binks
1945	R.D. Williams	B.C. Binks
1946	H.A. Stevenson	B.C. Binks
1947	J.Y. McCarter	B.C. Binks
1948	W.S. Owen, K.C.	(B.C. Binks
		(A.J. Brown
1949	W.S. Owen, K.C.	A.J. Brown
1950	A.H. Williamson	A.J. Brown
1951	A.H. Williamson	A.J. Brown
1952	R.B. Buckerfield	A.J. Brown
1953	R.B. Buckerfield	A.J. Brown
1954	R.D. Baker	A.J. Brown
1955	R.D. Baker	W.H. Kirby
1956	Leigh F. Stevenson	W.H. Kirby
1957	W. Manson	W.H. Kirby
1958	W. Manson	W.H. Kirby
1959	George O. Vale	W.H. Kirby
1960	George O. Vale	W.H. Kirby
1961	A.D. Bell–Irving	W.H. Kirby
1962	A.D. Bell–Irving	W.H. Kirby
1963	David R. Blair	(W.H. Kirby
		(C. Chapman
1964	David R. Blair	C. Chapman
1965	Thomas E. Ladner, Q.C.	C. Chapman
1966	Roderick M. Hungerford	C. Chapman
1967	Robert R. Keay	C. Chapman
1968	Alan M. Robertson	C. Chapman
1969	J. Douglas Maitland	C. Chapman

	President	**Secretary-Manager**
1970	P.R. Brissenden, Q.C.	C. Chapman
1971	Harold M. Gale	C. Chapman
1972	W. Thomas Brown	(C. Chapman
		(John P. Chutter
1973	G. Peter Kaye	John P. Chutter
1974	J. Norman Hyland	John P. Chutter
1975	Brenton S. Brown	John P. Chutter
1976	A.D. (Peter) Stanley	John P. Chutter
1977	Charles H. Wills	John P. Chutter
1978	D.Michael M.Goldie, Q.C.	John P. Chutter
1979	Lawrence Dampier	John P. Chutter
1980	Geoffrey H. Tullidge	John P. Chutter
1981	Graham R. Dawson	John P. Chutter
1982	William E. Whittall	John P. Chutter
1983	Sydney Wallis Welsh	John P. Chutter
1984	William G. Leithead	John P. Chutter
1985	George W. Hungerford	John P. Chutter
1986	Hubert O. Chapman	(John P. Chutter
		(George W. Smith
1987	Hubert O. Chapman	George W. Smith
1988	Hubert O. Chapman	George W. Smith

APPENDIX "B"

PAST PRESIDENTS OF THE FORMER UNIVERSITY CLUB OF VANCOUVER

	President	Secretary–Manager
1955	E.W.H. Brown	
1956	Peter J. Sharp	
1957	Peter J. Sharp	
1958	Charles H. Wills	Doug Dickie
1959	G. Dudley Darling	Doug Dickie
1960	Frederick W. Charlton	John T. Grierson
1961	Hon. Nathan T. Nemetz	John T. Grierson
1962	Donald A. Sutton	John T. Grierson
1963	Hon. J.D. Taggart	John T. Grierson
1964	William S. Jackson	John T. Grierson
1965	Herbert K. Naylor	John T. Grierson
1966	William H. Clarke	John T. Grierson
1967	David M. Brousson	John T. Grierson
1968	David A. Freeman	John T. Grierson
1969	William C. Gibson	John T. Grierson
1970	Kenneth W. McKinley	James Byrom
1971	Thomas C. Marshall	James Byrom
1972	Ronald J. Webster	James Byrom
1973	Michael C.D. Hobbs	James Byrom
1974	William B. Laurie	James Byrom
1975	Warren J. Brant	James Byrom
1976	David R. Sinclair	James Byrom
1977	John A. Pearkes	(James Byrom (George W. Smith
1978	Donald L. Wheatley	George W. Smith
1979	Sholto Hebenton	George W. Smith
1980	Stinson Clarke	George W. Smith
1981	David B. Leaney	George W. Smith
1982	Douglas C. Williamson	George W. Smith
1983	R. Clifford Wyatt	George W. Smith
1984	William S. Tully	George W. Smith
1985	Leonard A. Mitten	George W. Smith
1986	Edward H. Wallace	George W. Smith
1987	Edward H. Wallace	Act'g Sec–Manager Past President, Thomas C. Marshall

APPENDIX C

THE UNIVERSITY CLUB

The first University Club in Vancouver was founded in 1911 and survived until 1930 when it succumbed to the Great Depression.

The second University Club opened its door in 1958 and in the next thirty years joined the ranks of the most prestigious clubs in Vancouver and flourished as a separate entity until 1987 when it merged with the Vancouver Club. Following that union the new Vancouver Club commissioned Dr. Reginald H. Roy to update the history of the new Vancouver Club with a view to combining the two records. T. C. Marshall, who had been acting secretary manager of the University Club agreed to do this brief history of the University Club.

*   *   *   *

Those in attendance at the founding meeting of the earlier University Club in 1911 were citizens of Vancouver well known some sixty years later-- J. A. Clark, lawyer; G. B. Eldridge, geologist and G. E. Housser, lawyer.

The first club was established in quarters formerly occupied by the Terminal City Club in the Clarke & Stuart Building opposite the C.P.R. station. Facilities included a main lounge, dining, reading and committee rooms. The quarters were not luxurious but commanded a view of the harbour and the North Shore mountains.

The club was incorporated as a private company. Lawyers Leo Buchanan and E. A. (Eddie) Lucas, were signatories to the memorandum and articles and Alfred Bull, who was to become a senior partner in the law firm Bull Housser and Tupper, signed as a witness. The club's capital consisted of 10,000 shares with a par value of $10 each. Candidates elected to membership were required to purchase one such non-transferable share which was forfeited if the holder ceased to be a member. Each Resident Member (one living within a 15 mile radius of the clubhouse) was required to pay an entrance fee of $40 and a Non-Resident, residing beyond the 15 mile radius, an entrance fee of $10.

Among the early members of the University Club were men who became prominent in the development of British Columbia--Henry Esson Young, later Minister of Education and a moving spirit in the creation of the University of British Columbia; W. J. Bowser, who became Attorney-General and later Premier; George E. Robinson, the first Dean of Arts at the University of British Columbia; H. C. Shaw, for many years the senior magistrate in Vancouver; and H. S. Tobin, lawyer, who commanded the 29th Battalion, C.E.F., ("Tobin's Tigers") in the First World War.

Others in this distinguished list included D. E. McTaggart, the Club's Corporation Counsel; E. K. DeBeck, long time clerk of the legislature in Victoria; lawyers Cecil Killam, A. C. DesBrisay, Wendell B. Farris, W. R. Bray, Elmore Meredith, M. A. Macdonald; engineers J. A. Walker, W. G. Swan, Christopher Webb; clergymen Rev. J. W. Woodside, Rev. John Mackay, Rev. E. D. Maclaren, Rev. George C. Pidgeon, and physicians Dr. H. H. McIntosh, Dr. George Seldon, Dr. C. S. McKee, Dr. F. J. Ballem, Dr. A. B. Schinbein, Dr. G.H. Worthington, Dr. Wallace R. Wilson, Dr. A. S. Munro and Dr. R. W. Riggs.

Also on the early membership roll were Dr. S. D. Scott, editor of the *News-Herald*, the morning daily; Professor Charles Hill-Tout; archaeologist; W. Hamar-Greenwood; Professor J. A. Gillis, J. M. O'Brien and many others.

Professor Henry F. Angus, who joined the club in 1919 after his return from the battlefields of France, recalled that the club was then located at 908 Dunsmuir. He described the premises as being "very adequate" and only within the financial reach of the club because it had formed a temporary amalgamation with the Western Club which consisted mostly of men who had attended English public schools.

Sixty years later--on November 30, 1971--five members of the earlier club were honoured at a luncheon by the Board of Directors. They were Brig. Gen. J. A. Clark, Q.C., Gardner S. Eldridge, G. E. Housser, Q.C., A. Rutherford Thompson and Chris E. Webb. Many of the reminiscences of days gone by were both amusing and illuminating. Mr. Thompson recalled that the first manager had grandiose personal habits and entertained his friends lavishly with the club's fine cuisine and cellar until invited to depart. One prominent legal light stopped off every day after court for a cup of gin, which always ran handsomely over, to the club's loss.

The club provided a good table at a reasonable cost and had to break up two law partners, only one a member, who enjoyed luncheon frequently. The guest openly paid his partner the price of the meal, a practice which caused the directors to take action.

The club's stationery displayed a neat crest with the motto "Fiat Lux" (Let There Be Light) and the club once received a letter addressed to "Flat Lux" 312 Seymour Street.

Mr. M. P. Morris, the Chilean Consul and an avid chess player, promoted the first and only chess tournament. The young assistant city engineer, Dunc Mackinnon, had the temerity and luck to beat the old gentleman and that was the end of chess.

After a succession of managers in the early days, the club hired D.B. Robinson, an excellent administrator, who later went to the

Program

✤

GRACE

TOAST TO THE QUEEN

PRESIDENT'S REMARKS

TOAST TO THE UNIVERSITIES

Proposed by: C. H. WILLS   *Reply by:* DR. N. A. M. MacKENZIE

TOAST TO THE UNIVERSITY CLUB

Proposed by: COL. H. T. LOGAN   *Reply by:* DR. A. E. GRAUER

PATRONS REMARKS

THE HONOURABLE FRANK MACKENZIE ROSS

THE HONOURABLE ERIC W. HAMBER

THE HONOURABLE CHIEF JUSTICE SHERWOOD LETT

Program for the Inauguration Dinner of The University Club of Vancouver, held on March 4, 1958.

Point Grey Golf Club and from there to the Vancouver Club.

In 1923 when the University Club was on Howe Street, it arranged accommodation for the Military Institute and several well-known military men used the club frequently, including Col. J. F. Keen, Brig. Harold McDonald and Brig. Jock McLean.

When the club opened, 253 shares had been subscribed, so the enterprise started with a capital fund of $2,530. The membership reached 400 by early 1912. Records indicate that the largest professional groups were lawyers, engineers and doctors. Others included land surveyors--a profitable business in those pre-war days--architects, real estate and financial agents and lumbermen.

Directors listed in the first report to the Registrar of Companies dated May 31, 1912 were: W. F. Carter, president; R. J. Sprott, vice president; F. S. Keith, treasurer; T. S. Scott, Dr. J. W. Woodley, H. S. Robinson, H. C. N. McKim, Dr. A. A. Wilson and G. E. Meeker. During its early years, the club directorate included many men who became well known in British Columbia. In 1913, new directors included W. F. Coy whose address was simply "Shaughnessy Heights" recently opened by the C.P.R. In 1914 the list includes D. E. McTaggart; in 1915, Professor J. M. Turnbull; and in 1916, Rev. F. C. C. Heathcote, later Sir Francis, Bishop of New Westminster.

Others who served on the board included Dr. L. S. Klinck, president of the university, who joined the board in 1925. Sherwood Lett's name first appears in 1926 along with those of Elmore Meredith and J. L. Lawrence. Dr. R. E. McKechnie, noted surgeon, who served as Chancellor of the University of British Columbia for twenty-six years, was a director in 1927; along with S.F.M. Moodie, teacher; and Chris Webb, engineer. Mr. William E. Jenkins served as president of the club in these early days. His son, Bill, was a member of the committee of the Vancouver Club for some years, latterly serving as chairman of the House Committee during the amalgamation period.

THE WESBROOK YEARS

One of those who used the club frequently in the early days was Dr. Frank Fairchild Wesbrook, first president of the University of British Columbia. When he was appointed in 1913 he worked out of the office in the Carter-Cotton Building, later home of **The Province**, at the corner of Hastings and Cambie. Thus, he found the University Club a great convenience when starting to build an organization and recruit staff. His ambition was to serve overseas in the Canadian armed services. The Board of Governors of the university did not regard favourably his attempts to enlist. However, he attended the School of Commissioned Officers and completed all the courses. In addition he was active in the Military Committee established by the club's directors to recruit a defence unit officered and manned by members of the club.

Unfortunately, University Club records do not reveal what became of the Military Committee's defence unit, although correspondence indicates that when an auxiliary univeristy company was proposed for the 72nd Seaforth Highlanders of Canada there was an enthusiastic response. Later when the 196th Western Universities Battalion was recruited, a number of University Club members joined and went overseas.

In 1916 the University Club and the Royal Vancouver Yacht Club entered into an agreement for the exchange of privileges for one year.

The club remained at the 312 Seymour Street address for six years. In 1917 it moved to 908 Dunsmuir Street, where it shared facilities with the Western Club for five years. In 1922 the club separated from the Western Club and moved to quarters above the London Grill at 852 Howe Street. In 1926 it moved to 812 Robson Street, where it remained until 1930 when it fell victim to the Depression.

TWENTY-FIVE YEARS LATER

Twenty-five years after the first University Club ceased to function, Second World War veterans graduating from the University of British Columbia and others brought the dreams of many years to reality by founding the second University Club. Interest in the project was spurred by the enthusiasm and determination of a Special Committee. Its first recorded meeting was a luncheon in the Hotel Georgia on April 23, 1954, with C. H. ("Chuck") Wills in the chair and eight others in attendance--E. W. H. Brown, G. Dudley Darling, Dean Geoffrey Andrew, Nathan Nemetz, Q.C., Douglas MacDonald, Peter J. Sharp, Frank Walden and Frank Turner.

The next recorded minutes disclose a meeting held on November 8, 1954 at the Royal Bank board room attended substantially by the same group. This meeting soon got down to the nub of the matter, namely money, and each member deposited with Art Sager, the Secretary, a cheque for $25 "as a token of their willingness to accept membership in the University Club Society." Chuck Wills and Nathan Nemetz were appointed a Committee to arrange for incorporation.

The enthusiasm engendered at that meeting can be gauged by the fact that the next meeting, held at the Faculty Club, U.B.C., (then consisting of three Second World War army huts) was held on February 18th, 1955 with 39 persons present. It is of interest to note that three members of the original University Club were present: Messrs. J.

A. Walker, I. N. Angus and W. W. Ritchie. Others attending were: Chuck Wills in the chair, H. L. Purdy, G. Bradner, J. A. Crub, K.F. Pedlow, A. L. Pedlow, S. J. Crowe, C. M. Campbell, Jr., A. Kaplan, F. W. ("Ted") Charlton, K. W. McKinley, S. M. Cameron, P. Lauch, D. A. ("Don") Sutton, W. M. Ritchie, T. R. Watt, G. Dudley Darling, Peter J. Sharp, J. L. Davies, A. P. Gardner, Nathan Nemetz, D. A. S. Lanskail, L. Collins, D. A. ("Dave") Freeman, T. C. ("Tom") Marshall, Vernon R. Hill, M. M. MacIntyre, Eric Webb, C. B. MacKedie, G. Martin, J. A. Merchant, D. D. Reeve, A. L. Estabrooke, J. L. Miller, D. L. Johnston, F. B. Matson and A. H. Sager. Nathan Nemetz reviewed the draft constitution. It provided for 25 per cent of members from the business community and 75 per cent from university graduates, the professions, the armed forces and the clergy, a provision which remained intact over the years. The following officers were elected:

President	– E. W. H. ("Ernie") Brown
Vice-President	– Charles H. Wills
Honorary Secretary	– Nathan Nemetz, Q.C.
Honorary Treasurer	– Peter J. Sharp

The Honorable Eric W. Hamber, Lieutenant-Governor and former Chancellor of U.B.C., was named patron; Chancellor Sherwood Lett, Honorary President and Dr. Norman A. M. MacKenzie, Honorary Vice-President. Ernie Brown, the first president, shortly thereafter moved to the East and Peter Sharp became president, a post he held for a year and a half.

The Board of Directors met frequently during 1955 and considered numerous suggestions, such as an Extension Department--Faculty of Commerce Building downtown with club facilities, a joint venture with the Board of Trade, or with professional associations or a luncheon club only, attached to some existing restaurant facility. All were debated at length, merits and demerits weighed in the balance. Gradually the conviction grew among the directors that the kind of club they envisaged would require a new building with modern facilities for gracious dining and entertaining. A committee set out to find a suitable site and several were visited. It was estimated that the property would cost $100,000 and the building between $500,000 and $1,000,000.

The Pacific Athletic Club was seriously considered, being available from the estate of Jack Pattison who had operated the private club on Howe Street for more than twenty years. One of the most important factors considered was that the Pacific Athletic Club already held a liquor license. To start afresh without a license might entail a delay of up to three years, obviously an unthinkable hurdle.

"After we rejected the P. A. Club," Dr. W. H. ("Bill") Gibson

The University Club's main dining room over-looking the harbour.

Cedar carving by Lloyd Wadhams, well-known native artist, on the southern wall of the dining room.

recalls, "we visited the old Quadra Club Building at 1021 West Hastings, then occupied by the Royal Canadian Air Force Reserve. "We made an exhaustive tour of the five floors and our architect member, John Lovatt Davies, summed up our impressions: 'It's a gem.'"

Designed by local architects, Sharp and Thompson, and built by Hodgson, King and Marble for the Quadra Club which occupied it from 1930 to 1940, it was purchased by the Loyal Order of Moose for $10,000. The actual vendor was the City of Vancouver which had taken over the property through the default of the Quadra Club in payment of taxes. In 1950, the Federal Government purchased it for $150,000 and it became headquarters for the RCAF Reserve Wing.

What was to become the club's main dining room was the lecture hall and dance floor. One of the star turns at the mess dinners held there was to form a human pyramid from a standing start to see which squadron could put the first man on the ceiling beams. Due, perhaps, to the age of the members, this practice was not continued by the University Club.

Nathan Nemetz was considered the appropriate director to approach the Honorable Ralph Campney, Minister of National Defence, to propose purchasing the building for the University Club. Ralph Campney turned out to be a strong supporter of the University Club project. He toured the building immediately so he would know "as much as his Ottawa advisors." "We went through the building thoroughly and the Minister must have made up his mind then and there to help us," Bill Gibson recalls. Chief Justice Sherwood Lett, a past president of the Alumni Association and former Chancellor of U.B.C., suggested that a petition in support of the proposal be presented to the Minister of National Defence. The Hon. Frank M. Ross, Lieutentant-Governor of B.C., endorsed the project and did everything he could to help.

Later the directors outlined a plan which would allow the RCAF Medical Unit to remain in the basement, paying rent to the club, until it felt that a move was appropriate. This plan was eventually worked out, with the assistance of The Hon. George R. Pearkes, who succeeded Mr. Campney as Minister, the Hon. Howard C. Green, The Hon. Davie Fulton and Air Commodore C.F. Johns, Deputy Minister. By August 1957, negotiations with Ottawa had proceeded to the point where a lease could be considered, initally for eighteen months at $1,000 per month commencing November 1st. The RCAF Medical Unit would remain in the basement of the building, using a separate side entrance.

Other matters were moving ahead; a membership drive among graduates of U.B.C. and other universities, a budget of $75,000 for leasehold improvements and the setting of an entrance fee of $600 with $300 down and $300 later. Monthly fees were set at $12.00.

Foreseeing rapid action in the immediate future the directors agreed to a "temporary suspension of the Charter and Constitution until a membership of 300 had been reached." A purchasing committee was established to look into the question of eventually purchasing the building.

THE OPENING OF THE CLUB

Bill Gibson recalls that on Saturday, August 31, 1957, he was taking his turn as Medical Duty Officer at the RCAF Headquarters and playing the piano after lunch when a brigadier, just off a service aircraft from Ottawa, entered the Mess. Noticing Bill's medical insignia he went directly to him and mentioned that he was in some pain from a relatively minor but uncomfortable ailment. He added that he had come to sign the lease on the Reserve Headquarters Building downtown and wondered what it was all about.

Bell's professional treatment must have been just what the brigadier needed because the lease was prepared and signed in November 1957. Against the monthly rental of $1,000 was offset a monthly rental of $540 received from the RCAF Medical Unit which continued to occupy the basement.

At this time, with furnishings to be bought and remodelling to be done, the club's credit rating became crucial. The club had started with seven members at $25 each, later increased to $30, hardly a rich capital account. As Treasurer, Ted Charlton was asked if he could name one responsible person who could vouch for the new club. With great assurance he referred the enquiry to the Director of Development at the Royal Bank--Peter J. Sharp. As the RCAF withdrew from the building, they left behind Squadron Leader Charles Lindberg, a permanent force officer about to retire. He was appointed secretary-manager on a pro tem basis to make sure that no one took over the empty building while the directors were scouting for funds. He was succeeded by Douglas Dickie on January 1, 1958. His starting salary was $500 per month.

One of the first things the directors had to decide was the matter of racial or religious limitations to membership. Dean Geoffrey Andrew and John Lovatt Davies took a strong position against any form of discrimination. The other directors readily agreed and this became a guiding principle of the club.

W. H. ("Bill") Birmingham agreed to work with the secretary-manager on the kitchen layout. Bill was to become one of the most loyal members of the club, contributing lavishly of his time on many projects for the next thirty years, and participating in the joint planning for the renovation of the Vancouver Club following the sale of the University Club building in 1987. On March 5, 1958, the directors honoured the club's patrons at a black-tie dinner. Patrons were the Honorable Frank M. Ross, the Honorable Eric W. Hamber, and the Honorable Sherwood Lett; Honorary President was A. E. ("Dal") Grauer, Chancellor of U.B.C., and Honorary Vice-President Dr. Norman A. M. MacKenzie.

The Vancouver *Province* reported the next day:

> *Five years' planning and organization by a group of Vancouver businessmen came to a happy conclusion Wednesday when Lieutenant Governor Frank Ross officially opened the plush quarters of the University Club of Vancouver.*

Graceful winding staircase in the entrance hall of The University Club.

The spacious and comfortable lounge on the main floor.

PURCHASE OF THE BUILDING

Following the Federal election of 1958, Bill Gibson addressed a letter to Peter Sharp, outlining how the building at 1021 West Hastings might be available for purchase. Dr. Norman MacKenzie lent his support by writing to the Honorable G. R. Pearkes, then Minister of National Defence, asking his assistance in making the building available for the Club.

Peter Sharp submitted a brief to the Minister on June 10, 1958. He pointed out that the existing lease would expire in June 1959 at which time it was anticipated that the Club premises would be available for purchase. Ten days later Peter Sharp, accompanied by the club's John Lovatt Davies and the peripatetic Bill Gibson, waited on the government in Ottawa to negotiate purchase of the building. John Pearkes had briefed his father, the Honorable George R. Pearkes, Minister of National Defence. They then waited on the Honorable Howard C. Green, Deputy Prime Minister, and the Honorable Davie Fulton, Minister of Justice, to enlist their support. Bill Gibson recalls the meeting thus:

> *We were ushered into the office of the minister in charge of Crown Assets Disposal. We pointed out that the Prime Minister would be in Vancouver shortly and we wished to offer him hospitality in our own building, not in rented premises. The proposal fell on fertile ground, well prepared by our member, Leon J. Ladner, Q.C., and the deal went on to completion.*

In early 1959, the Club acquired title to the property for $178,000. The entrance fee had been set at $600 with one-half payable with application and one-half secured by promissory note. In order to meet the purchase price the notes were called in. The purchase of the property was made possible by sound management enabling the club to qualify for substantial bank credit.

GROWTH OF THE CLUB

Over the years many improvements were made. The Lower Lounge which was opened in October 1960, underwent extensive alterations in 1962 and 1985. The third floor private dining rooms were opened in May 1965. The main lounge was refurnished in 1971 and again in 1981 and windows were installed in the dining room, enhancing the spectacular view of the North Shore mountains.

With the steady increase in membership it soon became necessary to adopt a policy in regard to applications. It was agreed that all applicants be treated by the Membership Committee as individuals fitted or not fitted for membership. A policy statement issued by the directors provided that it should not be the responsibility of the

Membership Committee to consider the individual "in relation to his corporate, professional, business, religious or ethnic relationships but it shall be the responsibility of the Directors to make sure that the membership remains in reasonable balance."

It was agreed that members of the Consular Corps be admitted to membership with no entrance fee and dues of $17.50 a month. The club's close ties with U.B.C. were further strengthened by inviting as Associate members, teachers and lecturers from U.B.C. and later S.F.U. as well as those of the medical profession who were teaching at U.B.C.

By February 1959 the membership had increased to a grand total of 515, a great effort on the part of the early directors. New categories of membership were created over the years--one for sons of members in 1973, one for retired members in 1975. Upon amalgamation, retired members became resident members with reduced fees and the corporate members became resident members. The club was fortunate in its membership, attracting many younger leaders of the professional and business life of Vancouver. By affiliation with many other clubs in all parts of the world, it assured its members of a warm welcome when travelling abroad. A total of 2,034 had become members over the years before amalgamation.

The membership was always broadly based and represented a cross section of the life of Vancouver and indeed of British Columbia including many prominent military figures from the Second World War, the Judiciary, the Clergy, the business community and many well known local, provincial and federal politicians.

The club's close association with the universities is demonstrated in the club by the crests of 133 universities throughout the world, each one indicating the alma mater of some member or members. These are now displayed in the third floor corridor of the Vancouver Club.

The question of ladies' privileges at the club surfaced in 1971 when some members complained of ladies attending private meetings before 5:00 p.m.! After discussion it was agreed that members sponsoring a meeting at which ladies would be present would be expected "to escort the lady with all speed to the Private Dining Room." Early in 1982 the members were canvassed for their views on lady membership. Of 330 replies, 190 were in favour of lady members and 140 against. The matter was again raised in 1984. The Membership Chairman moved that the directors not proceed with any recommendation for female membership at that time. When the matter was put to the Annual Meeting in May 1984, the motion to admit ladies to membership was tabled. Just when it was thought that the matter had been laid to rest for all time, the board agreed again to canvas all members by mail. A questionnaire resulted in 236 members in favour of female members and 192 opposed--a lower percentage of "yeas" than would be required for a special resolution. This was still not the end of the matter. At the 1985 Annual General Meeting, the question was once again brought up and debated, with much the same arguments used in previous years. The male-only principle was again affirmed by a vote of 26 for and 50 against.

Membership figures remained fairly constant until 1982. The following three years, however, reflected the concern which the directors increasingly experienced concerning the club's long-term future. From the high of 826 members in 1981, membership dropped to 741 by the end of 1985. Despite a vigorous membership drive organized by W. deM. ("Monty") Marler, only a small number of new members resulted. It was apparent that the business recession and changing social habits were creating difficulties for private clubs. One area in which it was thought the club could gain new members was through the Downtown Vancouver Association, the president of which had expressed keen interest in some form of alignment with the club. The concept found little support, however.

With the opening of Expo '86, representatives of the following countries were granted temporary honorary membership for the period from May to October: Japan, Norway, France, Australia, Pakistan, Yugoslavia, Great Britain, Barbados, Mexico and Saudi Arabia. The long, hot summer, ideal for Expo, proved less than ideal for the club and the hoped-for increase in business failed to materialize. Clearly, the time was ripe for a new approach to assessing the club's future. Just how this materialized is recounted elsewhere in this history.

In October 1966, it became known that British Pacific Properties, owned by the Guinness family and owners of the Marine Building, had purchased the property to the west of the club and were considering a 23-storey building on the former parking lot. The Long-Range Planning Committee recommended that the interests of both the club and the Guinness group would be best served by a single development and, further, that possibly the club could be accommodated on the top floors of this or any other building in the immediate vicinity. Lengthy discussion failed to reach consensus, however, and it was felt that the club should remain in its own building. As the result of further discussions with British Pacific Properties, the club purchased a 12- foot strip to the west to provide an entrance and exit to the rear of the building and a parking lot used primarily by members of the staff. Equally important, it enabled deliveries to be made via the lane instead of through the front doors.

For the next twenty years the directors continued to keep an eye on the club's future. The purchase of some other building in the vicinity, the redevelopment of the existing property and in more recent years, the sale of the club's excess development rights, all came to be studied closely by the Long–Range Planning Committee. The Guinness interests were rumoured to be interested in developing property at Hastings Street and Thurlow Street and a possible redevelopment on the Customs Building site prompted further studies as to the value of the club's property in toto and the value of the excess development rights alone.

In his first address to the Board after election as president in May 1986, E. H. ("Ed") Wallace referred to the difficulties the club was facing–– high property taxes, higher anticipated maintenance costs and declining membership. He said the Long–Range Planning Committee was currently investigating the feasibility of the club remaining in its present premises. A report prepared by the indefatigable Bill Gibson was circulated. Essentially it dealt with the two most obvious choices: retaining the land and premises but selling the unused development rights or, alternatively, selling everything and relocating. The report favoured an outright sale of all assets and relocating the club elsewhere. The Long–Range Planning Committee concluded that this was the most viable course of action.

This, then, was the situation by mid–summer 1986. A great deal of time and effort had been devoted to considering all the various proposals. Many board members had been active for several months to ensure that no stone was left unturned in the search for an acceptable solution.

The thought of amalgamation with the Vancouver Club, first mentioned almost casually by Richard Mundie and then discussed enthusiastically and successively by Ed Wallace and Hu Chapman and then by the two boards, the past presidents and the members, gave a new direction to long–range planning and, thenceforth, as reported elsewhere, the preoccupation of both clubs became that of effecting the proposed amalgamation.

WORKS OF ART

Early on, it was decided as a matter of club policy that efforts should be made to acquire, either by purchase or loan, paintings and other works of art. No record is obtainable of the art collection but in 1977 the club's modest collection was valued at $25,000.

A Donations, Presentations and Loans Committee was established in 1966. Whether or not this committee was responsible for obtaining the impressionist nude by Plaskett that hung over the bar in the Lower Lounge is not clear but it hung there for many years. It is said that when the Children's Party was held each Christmas the painting was taken down in order to protect the little ones from a dangerous influence.

The large blank wall on the south side of the Dining Room was cause for concern from the earliest days. In 1971, with the help of Bill Gibson, a considerable improvement was made when a large modern French tapestry 16 feet wide by 11 feet high known as "Masters of Science" was obtained on loan from the Woodward Biomedical Library at the University of British Columbia for a period of six months. Special lighting was installed in the ceiling and this highly colourful post-war French tapestry was a great attraction. On it were depicted some fifty of the world's great scientists including Galileo, Newton and Pasteur.

Great consternation ensued when the tapestry suddenly disappeared from the club, and although it was covered by adequate insurance, the loss was keenly felt. But three months later the police of Vancouver received a tip that the tapestry was in a West End basement, having been miraculously recovered from under a stump in Stanley Park! The police were able to return it to the club in excellent condition, and it was speedily returned to the Memorial Room of the Woodward Library at U.B.C. What should be done to cover this wall became a challenge.

In July 1971 the President, Tom Marshall, reported he had attended the opening of a new hospital at Prince Rupert at which the Queen had expressed her admiration of a carved mural depicting the history of an Indian Band. He suggested that a carving might be suitable for the Dining Room wall. W. B. ("Bill") Laurie, took up the idea, made inquiries and reported that a 20' by 10' carving could be obtained at an estimated cost of $6,000 and would take six months to complete.

Mr. Lloyd Wadhams, a master carver waith the Kwakiutl Tribe of Alert Bay agreed to undertak the carving. A form of agreement was entered into with Tempo Canadian Crafts and Lloyd Wadhams to commence work on the projected yellow cedar carving. Through the kind assistance of Ted Taylor of Steele Lumber Ltd., the required quantity of yellow cedar was obtained. The wood had to be cut and kiln dried by a slow process and dressed to the necessary specifications. The total cost of the material and its preparation was $1,480.

On February 16, 1973 the wood was delivered to J. R. Bezanson Ltd., to dress the wood as required and make the 45 pieces of cedar into five four-foot panels, bolted together, with joints left loose and unglued.

Mr. William Braidwood, an engineer with J. R. Bezanson Ltd., then superintended the actual erection of the carving. It was unveiled at the club's Annual Meeting on April 18th, 1974 by the incumbent president, M. C. D. ("Mike") Hobbs, and his successor, Bill Laurie, who had worked so long to make the dream a realization.

The design reflects the Mah-Tag-Hulah people of the Salmon River near Kelsey Bay. Incorporated are various animals and fish, including the thunderbird and the whale which played such a prominent part in the lives of these native people. Following amalgamation, the directors of the Vancouver Club voted in favour of making a gift of the carving to the Vancouver Museum which had stated its intention to lend it to the Trade and Convention Centre at Canada Place where it is now to be seen.

In 1974, through the efforts of Bill Birmingham, the University Club obtained a ten-foot totem pole from the Hazelton area which stood in the main lobby of the club until its closure. It represents a giant beaver, one of the tribal figures of the Git-ksan people and is a typical interior house post designed to support the roof beams of a communal meeting place. It now graces the main foyer of the Trade and Convention Centre.

In 1977 Sholto Hebenton persuaded the Board to appoint an Art Acquisition Committee to investigate the possibility of purchasing works of art. In 1980 the painting "A House on Prior Street" by Geoff. Rock was purchased. "Intertidal Barclay Sound" was acquired by purchase from Robert Genn in 1980 and graced the south wall of the Dining Room Lobby. Both paintings were subsequently transferred to the new Vancouver Club.

ENTERTAINMENT

After the official opening in March 1958, the organization of the club, including hiring of suitable staff, appointment of committees and development of a social program proceeded with dispatch. An entertainment committee was formed under the chairmanship of Chuck Wills. This committee would, over the next thirty years, be instrumental in organizing many social functions and bringing to the club some famous entertainers.

It was the custom of the club to hold an Anniversary Party. This was always a popular event. In 1965 the club invited George Feyer, noted pianist singer of the Carlisle Hotel in New York, to entertain and he packed the house for three nights. His visit was so successful that he returned in 1966, 1968 and 1975. Others who entertained at Anniversary parties were Anne Mortifee, the famous Vancouver singer; Kathleen Payne, actress-singer; the Ormiston Concert Party; Dal Richards and his Big Band; singer Juliette of T.V. and radio, and many others.

Another special occasion on the club calendar was the Directors' Dinner held annually when the president and the board were joined by past presidents and honorary officers to recall the past and toast the future.

At the annual meeting in May 1980, the president, R. C. Wyatt and directors paid special tribute to the charter members and named them Honorary Life members. Special tribute was paid to the late Chuck Wills whose lively spirits and keen wit had enhanced many a directors' dinner.

The last of these gala dinners took place on March 25, 1988 following the amalgamation and was co-hosted on this occasion by President Hu Chapman, Vice-President Ed Wallace, and the Board of Directors of the new Vancouver Club, with 29 Past Presidents of both clubs and their ladies in attendance. Air Vice Marshal Leigh Stevenson praised the amalgamation and as senior member present, at age 93, received a standing ovation. It was a memorable occasion which did much to bring the members of both clubs together.

Football nights were instituted in the early days. B. C. Lions coaches, Wayne Robertson, Dave Skrien and Don Branby were offered transient membership. As early as July 1958, a smorgasbord dinner was offered the members prior to an exhibition game between the Lions and the Calgary Stampeders. The price of $4 included parking, a smorgasbord dinner and bus transportation! This experiment proved so popular that, for all the B.C. Lions' home games and the Grey Cup finals held in Vancouver in subsequent years, similar dinners would be held but not for $4.

Golf tournaments were started in 1960. Although these proved popular for a few years and undoubtedly generated a few more golf stories, they were discontinued after 1972.

Children's Christmas parties including lunch, entertainment and a visit from Santa Claus in the person, latterly, of Paul Diemer, now in charge of maintenance at the club, were commenced in 1960 and proved a great success, not only for the children but for proud parents and grandparents alike. Years later sons and daughters of members were able to recall, with pleasure, the good time they had enjoyed at these parties.

The club itself always looked particularly festive, warm and inviting at this time of the year with a big fire crackling in the main fireplace in the Lobby and Christmas trees throughout the three floors. Often a large tree would be placed in the curve of the stairway on the main floor, reaching as high as the second floor. Receptionist Dorothy Cooper headed the group of staff decorators and the tall tree proved to be a challenge to all.

Many members recall bringing their families to dinner and holding wedding receptions at the club as well. Many groups and organizations held private functions at the club including professional groups, university reunions and regimental dinners. The President's Room and the three private dining rooms on the third floor proved ever popular and were put to good use.

Epicure dinners proved popular over the years. Always well patronized they featured the food, and sometimes the wines, of foreign countries. David Freeman, an avid collector of good wines, served for many years and the club's unofficial advisor and the club was able, through his efforts when visiting France, to maintain an excellent cellar. Thankfully he has taken his expertise to the new club and again has been asked to advise the directors.

Guest speakers over the years included the Honorable Lester B. Pearson and the Honorable E. Davie Fulton (1961), the Honorable Maurice Lamontaigne (1963), the Honorable H. P. Bell–Irving (1983) and the Honorable A. R. Huntington (1986). Those associated with U.B.C. and Simon Fraser University included Dr. John B. Macdonald (1963), Dr. Gordon M. Shrum (1980), Dr. E. Kenneth Hare (1968), Dr. Kenneth E. Strand (1975), Dr. William G. Saywell (1985), and Dr. D. W. Strangway (1986). The last speaker was Peter G. Stursberg, former well-known news analyst and journalist.

Special trips were arranged for members. In September 1965 a large number went by chartered plane to view the Bennett Dam near Hudson Hope. In October 1966 sixty members and guests visited the Boeing plant in Seattle, Washington to view a prototype of the famous "747", destined to become one of the most popular aircraft in the world. The cost for that trip, including air fare, bus and meal at the College Club--$25.

Other events were held on a regular basis. Every January, the Scottish Bard was celebrated in fitting style with the club's real or imaginary Scotsmen addressing the Haggis and toasting Robbie Burns. Every Christmas the kitchen staff arranged magnificent buffet for the week before Christmas Day. These proved to be popular for members entertaining their office staffs. And each Christmas also, for several years, an old fashioned "Shoppe" was installed in the Main Lobby where the members could purchase from a wide variety of gourmet foot items and delicacies.

RELATIONSHIP TO UNIVERSITIES

The first University Club had avowed itself to be interested in and anxious to establish a liaison with universities. So, also, did the second University Club which from the outset was determined and eager to establish close ties with U.B.C.

By May 1958, there were 34 "Associate" members from U.B.C. Later, with the establishment of Simon Fraser University additional Associate members were added. By 1983 the number had reached 102 out of a total membership of 820. The numbers then commenced to decline as these busy academics found it increasingly difficult to get down to the club. By the close of 1987, the total had fallen to 64 out of a total membership of 645. All of them automatically became Associate members of the new club.

The presidents of both universities were invited from time to time to address the members and members were kept informed of the growing problems of both institutions.

By 1962, the club seemed financially well-launched on its way and the directors agreed to make a $10,000 donation to U.B.C. for scholarships and bursaries. A close link was maintained with the U.B.C. Alumni Association, its president being granted temporary membership during his term of office.

The club also contributed $1,000 per year to what became designated as the Walter Gage Fund in honour of that popular and respected member of the teaching staff of U.B.C. and latterly president.

Over the years the club faithfully lived up to its promise to maintain a close liaison with the universities of British Columbia and to foster interest in and support for the work of those institutions.

STAFF

The success of the second University Club's 30 years was due in large measure to its secretary–managers and staff. Total dedication to service was exemplified by everyone who worked for the club which was blessed with good leadership. John T. Grierson, the late James A. Byrom, and latterly George W. Smith all left their mark indelibly imprinted on the history of the club.

The kitchen staff saw a number of Chefs de Cuisine, each with his own style but one common bond--superb preparation and presentation of food. Whether it was only a handful of members for dinner on a Monday night, a gala banquet or a Christmas buffet the kitchen staff gave it their all. With aging equipment and cramped space they nevertheless solved problems as they arose and always upheld their tradition for serving good food.

The service staff supplemented the kitchen staff and to them fell the challenge of serving the members quietly and efficiently. Understandably the members did not come to know the kitchen staff as well as the service staff. The waiters, barmen and waitresses came to know the special wishes of the members and strove to provide high quality and attentive service.

The unseen maintenance staff ensured that the club was kept in perfect condition. Latterly, with many equipment breakdowns, leaking roof and defective plumbing occurring all too frequently, Walter

Gitschman and his assistant were kept busy, often having to use a "band-aid" method to keep out the leaks.

Accounting and office staffs ensured efficient administration. All the club's receptionists had a greeting and a cheerful word for every member and guest and did much to enhance the club's reputation for friendliness.

Nothing in this brief history can be emphasized more than the loyal, efficient and friendly service of the club staff over the period of 30 years. It is to them that this history is dedicated.

EPILOGUE

When the University Club closed its doors on June 4, 1988 it left behind 30 years and five months of successful operation. To measure that success in terms of dollars would avoid the club's chief role--to provide first class food and beverages, attentive service, an atmosphere of quiet relaxation and above all, to foster friendship among its members.

The more than two thousand gentlemen whose names were posted to the membership roll attest to the attractiveness of the club. In the majority of cases a new member became an old member. Hundreds took their turn to serve on the board or the committees so that member participation was always a prominent feature.

It was with regret that the directors, acknowledging the hard facts surrounding the club's future, recommended amalgamation. However, despite the emotional trauma experienced by so many members, it is a tribute to their sound judgement that the mandate given the directors was unanimous.

The new Vancouver Club combines the personalities, the skills, the talents and the background of the two clubs to form one of the finest clubs in Canada.

APPENDIX "D"

DONATIONS TO THE CLUB HISTORY FUND

Ian M. Adam
H.W. (Spud) Akhurst
Bank of Montreal
Ian M. Bell-Irving
Winslow W. Bennett
Raymond P. Bergen
Ronald M. Brown
Alexander Campbell
John K. Campbell
Archie H. Cater
Arthur J.E. Child
Donald M. Clark
CP Rail
Mortimer S. Duffus
Claude F. Dunfee
Donald R. Dunfee
Edward Chapman Ltd.
   & Chapy's
Hon E. Davie Fulton
D. Michael M. Goldie
James B. Grinnell
Alan F. Hackett
George W. Hungerford
Roderick M. Hungerford
J. Norman Hyland
Derek Lukin Johnston
John C. Kay

Thomas E. Ladner
Arthur F. Lungley
Gordon C. Lyall
Ian W. McDonald
George B. McKeen
Victor F. MacLean
William deM. Marler
Roy S. Minter
L. Reed Naylor
William T.H. Negus
A.J. Patrick Oswald
Philip W. Owen
Phillips, Hager & North Ltd.
Family of Russell J.G. Richards
John M. Rose
Royal Trust
Royal Bank of Canada
Ralph A. Smith
Donald F. Spankie
Mrs. Douglas M. Stewart
Thorne Ernst & Whinney
Richard W. Underhill
John W. Walsh
Franz M. Wilhelmsen
John D. Wilson
Edward T. Winslow

INDEX

Listings in *boldface italics* indicate "thumbnail sketches" of a member.
Listings in **boldface** indicate illustrations.